Moonlighting on the Internet

Moonlighting
on the Internet

5 World-Class Experts Reveal Proven Ways
to Make an Extra Paycheck Online Each Month

Yanik Silver
Robert Olic

EP
Entrepreneur₀ Press

Publisher: Jere Calmes
Cover Design: Desktop Miracles, Inc.
Editorial and Production Services: CWL Publishing Enterprises, Inc.,
Madison, Wisconsin, www.cwlpub.com

This publication is designed to provide accurate and authoritative information in regard to the subject matter covered. It is sold with the understanding that the publisher is not engaged in rendering legal, accounting, or other professional services. If legal advice or other expert assistance is required, the services of a competent professional person should be sought.

> —From a Declaration of Principles jointly adopted by
> a Committee of the American Bar Association
> and a Committee of Publishers and Associations

ISBN 13: 978-1-59918-157-8
      10: 1-59918-157-6

Library of Congress Cataloging-in-Publication Data
Silver, Yanik.
  Moonlighting online / by Yanik Silver.
    p. cm.
  ISBN-13: 978-1-59918-157-8 (alk. paper)
  ISBN-10: 1-59918-157-6 (alk. paper)
  1. Electronic commerce. I. Title.
  HF5548.32.S554 2007
  658.8'72—dc22

                                        2007023366

Printed in Canada

11 10 09 08 07   10 9 8 7 6 5 4 3 2 1

Contents

Introduction   **xi**

Part One. Moonlighting on the Internet Method #1   **1**
Section 1. *Selling Digitally Delivered Information*

  1. **Creating "Digitally Delivered Information Products"**   **3**
     Seven Reasons Why a Digital Information Product Is the
        Best Way to Build Your Fortune on the Net   4
     "But Everything's Free on the Internet—
        So How Could I Possibly Sell Information?"   5
     Here's What You Don't Need to Get Started   6
     How about Multiple Web Sites Funneling Money
        into Your Bank Account?   7

  2. **What Is Information Marketing?**   **9**
     Here's How I Stumbled onto This Weird Little
        World of Information Marketing   12

  3. **Top Seven Information Topics**   **17**

  4. **How to Figure Out What Information to Sell**   **27**

  5. **Researching the Online Marketplace**   **35**
     Finding Ideas When You're Clueless on What to Sell   40

Contents

6. Evaluating Your "Brilliant" Idea   **43**
Research Using Search Engines   44
Picking a Winning Project   46

7. Creating Your Information Product   **49**
You Write or Create It   49
Your Outline Is the Key   50
Power of Mind Mapping   52
Speak Your Product   55
Ghostwriter   55
Do What You Do Already   56

Section 2. *Where to "Steal" Your Bestselling Idea*   **59**

8. Licensing   **61**

9. Joint Ventures   **65**

10. Public Domain   **71**
Your Public Domain Cheat Sheet   72
Finding Your Public Domain Gold Mine   74
Clearing Rights of Public Domain Works   76

Section 3. *Building Your Web Site*   **87**

11. Getting Your Site's Foundation Built   **89**
Registering the Right Domain   89
Domain Hosting   90
Putting E-Mail Robots to Work for You   96
Taking Money   97
Shopping Cart   99

12. Creating Your HOT Offer   **101**
How Can You Make Your Offer as Irresistible as Possible?   102
The Real-World Offer for *Anatomy and Drawing*   103
How to Price Your Information Product   106

13. Setting Up Your Site   **111**

14. Headlines That Sell   **117**
Bullet Points   119

Contents

Part Two. Moonlighting on the Internet Method #2: eBay   123

15. **The eBay Machine**   125

16. **Finding the Right Products and Setting Up Business**   129
  The eBay Experience: Getting Your Business Straight
     and Making Money Without Risk   131
  Why People Buy on eBay   133
  Product Sourcing—Drop-Shipping, Wholesale, or Closeout?   134

17. **"The Flood"**   137
  The Three-Part Formula   140
  Beating the Competition   144
  Using the Right Keywords   148

18. **Your Listing**   151
  Getting the Headline Right   151
  Personalizing Your Listing   154
  To Specialize or Not to Specialize   158
  Getting People to Bid   160
  The eBay Auction: How Long Must It Be and When Do I Start?   162
  Feature It!   163
  Buy It Now   165
  After the Sale   165
  Auction Management Software   166
  Keeping the Buyers Interested   168
  Dealing with Non-Paying Buyers   169
  Feedback   170
  Accepting Payments   172
  Managing Customer Orders   173

19. **What Makes a Successful Seller?**   175
  More Cool Secrets to Success on eBay   178

Part Three. Moonlighting on the Internet Method #3:
Affiliate Marketing   181

20. **The World of Affiliate Programs**   183
  What Exactly Is Affiliate Marketing?   183
  Many Ways of Getting Paid   185
  How I Got Started   187
  A Business for the Lazy   189

Contents

21. Finding an Affiliate Program and Working It   **191**

Choosing an Affiliate Program   194

Read the Agreement   196

The Business of Affiliate Marketing   197

Don't Sell, Presell   198

KISS   200

Narrowing Your Focus   202

Driving Traffic   202

List + Autoresponder = Repeat Business   205

Offline Marketing   207

Tracking   208

Part Four. Moonlighting on the Internet Method #4: Yahoo! Stores and E-Commerce Stores   **211**

22. The Yahoo! Stores Phenomenon   **213**

What's So Special about Yahoo!?   214

It All Started with a Sword   214

Getting Others to Do the Hard Work   217

Sold on Yahoo! and How You Can Get Started   219

Business License   220

You Are Going to Need a Web Site   222

Deciding What to Sell   223

Checking Out the Competition   223

23. Establishing Your Niche   **227**

Marketing to Your Niche   229

Drop-Shipping in Depth   231

Beware of Middlemen   234

Taking Payments   234

Running a Part-Time Store   236

Traffic Value of Suppliers and Affiliates   237

Adding Your Own Affiliate Programs   238

Repeat Sales   239

Cross-Selling   240

Exclusive Packages   242

Finally …   243

Contents

Part Five. Moonlighting on the Internet Method #5: Blogging **245**

24. Why Blogging? **247**
What Is a Blog? 247
Qualities of an Ideal Blogger 249
Getting Started 251
Deciding on a Blog Platform 254

25. How to Set Up a Blog **257**
Five Steps to Setting Up a Hosted Blog at Wordpress.com 257
Set Up a Custom Standalone Blog Using One-Click-Install 258
Your Own Domain Name 260
Blog Design 262
Tools of the Trade 263
Writing Good Content 263
Different Styles of Blog Posts 268
Miscellaneous Content Writing Tips 270

26. Making Money with Blogs **271**
Direct Income Earning Methods for Bloggers 272
Indirect Income Earning Methods for Bloggers 275
How Much Money Can a Blog Earn? 276
How Much Do I Spend? 281
Ad Relevancy 281
Ten Tips for Using Affiliate Programs on Your Blog 282

Conclusion: What Am I Doing Now? **285**
Secret #1: Cheerful Expectancy 286
Secret #2: Do One Proactive Thing a Day 287
Secret #3: Decision 288
Secret #4: Deadline 289

Index **293**

Introduction

Moonlighting on the Internet: How to Get Rich SLOWLY Online

"What the hell do you do exactly?"

That's the typical response I get from people I just meet. Well, if I'm being honest, even my family and good friends still don't quite "get it." If I tell people I'm an "internet marketer," they think I build web sites. If I say, "I'm an online publisher," they make me out to be some kind of porno operator. So I still haven't really been able to come up with a good explanation. Hopefully, in the pages of this book you'll get a glimpse of my bizarre little world and see how you can truly create money while you sleep.

But before I get to that, I want you to picture something . . .

Imagine waking up every morning and finding orders waiting for you in your e-mailbox. While you were sleeping, customers from all over the world were giving you money. And you don't have to do much at all, because your computer does all the dirty work for you and then deposits money in your bank account—all without lifting a finger.

It's like having your own perfect moneymaking machine working for you tirelessly day and night.

Think about having your car payment taken care of . . .

Think about your mortgage getting paid off . . .

Think about your bills and debts disappearing . . .

Or what about some extra spending money for vacations or cool gifts and gadgets ...

All this and more from moonlighting on the internet and setting up your own little web business in your spare time that keeps throwing off cash, month after moneymaking month!

It's all possible, like it has been for my good friend Jim Edwards. Jim started off in 1999 and put up a site helping homeowners sell their houses alone and another site that explained the tips and tricks to securing the best mortgage. By Jim's own admission, he hasn't touched the sites in years, but they still keep bringing in enough money to pay his mortgage, his utilities, and two car payments.

If you have basic computer skills and follow these simple directions, I'll show you five legitimate, down-to-earth methods to make a little extra money each month online ... in your spare time.

Keep reading because you'll be handed five different roadmaps for making $500–5,000+ per month online like clockwork in your spare time. These are five proven ways to earn a second paycheck online without another daily 9-to-5 grind . . .

- ◆ Even if ... You HATE computers
- ◆ Even if ... You're a complete computer dunce and don't really feel like learning anything else about them
- ◆ Even if ... You only have a few dollars to get started with
- ◆ Even if ... You're totally lost on the web and don't have time to play catch-up
- ◆ Even if ... You have no clue what you want to sell online
- ◆ Even if ... You only have a couple of spare hours each week

I promise you'll get so excited by the endless (and very real) opportunities online that you'll have a tough time sleeping. The best way I know how to prove it really works is to simply show you . . .

I'm writing this introduction at 11:48 a.m. on Sunday, April 29, 2007. My wife Missy and I went out to dinner last night for her birthday. We stayed out for our first "sleepover" without the boy. Our son, Zak, is 20 months old and I finally coaxed Missy into staying out the night. So we left at about 7:30 p.m. (after he went to bed—I know that's cheating a little) and returned around 11 a.m. this morning. I logged on to my e-mail and woke to $2,312.17 in my inbox when we returned (Figure A-1).

	Check Mail	Stop	Process Mail	Mail Program	Spam Tools	

Delete	Bounce	Size	From	Subject /	Sent
☐	☐	1.7KB	surefireadmin@surefiremarketing.co	080314645 New Order Received	28 Apr 2007, 6:33pm
☐	☐	1.7KB	surefireadmin@surefiremarketing.co	08031466J New Order Received	28 Apr 2007, 8:21pm
☐	☐	1.7KB	surefireadmin@surefiremarketing.co	08031467G New Order Received	28 Apr 2007, 11:56pm
☐	☐	1.7KB	surefireadmin@surefiremarketing.co	08031468e New Order Received	29 Apr 2007, 12:51am
☐	☐	1.8KB	surefireadmin@surefiremarketing.co	08031469k New Order Received	29 Apr 2007, 1:12am
☐	☐	1.7KB	surefireadmin@surefiremarketing.co	08031471s New Order Received	29 Apr 2007, 2:51am
☐	☐	1.8KB	surefireadmin@surefiremarketing.co	08031475q New Order Received	29 Apr 2007, 7:35am
☐	☐	1.7KB	surefireadmin@surefiremarketing.co	080314774 New Order Received	29 Apr 2007, 10:45am

Figure A-1. SureFireMarketing—Orders received on April 29, 2007

I've been at it for seven years now, and I have to tell you that you probably won't start off like this, but from the first few days my site was up, I started receiving notices of money hitting my inbox. I tell you, there's no better feeling in the world. In fact, I can still remember the customer's name (Ron K.) and his state (New York). There's just an incredible joy to discovering this stuff actually works!

Even my wife was shocked when she tried my simple, down-to-earth system and just 18 days later started cashing her "extra shopping money" checks.

And that's what my job is here!

I want to shatter any excuse you might have and help you get to $500 per month as quickly as possible in a REAL online business. And then I want to show you how to keep building to $1,000, $2,000, $5,000, or way more per month, just like I have for thousands and thousands of students.

I have to pinch myself sometimes, because we are truly living in the best time ever for everyday people to moonlight online. All you need is a computer, an internet connection, motivation, and the right know-how. The internet has changed everything, from the way we order pizza to the way we

Introduction

file our taxes to the way we find our mates, and in the process, created an exciting, new world of opportunities for ways to make money.

It's the first time in history that any average Joe with a web site can be on equal footing and have the same presence as a multibillion-dollar corporation.

There's way too much BS about "Here's how to make millions online in your underwear."

Yes, I truly have made millions (I'm a little more modest with a pair of jeans and a T-shirt), but frankly, it's not as easy as most people might want you to believe. However, getting to an extra $500, $1,000, or even $5,000+ per month is *very* doable.

I'm not saying you won't have to work. You will. But the work you put in will keep making you money for years to come. I have a few of my "online oil well" sites that I literally have not touched since 2001 (that's six years ago) and they're still making me thousands of dollars each month. It's about leverage and putting in the hard work once instead of trading time for money!

> Truly, the internet has changed everything, and it doesn't require you to be a "techie" or incredibly smart.

Truly, the internet has changed everything, and it doesn't require you to be a "techie" or incredibly smart. I'm neither. I'm a self-proclaimed computer dunce, and I literally cannot put up my own web site if you put a gun to my head. Guess what? You don't need to—there are plenty of people who can do anything you need done. When you flip on the light switch in your house, do you care how the power gets to your home from the substation across wires in your neighborhood? Of course not! That's the same with your site. I have no idea how any of the technical stuff works—I just know whom to ask and what should happen. That's it!

With virtually no barriers to entry, a level playing field, and an investment of a few hours a week, almost anybody can make a full-time income working part-time … in fact, thousands of folks are already doing so, and I'll share their exciting stories with you right here. Or if you only want to make a few hundred dollars extra, I'll get you there, too! But who am I to teach you?

Proof That I Really "Walk My Talk" (Figures A-2 and A-3)

Only six months after starting my first web site, our daily deposits were ranging anywhere from $384.79 to $789.61:

▶	1261	11/2/2000 4:03:10 AM		0016	$764.55	A
▶	1260	11/1/2000 4:03:31 AM		0013	$449.73	A
▶	1259	10/31/2000 4:03:42 AM		0026	$759.61	A
▶	1258	10/30/2000 4:02:08 AM		0024	$789.61	A
▶	1257	10/29/2000 4:02:13 AM		0013	$639.61	A
▶	1256	10/28/2000 4:02:20 AM		0009	$394.76	A
▶	1255	10/27/2000 4:02:15 AM		0015	$384.79	A

Now, today it's not unusual to take in $1,500 to $2,000 a day or more:

Settlement Date/Time : 22-Sep-2002 19:19:04

Payment Method	Charge Count	Charge Amount	Refund Count	Refund Amount	Total Count	Total Amount	Net Amount	Decline Count	Approval Percentage	Void Count	Void Amount	Error Count
Visa	11	USD 1,114.84	0	USD .00	11	USD 1,114.84	USD 1,114.84	1	91.67%	0	USD .00	0
MasterCard	8	USD 480.88	0	USD .00	8	USD 480.88	USD 480.88	1	88.89%	0	USD .00	0
American Express	1	USD 136.00	0	USD .00	1	USD 136.00	USD 136.00	0	100%	0	USD .00	0
Totals	20	1,731.72	0	.00	20	1,731.72	1,731.72	2	90.91%	0	.00	0

Settlement Date/Time : 08-Aug-2002 23:00:16

Payment Method	Charge Count	Charge Amount	Refund Count	Refund Amount	Total Count	Total Amount	Net Amount	Decline Count	Approval Percentage	Void Count	Void Amount	Error Count
Visa	29	USD 2,177.49	1	USD 39.97	30	USD 2,217.46	USD 2,137.52	4	88.24%	2	USD 34.00	0
MasterCard	3	USD 128.94	1	USD 39.97	4	USD 168.91	USD 88.97	1	80%	0	USD .00	0
American Express	4	USD 210.94	1	USD 29.00	5	USD 239.94	USD 181.94	0	100%	0	USD .00	0
Discover	1	USD 127.00	0	USD .00	1	USD 127.00	USD 127.00	0	100%	0	USD .00	0
Totals	37	2,644.37	3	108.94	40	2,753.31	2,535.43	5	88.89%	2	34.00	0

Figure A-2. Daily earnings from 2000 to the present

And the money has kept coming in and even increased year after year:

Transaction activity summary report for settlement batch: 23-Nov-2005 19:24:23

Transaction Volume Statistics

	Visa	MC	Disc	Totals
Charge Count:	10	5	1	16
Charge Amount:	4,849.89	367.91	504.00	5,721.80
Refund Count:	0	0	0	0
Refund Amount:	0.00	0.00	0.00	0.00
Total Count:	10	5	1	16
Net Amount:	4,849.89	367.91	504.00	5,721.80

Figure A-3. Transaction volume statistics

Figure A-3 shows documented daily deposits from one of our accounts. And all this is actual money that was deposited in my account automatically from my web site while I was sleeping, working on other projects, or just hanging out. (Now, keep in mind that these amounts are gross figures, not net figures, but I do have a *very* healthy profit margin with an extremely low overhead that I'll explain to you in the next chapter.)

Of course the money is great, but there's actually a much bigger benefit to having an online business that runs itself almost on autopilot—and that is the freedom of living the "internet lifestyle."

Now I have the time to do pretty much whatever I want to ...

Time to have fun ...

I go play beach volleyball, work out at the gym, paint, or goof off whenever I want. The internet pays for my wild adventures from bungee-jumping, Baja racing, zero-G flights, and rafting to exotic car rallies and more.

Actually, most of my friends still wonder how I'm driving around in a brand new Aston Martin and how my wife, Missy, and I can take off for so many trips. In fact, the most recent ones that come to mind are Hawaii, Australia, New Zealand, Italy, a Caribbean cruise, Aruba, and we even spent

Introduction

2½ months living on the beach in California where we rented a house and brought only our laptops. All this while my web sites kept pouring out orders and putting more money into the bank account.

Plus, now that I'm a father, I have time to watch my son, Zak, grow up. I get to witness every little moment, from his first real smile to his very first steps. I'm usually one of the few dads who regularly show up to his "My Gym" class.

It's truly about having more options in your life, like one of my Underground™ Millionaire MasterMind members, Mike Oshsner, shared with me:

> In a nutshell, the best part of internet marketing for me isn't all the neat stuff that's happening right now. The best part is that four years ago, I was able to drop everything and go to Colorado to be a volunteer mountain climbing guide at a church camp. Over the course of the summer, I helped 600 kids rappel a 180-foot cliff, learn rock climbing, backpack for a week at a time, summit 14,000-foot peaks, and straighten out a lot of their lives. The amazing thing is that I was able to do all of this while running my business 30–60 minutes a day from my PDA phone with no office and no employees.

I stumbled onto all this by accident back in February of 2000. My first site (still making money hand over fist) is called Instant Sales Letters. Just last month it brought in $18,732.37 (Figure A-4).

Combined, all my web sites raked in over $3 million last year. Don't worry if you can't relate to that kind of number yet, because I started off small. My first site brought in about $1,800 in the first month and then roughly $3,400 in the second month … and finally grew to a solid six figures over time.

I have web sites on all sorts of subjects, from fitness to artistic techniques to business subjects to houseplants and more. Even my wife sells a "thank-you letter" product that started making her money within one week of putting it up. All these are just additional, passive "online oil wells." I only started teaching my techniques based on what I've done, and I've helped students all over the globe sell their ideas online and achieve the

Version 2.12

Total Product Sales

March 01, 2007 through March 31, 2007
(Important Note about this Report)

Product ID	Product Name	Total Quantity	Gross Sales	GS + S/H	Commission	Net Sales
ISL1	Instant Sales Letters	96	$3837.12	$3789.12	$867.36	$2969.76
ISLG	Instant Sales Letters Gold	149	$8190.53	$8190.53	$1776.38	$6414.15
ISLGU	Instant Sales Letter Gold Upgrade	1	$15.00	$15.00	$7.50	$7.50
ISLHCP	Instant Sales Letters and Headline Creator Pro	20	$1539.40	$1539.40	$493.78	$1045.62
ISLHCPG	Instant Sales Letters Gold and Headline Creator Pro	56	$5150.32	$5246.32	$1385.78	$3764.54
	Grand Totals	322	$18732.37	$18780.37	$4530.80	$14201.57

Figure A-4. Total product sales for Instant Sales Letters

excitement and financial freedom the internet can provide, making themselves six, seven, or even eight figures online.

As Andrew Koblick, who teaches guitar lessons online (**www.guitar5day.com**) says:

In ten months I sold more than 1,000 copies of my product! My site is now in the top 2 percent of site traffic according to alexa.com. I now have several super affiliates sending me orders every day. I control my life instead of a "boss." I now have time for my children. But I will be truthful. I have only gotten around to using about 10 percent of your ideas. The reason: I started getting orders immediately! In the three years while all of my other investments were free falling, this was the best investment that turned into $24,000!! And this year I plan on doing $100,000 in sales! ... I am rolling out my Amazing Guitar 2.0 this month and estimate I will bring in over $40,000 using five simple e-mails. And now I can also spend time with friends and family, because I know my automated business that Yanik has helped me produce has the power to grow. I have made over $275,000 in about three years! That's amazing for a business that runs itself. Talk about freedom. Thanks, Yanik!

Introduction

Or Fernando Cruz, who is selling salsa lessons online (**www.salsa-rhythms.com**):

> I get about 80,000–100,000 visitors a month. Frankly, I can't even put a number on it for future earnings, but as of the last two years I would say we have earned a solid $300,000. Well, today I own property in two states. I've got a beautiful wife and a baby daughter. In the last two years we've been on five vacations. We've been to Mexico, the Dominican Republic, and Fiji. We each have our own car, plus a nice SUV for the baby. But most importantly, neither my wife nor I have to miss a single event in our baby's life, because we can now both stay at home.

It's exactly these kinds of life-changing stories that get me so excited! I could easily retire from teaching internet marketing and live very comfortably from my sites. The thing is, you will *not* see me on endless road trips pitching my products to audiences around the world. I rarely speak and only when I want to. I don't need to make my money by selling my "How to Make Money on the Internet" information from stage, and I'd be wary of those whose only success is in that area. The reason I still teach is because I love being able to hear from successful students around the globe.

Talking to so many people, I realized that banking hundreds of thousands of dollars online might be a real stretch for some. They wanted something to bring in a few hundred extra dollars without being a computer geek, and they wanted to do it in their spare time.

In fact, in one shape or another, I get this same question asked hundreds of times. Take a look at a few actual e-mails from my inbox over the last few days (yes, these are all from real people, but I've removed their names so as not to embarrass anyone):

> I've read the letter that you wrote on how to make money on the internet. My question is what if you have nothing to sell. I'm a mother of 5 girls, and I've been laid off because of my disability. I want to make enough money so my husband doesn't have to work all the time. We live in a small farm town, and there is nothing I can work at around here. In most of the post I read about where the person had something to write about, but what if you don't. Can you help me? Now your site has me intrigued.

Introduction

> So, with not much money, but tons of enthusiasm, no writing skills, and cannot figure out what to sell online, what would you suggest I try with all the things you sell? I am 45 years old and sick of the rat race. I am broke, deep in debt, but I know I can succeed; it's in my head and heart. Please show me the way to make big bucks so I can get out of debt, out of the rat race by making a living online, and then help others too. Thanks very much for your time and any help. Please advise which of your items to start with.

> I am 72 years old and would like to make some real money on a home-based program. I joined xxxxMall and have made some progress. However, it isn't the easiest thing they promised it would be. Are you involved with xxxxMall in any way?
>
> Would you, since you've made it, literally "hold my hand" and help me get my web site, and then how to set it up, and then show me how to promote it and what the attendant costs might be?

> For some time now, I have wanted to get a business going on the internet. I need your help. My problem is that there are too many products, and I have no experience in building a page or anything like that. I also don't at this time have a product in mind to sell, although I do think that some kind of information product is what I will sell.
>
> My question to you is if I have a limited budget and need a detailed road map right from step one—how do I start?

Do these stories sound familiar?

I've talked to so many people who have told me something like this: "I don't need to make millions online like you have—just show me how to make a few hundred dollars extra."

That's how the idea for this book developed.

Now I know my way (Moonlighting Method #1—Selling Digitally Delivered Information) works, since I'm living proof along with the hundreds and hundreds of success stories I've helped create. But I also know

Introduction

that one way isn't right for everyone, although having more choice for the sake of more choice is a big mistake. Of course, I could have created a "237 Ways to Make Money Online" book, but that would never fly. Probably 219 of them are mostly worthless ways such as "get paid to surf," "get paid to read e-mails," or "get paid to pick your nose." That's pure, unadulterated crap! Sadly, some people fall for it.

Here are the criteria I used for a real "Moonlighting Online" business:

- **Moonlighting Business Criterion #1: HUGE DEMAND.** For any business to be successful, it must have a product that someone wants and needs. The internet has made it possible for someone in the middle of Kansas to sell their product to someone who is looking for it in Tokyo, Japan.

- **Moonlighting Business Criterion #2: NO NEED TO BOTHER YOUR FRIENDS.** Who wants to bug their friends with their newest money-making scheme? (None of that here!)

- **Moonlighting Business Criterion #3: NO INVENTORY.** Do you really want to fill up your garage, your basement, or half your bedroom with a bunch of products that no one will buy? No way.

- **Moonlighting Business Criterion #4: NO EMPLOYEES.** Avoid the cost, the hiring headaches, the training ... enough said.

- **Moonlighting Business Criterion #5: RESIDUAL INCOME.** You do the work one time and get paid over and over again. No trading time for dollars.

- **Moonlighting Business Criterion #6: LOW COST & LOW RISK.** One of the cheapest investments you'll ever make, and you won't carry a big risk of losing what you put in.

- **Moonlighting Business Criterion #7: LOW MAINTENANCE.** Can keep running on autopilot with minimal direct involvement.

- **Moonlighting Business Criterion #8: DON'T HAVE TO BE SUPER-TECH-NICAL.** If you have basic computer skills, you can still do this.

- **Moonlighting Business Criterion #9: REAL BUSINESS.** Has the potential to turn into a substantial and lucrative business.

Introduction

Truth is, in most businesses it's hard to find even three or four of these together—but as many as all nine, that's something else! And actually, I've got one more criterion I haven't added to the list, and that's my most important one: IS IT FUN?

There you have it! When I narrowed down the list of ways to truly profit online, I had a very short list. Then I decided to rule out any fad, anything based solely on technology, or anything with an unproven track record.

That left four other ways to moonlight online. As I wasn't an expert in these four other ways, I called on the real experts in these fields and asked for their help. These are guys and gals who are actually "doing it" and talking about it like I do. I told them to pretend they were sitting down with you for a beer and explain how you could get to $500/month as quickly as possible. Each one has a unique style and twist, but it all gets you to the same spot. Review each method and see which one feels right for you.

Maybe it's selling other people's products or services as an affiliate …

Perhaps it's selling on eBay …

How about hard products that are drop-shipped for you from orders made on your e-commerce store?

Or it could be writing your own blog and profiting that way …

Or my personal method … the 21st-century electronic vending machine!

It doesn't matter which method you choose as long as you follow a proven road map and "recipe" to get there.

There's a revolution taking place, and there's no better time than today to start moonlighting online. You don't have to leave your job; you can easily start part time, investing a few spare hours—you just need to start!

About Yanik

Yanik Silver truly leads the ultimate "internet lifestyle" of fun, freedom, and financial independence funded by the internet. He runs his multimillion-dollar business out of his house with zero employees except his wife, Missy.

He is recognized as the leading expert on creating automatic, money-making web sites . . . and he's only been online full time since February 2000. He's been featured on the cover of *Millionaire Blue Prints* magazine, inside Business 2.0, *TIME*, About.com, Staples.com, Internet.com, the *Denver Business Journal*, and others.

Yanik's friends were rolling on the floor laughing when he told them he was going to put up a web site. And they had every right to be amused, since he had absolutely no web site design skills, zero HTML or coding knowledge … in fact, not much computer "know-how" whatsoever (still doesn't). He's a self-proclaimed computer dunce, but that didn't stop him from going ahead with the simple two-page web site idea he got at three o'clock in the morning. That site was www.instantsalesletters.com, and the flood of orders hasn't stopped since.

Starting from his one-bedroom apartment with just $1,800 invested, Yanik has personally made over $10 million online and counting from e-books on fitness, drawing techniques, and houseplants to $20,000+ "MasterMind" programs. After hearing of his success, students from all around the world began asking Yanik to share his inside secrets. Now they've gone on to sell tens of millions in nearly every type of market on the internet, from potty training to guitar to salsa dancing lessons. He drives more traffic to his sites than huge multinational conglomerates.

He is the author, co-author, or publisher of several best-selling online marketing books and tools. Yanik is also the creator of the new Underground™ Online Marketing Seminar, which brings in under-the-radar success stories to share information about how people are profiting online.

Personally, Yanik gets his thrills from any kind of extreme activity he can find. He's taken part in the Running of the Bulls, bungee-jumping, sky-

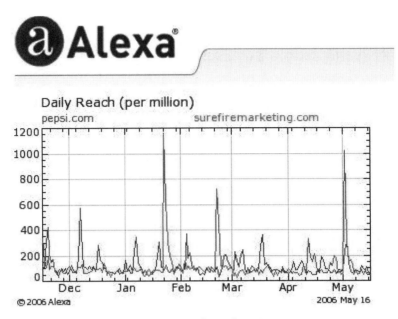

Figure A-5. Measurement of traffic at one of Yanik's sites

diving, Baja racing, exotic road rallies, zero-G flights, and more, document-ing it at www.internetroadtrip.com. But his biggest extreme activity is rais-ing his two-year-old son, Zak.

About Robert Olic

Robert Olic is the co-founder of moonlightingontheinternet.com.

In 1996, Robert stumbled onto the world of direct response marketing by accident when he discovered that he could mail letters and get back money in the mail. This led to his total immersion in the field, and he quickly became a sought-after marketing expert.

Robert is a former director of marketing for the Small Business Development Center at the Wharton School of Business, where he was exposed to businesses in just about every industry and every phase of devel-opment. There he developed a passion for working with small businesses and driven entrepreneurs.

He is now a marketing consultant helping his clients with results-driven copywriting and cutting-edge marketing strategies through www.extremeprofitsmarketing.com. Clients typically pay a fee plus a percentage of increase in business or equity interest and sometimes wait several months to get access to Robert.

Aside from sharing some business interests, Robert is also a thrill-seeker and shares Yanik's propensity for extreme activities such as bungee-jumping, skydiving, Baja racing, zero-G flights, etc.

Moonlighting on the Internet Method #1

)

Section 1

Selling Digitally Delivered Information

Chapter 1

Creating "Digitally Delivered Information Products"

Did you know that 92 percent of what everyone searches for on the internet is information?

For those of you who like numbers, that works out to about 200 million searches per day for anything from what's the weather like to how to build a treehouse to how to get a stain out of your carpet. It could be anything, really.

Now, if we know that there are people (lots of them) looking for information, might it make sense that some of them are willing to pay for that information? You betcha!

I create what I call "Digitally Delivered Information Products."

Let me give you a simple example of what happens on my web site so you'll get the idea. To start with, a visitor comes to my site and he'll read my homemade web site. Then, once he decides to order, he'll click over to my order page and give me his credit card number. That credit card is processed in real time to make sure it is valid, and after it's approved, the customer accesses my digitally delivered product. Once the money is deposited in my account, I get an e-mail confirmation of the order. Simple, right?

Did you catch what I left out? Exactly. No personal involvement on my part. My computer and systems I've set up handle everything on complete autopilot. Trust me, it's very cool when you wake up to more money in your bank account than when you went to bed.

Seven Reasons Why a Digital Information Product Is the Best Way to Build Your Fortune on the Net

Reason #1

You have no competition. Everything you sell is copyright-protected, so you can't be "knocked off." If you manufacture a product, someone can knock it off in a few weeks, but information is unique and you are legally protected.

Reason #2

Incredibly huge profit margins. People aren't paying for bits and bytes; they are paying you for the value of the information. With a digitally delivered or downloadable product, your profit margin is nearly 100 percent. (Actually, it's about 97 percent, because you'll pay 3 percent to your merchant account provider to be able to let customers use their credit cards.) Now compare that to any giant online retailer who can only compete on price and ekes out a slim single-digit profit margin.

Reason #3

You can work from anywhere you wish. It doesn't matter if you're playing beach volleyball in Aruba or skiing in the Rockies (like I frequently do). You can run your digital information site from any place where you can find an internet connection. My family and I typically head to Aruba for the week of Thanksgiving, and during the last trip, $12,352.89 was deposited in my account. I didn't even bring my laptop because I could use any random internet café to run my business. Or a few years back my wife, Missy, and I decided to go off to Manhattan Beach, California. Our house is in Maryland, so this is the other side of the United States for us. We spent 2½ months there—for our trip we packed up our laptops and a couple of files and ran our business from a rented house right on the beach. We didn't skip a beat. We actually probably made more money while we were out there, surprisingly enough. It just kept running on autopilot.

> *My family and I typically head to Aruba for the week of Thanksgiving, and during the last trip, $12,352.89 was deposited in my account.*

Reason #4

You can set up your business so it works on complete autopilot. I'll be sharing with you some of the cool tools and resources I use to make your computer do all the dirty work for you.

Reason #5

No need for employees. I have absolutely zero employees (it's just Missy and I running the whole show), and I couldn't be happier not to deal with all those headaches and hassles.

Reason #6

Incredibly low start-up costs. You don't need a factory or even a storefront because you can run your business in any spare space where a computer fits. I'll tell you about how I started from a tiny one-bedroom apartment.

Reason #7

You get paid over and over again for work you do one time. Once you create your digital product, you can keep selling it over and over again. It's now been seven years since I started my first web site, and I've only updated the site about four or five times. It's been years since I just touched it, and the orders keep coming and coming!

> *Once you create your digital product, you can keep selling it over and over again.*

By now you might be thinking …

"But Everything's Free on the Internet—So How Could I Possibly Sell Information?"

Not exactly. There is plenty of information available for free on the internet, but the problem becomes information overload and lack of time. Believe me, people will gladly pay for information that will save them time and money searching around. How do I know? Easy—people buy from our sites every single day of the year (even during the Christmas and New Year season).

It's easier than you think, especially when you see what you don't need.

Here's What You Don't Need to Get Started

◆ **Lots of money to design your site.** Nearly anyone can design a simple two-page web site for you if you can't do it yourself. (Because I didn't know any HTML, I paid for my site to be designed—but with the easy web design tools available now, you could be up and running for a couple hundred bucks.)

◆ **Lots of time.** I only work a couple of hours a week in the business, so this is the perfect home-based business to start with even if you're working at a full-time job.

◆ **An idea.** I'll share lots of easy ways to brainstorm a great project idea. In fact, it's better if you don't have an idea, because that way you can locate a hungry market first, which is more important. Plus, I'll even give exact details on how you can tap into the incredible repository of public domain information available for anyone to pillage. (One of my friends told me in confidence about a public domain manual put out by the government that he repackaged and sold to the tune of an extra $250,000 in revenue!)

◆ **Lots of free content.** Trust me on this one. My web site is a simple two-page site because I didn't have time to create lots of free content like many experts advise you to do. You don't need it—in fact, in many cases it even hurts your sales.

◆ **Lots of money to advertise.** I'll show in exact detail how I've managed to drive thousands and thousands of visitors to my site using free and very low-cost marketing methods. In fact, one of my favorite secrets is setting up a whole network of hundreds, even thousands of sites all selling your product. And the best part is that you only pay these resellers when they make a sale. (Therefore, it's zero out-of-pocket expense until a sale is made and the money is already in your bank account.)

> *... one of my favorite secrets is setting up a whole network of hundreds, even thousands of sites all selling your product. And the best part is that you only pay these resellers when they make a sale.*

Frankly, there are so many hyped-up "get rich quick" schemes floating around the internet—it drives me crazy! You'll find all kinds of people running around touting themselves as internet "experts," making wild claims about how easy it is to become the next internet millionaire.

Yeah, right.

I say, "*Put your money where your mouth is.*" Let all of us see what you are selling on the internet that isn't "how to get rich quick on the internet."

Sadly, I don't think you could find many takers for this challenge.

But that's exactly what I've done. I've been making money hand-over-fist on the internet. In my first 6½ months going at it haphazardly, I banked $51,351.94, working part time out of the corner of my living room. Now I've refined the process I use. I've honed it down to a science.

How about Multiple Web Sites Funneling Money into Your Bank Account?

At this moment I have 14 different internet profit centers (or "online oil wells," as my friend Bill is fond of calling them) that crank out cash day-in, day-out.

But do you know what my biggest problem is?

Telling you about my proven internet strategies and techniques (and what kind of lifestyle it can give you) without sounding like some shady rip-off artist! Listen, I'm not going to BS you and insult your intelligence by telling you how I make $25,000 a day in my underwear. I'm going to give it to you straight.

Yes, I've made millions each year online, but I also started out small like you probably will. My first month online, I made $1,830.00; month #2 added up to $2,725.45, and month #3 grew to $4,714.37. But even more exciting than my own success is the success of my students, who have gone on to build part-time and full-time incomes selling information in every conceivable field. My students have succeeded in these subject areas:

> *My first month online, I made $1,830.00; month #2 added up to $2,725.45, and month #3 grew to $4,714.37.*

- ◆ Self-Help
- ◆ Fitness
- ◆ Natural Medicine
- ◆ Music Lessons
- ◆ Sports

- Multi-level Marketing (MLM)
- Child Development
- Business-to-Business Training
- Cars
- Investing
- Business
- Professionals
- New Age Development
- Dieting
- Dancing
- Dating/Relationships
- Real Estate
- Pet Training and Care
- And lots more that I'll be sharing with you!

Okay, let's get to it …

What Is Information Marketing?

In simplest terms, information marketing is what it sounds like: the marketing of information. To get your brainstorming started, let's talk about different formats you can use to deliver information over the web.

1. E-books. An e-book is an electronic book. Most of the time it's delivered as a PDF file. It works like a regular book, but you download it and read it on your computer or print it.

2. Membership Sites. Access to a private membership site protected by a password. This is where people either pay a one-time fee, where it could be $30, $40, $50, or whatever it is, perhaps $100, and they get the membership site for life. Or, a really cool way is where people will pay every single month. The fee could be $14.95 a month or $29.95 a month or any other amount. The great thing about that is that you get paid every single month. So you get 100 members paying you $30 a month; pretty soon that will add up to some good money.

And the sky's the limit on membership sites. My good friend, Ryan Lee, is an ex-gym teacher who put up a simple site a few years back and realized he didn't have to teach kids in the Bronx anymore. Today, he's making over six figures each month, but he started off small:

Moonlight on Ryan Lee

Ryan's Moonlighting Story

I got started in October 1998 when I built a simple web site with fitness articles to promote my personal training business. Before Moonlighting, I had long, grueling hours. Trained my first client at 7 a.m., then went to my full-time job until 5 p.m., after which I trained another two or three clients until 7 p.m. And at the same time I took night classes for my master's degree in exercise physiology.

Today, I run almost 100 different web sites. I have 45 paid membership sites, a nutritional supplement company, and dozens of books, DVDs, CDs, and information products. I have well over 12,000 active subscribers and customers. I'm married and have two beautiful daughters. I no longer set my alarm clock. I have my own office and I'm home by 5 P.M.—at the lat-

www.RyanLee.com

est. We take a lot of vacations and we live comfortably in a house worth almost 2 million dollars. But the most important part for me is the ability to spend more time with my family. And I no longer have to worry if I can afford to travel or eat at an expensive restaurant for dinner.

Ryan's Advice

My "aha" moment came when I realized that people would pay for my information on the internet. It was amazing to help so many people and create passive revenue at the same time. It gave me the confidence to put more programs out there and declare myself an expert. I continue to educate myself and NEVER rest on my laurels. If you have an idea—don't overanalyze it. Just TAKE ACTION TODAY!

3. Templates/Tools. These are premade tools and templates for people to use right away. You can sell templates and tools, and that's one of the first things that I sold with my **instantsalesletters.com** site. There you could find fill-in-the-blank sales letter templates. This is one of the best things to sell, because everybody is lazy and everybody wants a shortcut, and everybody wants it done for them.

We live in the instant microwave age, so the better you can make it for people so they can fill in a couple of blanks, the more perceived value your product has and the more likely it will sell.

Now, I don't know if you remember this, and I don't even know if any companies still do this, but buying a product and seeing the little thing on the bottom that says "Please allow four to eight weeks for delivery"—well, nowadays, this particular thing won't fly.

Even my wife has her own web site selling templates. I'm telling you, this stuff is easy. She makes an extra $500, $600, $700 a month. Her site is called **instantthankyouletters.com**. She told me one night, "I want my own product out there. But I want the checks going out to me." She wrote some thank-you letters and we hired some people off of **elance.com** to write some letters. Then we created this product, which sells fairly well month-in, month-out for $14.95.

She loves going to the mailbox when these checks come twice a month. That's her extra shopping money and she can do whatever she wants with it.

4. Newsletter. Deliver your newsletter content online to a subscriber-only area of your web site.

I like to fly first-class as much as I can, but I don't always like to pay the first-class fees. So I subscribe to an online newsletter called First Class Flyer by Mathew Bennett, who shows me how to get great deals with my frequent flyer miles and in other ways. He keeps abreast of all of the deals that the web sites are running, and so on. He doesn't even really have that much of his own original content. A lot of it is only research. What's the cool deal on Air New Zealand this month? Or what's the best deal United is running this month? It costs $100 a year, but it saves me more than that.

5. Directories. You can sell access to useful directories of information people are looking for. In Part Two on eBay, we'll introduce you to a regular guy doing extremely well who created a directory of drop-shippers that eBay sellers could use. He's done a lot of research and compiled the best drop-shippers for all kinds of products.

> *In Part Two on eBay, we'll introduce you to a regular guy doing extremely well who created a directory of drop-shippers that eBay sellers could use.*

6. Audio Files/Mp3s. Deliver audio content to paying customers over the web. You can also sell audio online via mp3s. Look at one of the biggest ones, Apple with **itunes.com** that supports their iPod. They sell songs for 99¢ each. It doesn't cost them 99¢, obviously, to sell a song. And they can sell as many of those as they want. So digital downloads of audio or even music are really possible. Very easy to do that.

7. Online Learning. Provide valuable learning advice to students, anytime, anywhere. One of the cool tools that has come out recently is something called Camtasia. This application lets you record everything that's going on on your computer, including your voice. You just have to have a microphone. And you can walk people through all kinds of things on their computers, from a piece of software to teaching them via PowerPoint. For example, you could be teaching them how to use Microsoft Word, and you have these Camtasia videos that go into all aspects of using Microsoft Word. People will pay you for that. One of my friends did this with Photoshop and is doing quite well.

8. Software. Can be a little more complicated to produce, but still fits our model. You can also create software. There are lots of ways to create software, and even if you're not a techie-type person, you can do it yourself. There are places such as **rent-a-coder.com** and **elance.com**, where you can hire someone to write a piece of software for you.

In the following pages, I'll introduce you to some real-world moonlighters who will share their own information marketing success stories to inspire you.

I may be biased, but I think that this is the best business in the world. I don't know any other business with such incredible profit potential and such low time and money requirements . . . and most importantly, one that can be done part-time.

Here's How I Stumbled onto This Weird Little World of Information Marketing

When I got started, I had a regular job. I was working, selling medical equipment, and I was working with a lot of doctors. One type of specialist that I did a lot of work with was dermatologists. So, I was talking to some of my dermatologist clients and they were explaining their business to me and told me how they really wanted to get more patients to do cosmetic procedures. And I thought, "Well, I've learned a lot about marketing, maybe I can help you."

So I started doing a little bit of freelance, actually consulting, with a particular dermatologist, and my methods worked well. I decided I could make a little bit of money working one-on-one with the dermatologists, but what if there were some way I could package it all up and sell it to doctors all across the country to help them build their practices?

And that's what I did. I bumbled along and turned what I did for my client into a manual. You might not believe this, and you might want to be sitting down—it sold for about $900 per package. Really. It was just a three-ring binder full of information that was intended to help them get more cosmetic patients.

I put together a little classified ad that cost me about $50 to run in the *Dermatologic Surgery Journal* saying something like "Free report reveals the secrets to exploding your cosmetic practice," and told people to call a 1-800 number. I got 10 doctors to respond and I sent them a long sales letter explaining my program that I was selling for $900. It was a package consisting of everything I was teaching this other doctor. At that time, I didn't have the package done, just the sales letter and an outline! I sent the letter, and nobody responded. I sent another letter to those 10 people 10 days later. Nobody responded. I sent another notice seven days later with a deadline that was prominent on the order form. Literally, the last day of the deadline, finally, while standing over the fax machine, I heard this ring followed by the familiar tones and the mechanics of the fax being printed.

A fax came in with an order for $900!

I started jumping up and down for joy. I was, like, "Yes! I can't believe someone finally ordered one of these!" And then I realized I had to put together this package! For the next three weeks I worked until 2 or 3 o'clock in the morning getting this manual together. I ran that business selling to the doctors and cosmetic surgeons out of a one-bedroom apartment. (I know it sounds like an infomercial, but this is true!)

> *I was, like, "Yes! I can't believe someone finally ordered one of these!" And then I realized I had to put together this package!*

That was before we moved to the house that we're in now. It didn't even take up any room. I kept it all in a tiny bit of a closet, where I had a couple of original copies of the manuals. And when I got an order, I walked down to my local printer and said, "Hey, make this, make this and make this by tomorrow."

Moonlighting on the Internet

Pretty soon it got to the point where I was making more money selling this kit than I was at my regular job, and I decided to quit. Shortly after, in late 1999, I could see people selling legitimate products online, such as e-books—products with no delivery cost and no product cost. People paid for it with their credit cards and downloaded the product right there. I became completely enamored of that business model.

I firmly believe that the types of questions you ask dictate the kind of results you get. I asked myself, *"How do I create a fully automatic web site that provides an incredible value and makes me money while I sleep?"*

I wanted to create something that worked on autopilot and made money regardless of where I was in the world. I also wanted to provide incredible value.

I literally woke at three in the morning and it came to me. I poked at my wife and said, "Missy, Missy, get up! I've got the idea!" I always have ideas, like any entrepreneur. She said, "Just go back to sleep." And I said, "No, no. This is going to be great ... Instant Sales Letters®!"

I jumped out of bed, registered the domain **www.instantsalesletters.com**, and got to work. I created some simple "fill-in-the-blank" sales letter templates for any kind of business. Let's say you need a sales appointment. You click on the appointment letter, and you've got a couple of letters to choose from, each with spots where you fill in the blank for the benefits of the product you're selling. The package reduces it to simple formulas that I've tested.

I remember the first e-mail coming in that told me I had $29 in my inbox. It was one of the best feelings in the world. And an even better feeling is waking up and looking in your e-mailbox and instead of having spam and dumb jokes from your friends, you have little notices that people had paid for something from you, given you a credit card or a PayPal payment, anything like that, and purchased your product and self-serviced themselves.

The money is waiting for you in the bank account, and you didn't have to do anything. You don't have to go wait in line at the bank.

The money is waiting for you in the bank account, and you didn't have to do anything. You don't have to go wait in line at the bank.

All I can tell you is that once you experience orders (and money) coming in like this, you'll feel like it is Christmas every day!

Now, I know what you are thinking: If I go online and I start doing searches, everything is free online. So why would anyone pay for information? That's a great question, and I agree, there's so much stuff online that's free. But here's what I say: "Free sucks!"

And the reason I say that is this: Try going to the bank and depositing free. Say, "Oh, I give away free information on my web site." See if they'll let you deposit that in your bank account. I don't think that will happen. But seriously, this misconception that so much stuff is free and that nobody will pay for anything is absolutely not true.

Trust me, people will pay for information that's readily available to them. I know of one marketer who sold information to people about how to collect from Social Security at any age. This information was hidden away in some government publication that most people didn't know about. So he showed them how to find out this information, and they bought it—even though anyone could have done the research and found out for free.

Or how about **consumerreports.com**? They actually have over a half-million people paying them $5 every month to get their ongoing consumer reports information, like what's the best TV, washing machine, or whatever. That's some pretty regular information. You could find that on **epinions.com** or some other sites that provide people's feedback and research. But **consumerreports.com** has over 500,000 people who are paying them $5 a month. That's pretty good money. That's $2.5 million a month, I believe, if my math is correct.

In my case, there are a lot of people giving away free sales letters and advice on direct mail, and different things like that. But most of the time, that information is pretty poor quality. So you want to have something better, and it's not that hard to do. One other thing to keep in mind is that if you worry that people are still concerned about so much free information, the thing is that people are in information overload. So they'll pay for solutions, ones that will let them have quick solutions to their problems.

> *… people are in information overload. So they'll pay for solutions, ones that will let them have quick solutions to their problems.*

Now, some of my sites bring in a couple hundred dollars a month, but I have a whole conglomerate of sites making me really good money. You are probably saying to yourself, "That's all fine and good, but I am just starting out and I don't know what to sell, or where to even look for ideas!" No worries; I believe everybody has useful information they can share, and it is just a matter of uncovering it.

Chapter 3

Top Seven
Information Topics

I want you to focus on something you can sell over and over again for many years, so don't look for the next fad. Here are seven big moneymaking topics:

1. How to. "How To" is one of the best sellers. If you know how to do anything—if you know how to fix your bathroom sink and make sure it stops leaking forever—that would sell. "How To" is great.

There are over 7,000 books in print with titles starting with "How To," and there's a reason for that. It's because "How To" books sell! Also, if you start with "How To" in the title, you are almost forced to put a benefit after that.

Moonlight on Lee Cornell

Lee's Moonlighting Story

I started on the internet in 1997 ... I have had a lifelong love for the art of ventriloquism, and even though I knew this was a very small niche market, it was a project and subject I was passionate about. I think I sold 25 videos the first year I was online for $29.95 each, but that was OK. It was just kind of for fun. I had no shopping cart or merchant account, which I did add quickly as soon as I realized that I was selling some of these, and I only had a one-page web site that looked like crap.

www.ventriloquism101.com

Today, after ten years and using ideas I've learned from Yanik, Dave Dee, Dan Kennedy, and others who are real experts and pioneers in direct and info marketing, my site is consistently in the top five for the keyword ventriloquism on Google. I average 12,000 page views per month, which is a lot for the small market ventriloquism is. There aren't a million people a week wanting to learn how to make a piece of wood talk. My one core product, "The Ventriloquism 101 Video Course," sells around 300 copies per year at $97 a pop … I have used the bonus technique and added a lot of free bonuses to the course that cost me hardly anything, but really pump up the perceived value of the course. My little one-page sales letter with my one video has turned into a large web site that now additionally offers other books, DVDs, puppets, and dummies. I started a blog about six months ago and also implemented a newsletter opt-in form on my home page, which now has about 600 subscribers. Am I getting rich from my web site? No. But it's a really nice additional income that totaled around $35,000 last year, and because these techniques I have learned from Yanik and others will work for any online business, I know I can replicate this again with other products … Heck, if I can sell a fair amount of products to such a small market as ventriloquists, I sure could sell many other products!

I still work my day job as I continue to try and come up with ways to replicate the success I've had with my small niche ventriloquism web site, but it generates enough to have allowed my wife to cut back on her work hours. It has given us money for nicer vacations and it allows me to purchase a lot of the toys I want, such as guitars, new dummies, electronics, etc., without having to dip into our job money. I'm not as worried about someday leaving my corporate job. It's actually my goal, as I know I can succeed online and offline with what I know now.

Lee's Advice

For me it was important knowing that I had an area of knowledge that very few people had any idea of and knowing that there would be people interested in learning how to be a ventriloquist. I used a subject I was interested in, which made it fun and easy to market. I also realized that I needed to invest in marketing knowledge to help me sell my product. I found a product first that I knew would sell even though I knew the market would be small and took action to create the video course and then market it. The biggest "aha" moment that made me realize this would work was when I got my first order … Seeing results from your marketing efforts and cash coming in is such a rush and really makes you want to keep moving forward.

2. Self-Help/Relationships. There are lots of people wanting to improve themselves. Topics you see in the "Self-Help" section of your bookstore are good sellers—anything from goal setting to self-hypnosis to relationship advice.

Moonlight on Debby Hirschhorn, Ph.D.

Dr. Hirschhorn's Moonlighting Story

I absolutely didn't have a clue how to use the internet to market. I am a family therapist and therapists are notoriously bad businesspeople. I was no exception. But my husband (a.k.a. my research assistant) kept pushing me to buy this book by this guy named Yanik, so finally I did.

www.abuse-recovery-and-marriage-counseling.com

I launched my web site, and here's a key point: I never took insurance, so my entire living was going to come from this one web site! And it did! I went from making $20,000 per year to $60,000 to well over $80,000—all because of the traffic at my web site. For the years 2000–2005, I was either #1, #2, or #3 on Google for the keywords *marriage counseling*. At present, I am #7 on Yahoo! for the keywords *verbal abuse*. My spot has shifted down, but I'm working to get it back up. Three years ago, I wrote an e-book that I put up on my web site, and I recently put a second one up. These books have been bringing me an extra $800/month—and that's without affiliates! I used to have the wrong idea that therapists cannot have affiliates. What nonsense! My goal is to have more income from the internet than from my private practice.

Before Moonlighting Online, we struggled for years. We even lost our house. I cried because I didn't have airfare to visit my children out of town. My husband was disabled and went through a serious operation at that time, so he not only couldn't help, but he also relied on me. It was horrible, and I don't want to look back. Today we are paying our bills, and my husband and I can travel to see our children and grandchildren. In addition, one child studies in Israel and we can pay for him to come back and forth. We just made a wedding for our second child. But even more important than all this, I can see a future where I can both radically multiply my income and disseminate my ideas to large numbers of people.

Dr. Hirschhorn's Advice

My husband kept nagging and nagging: "You're smart! You can do it! You SHOULD do it! Just read what this Yanik guy says, will you?" I truly didn't see myself as BIG, at least not back then. It was only last year when I sat down to do my income taxes that I realized I had grown in more ways than can be indicated by a dollar figure: Yes, that dollar figure was nice, but more significantly, I saw my potential for it to be even nicer. I feel blessed and grateful to God for a nagging husband!

3. Financial. Money and financial topics are another evergreen best seller. There are lots of top titles with the word "millionaire" in them. *The Millionaire Next Door* and *The Millionaire's Mindset* are two. Readers are always looking for ways to increase their revenues. It could also be something related to financial savings.

Moonlight on Wayne Davies

Wayne's Moonlighting Story

In January 2003, I started selling an e-book I wrote called *The Tax Reduction Toolkit: 29 Little-Known Loopholes That Will Reduce Your Taxes by Thousands for Small Business Owners and Self-Employed People Only*. I had written this as a regular offline book in fall 2002, but didn't have a clue how to get it published. So I started reading e-books by Yanik Silver, Jim Edwards, and Joe Vitale that explained how to market a book online as a digital information product at a fraction of the cost of getting a book published offline. I'm not a tech-savvy person at all. But I read Yanik's, Jim's, and Joe's e-books and literally followed the directions as if I were reading a recipe and doing exactly what it says to do on the back of the box. And much to my amazement, it worked!

Today I spend very little time on my online business—maybe two or three hours a week, tops. I'm a tax accountant by trade, and most of my time is devoted to my offline business. So, for such a part-time activity, I know these numbers may be hard to believe, but I'll give them to you anyway. Over the past four years, I've sold over $70,000 worth of information products. And I've picked up quite a few new tax clients from selling the e-books—over $30,000 worth of tax consulting and tax preparation fees have been generated as a direct result of running this web site. You know, it really is unbelievable to me that a short, bald, stuttering tax accountant could make over $100K from the internet by working a few hours a week. Those numbers really do seem too good to be true, don't you think?

www.yousaveontaxes.com

Like most tax accountants, I worked hard during tax season and then didn't have that much to do the rest of the year. Now I have a steady stream of business all year-round. And I have much more control over my time. I can work as much as I want to or as little as I want to, whenever I want to.

Wayne's Advice

I'll never forget the day I sold my first e-book. It was incredible. I ran this little pay-per-click ad that drove people to my sales page and I thought, "Hmm, I wonder how long it will take before somebody actually buys my e-book." I was sure it would be weeks or even months before anyone would buy it. Man, was I ever wrong!

Within a couple of hours, a visitor to my site bought the e-book. And people have been buying it ever since. You know, the whole online sales process still boggles my mind! Another big "aha" moment was the day that Jim Edwards sent an e-mail to one of his lists promoting my e-book. I had heard about the power of joint ventures before but had never done one. Well, I found out firsthand that joint venture marketing works just as well online as it does offline—maybe even better. Within minutes of his e-mail going out, orders started coming in like crazy. It blew my mind.

---

4. Business/Moneymaking. This is pretty straightforward. Since mail order began, there have been ads and courses for how to make money doing all sorts of things. So there might be topics like how to make money sending out envelopes, how to make money as a consultant, how to make money with an answering machine, how to make money as a pharmaceutical salesperson, and so on and so forth. Information on making money has been one of the oldest and definitely most popular ways of selling information. And it could be industry-specific, like we talked about with my cosmetic surgeons and dermatologists, or it could be targeted to the masses, as is the case with topics like "How to Make Money with Your Computer."

Moonlight on Daniel Levis

Daniel's Moonlighting Story

In 2003, I started using the internet, and in the process of learning how to do that, I encountered a number of people selling e-books online that I bought and used and found useful. Well, it didn't take long for me to put two and two together and realize that this was a compelling business. I had effectively slashed my marketing costs to the bone by shifting over to the internet from direct mail, and here were these guys basically selling electrons for $30, $50, even a hundred bucks a pop with essentially no fulfillment cost whatsoever.

So I started doing it, too. It was almost too good to be true. Here was a business that I could start up for next to nothing that would allow me to immediately begin generating revenue, and aside from marketing costs, the revenue was nearly pure profit. It still blows my mind to this day, because for years I had been racking my brain looking for a business opportunity that made sense for me, but had never found anything serious that didn't involve

www.sellingtohumannature.com

forking out wads of cash to get started. The first thing I did was research the market to see who the big dogs were in the field that I was interested in. I signed up for dozens of e-mail lists that were related to the prospect I was after and that I found appealing, and started watching the marketing. I started getting to know the positioning of the various players, and in particular, some of their personal preferences and business passions. And of course, one of the people who I came across was Joe Vitale, and after getting Joe's stuff, it wasn't long before I discovered that he was a really big Robert Collier fan. So we had that in common, because I've been a fan of Robert Collier, too, and have studied him for years. So Joe and I had a common bond, even though he didn't know me from Adam. I mean, nobody knew me from Adam in the online world at the time. So I sat down over the course of a couple of weeks and put down everything I had learned about online marketing and everything I'd learned about copywriting from Robert Collier and turned it into an e-book.

Before Moonlighting, I was making good money, since I had started in corporate sales, but I hated the daily commutes and the boneheaded sales managers that I had to deal with, and most of all, I hated wearing a suit and tie. Today I've got a list of about 30,000 prospects, I'm generating close to a quarter million in sales, and I'm pulling an approximate 75 percent margin, all from home and with zero employees. I still work very hard—but I love what I do. I can get up anytime I please, work as much or as little as I like, hang out with my family all day long, and dress as I please. The difference is night and day.

Daniel's Advice

The best advice I could give to anyone interested in becoming successful in information marketing is this: First, put some serious effort into learning about marketing, sales copy, and personal selling. Those skills, more than anything else, will determine your success and your income. And second, dive in with both feet right away. The fastest way to break into this business is to just do it. Start-up costs are low, and the results can come quickly. So, in my humble opinion, like William the Conqueror in the Battle of Hastings, the best thing is to burn your bridges and go for it. There's nothing like being dependent on success to bring it to you quickly. All you need is the know-how, and it's readily available.

5. Health/Fitness/Diet. Health and fitness is a HUGE market. If you think about beauty tips, weight-loss topics, and fitness, you'll quickly realize how vast this market is. It's hard to compete against the South Beach Diets of the world—which I why I always suggest targeting a small subset market just like this success story:

Moonlight on Zach Even-Esh

Zach's Moonlighting Story

I got started in 2003 after reading a product from Ryan Lee on earning a six-figure income as a personal trainer. I was training athletes in field parking lots, backyards, and garages, using homemade stuff from Home Depot or leftovers from junkyards. I started taking pictures of all our workouts, recorded the workouts, and turned this material into an e-book in less than three weeks. It was selling four or five copies a day all over the world, with especially heavy sales in the UK. Every night I sat down and typed five to ten pages and added a few pictures. In no time at all it was finished, and I contacted a major martial arts web site to review it. They interviewed me and reviewed my book, and it took off big time in the UK! After seeing the power of publicity, I contacted the largest martial arts and strength web sites and offered to write articles and do interviews for them. Things took off quickly!

Now I have a web site and almost ten products dedicated to this style of underground training. I have a membership web site that makes $5,000 per month, plus product sales, which earn another $1,000 to 2,000 plus a month.

Before Moonlighting Online, I was a teacher, but I was heavily in debt, approximately $12,000 worth, and living at home with my parents! Now I own a home, have my own underground gym, and have a following around the world, even from countries I never heard of! I own a timeshare for three weeks right on the water in Lake George, New York. I have people consulting with me from around the world on

www.undergroundstrengthcoach.com

how to start their own underground training businesses. In 12 months' time, I plan to license my gym and methods! Last year, I also bought my first brand-new, fully loaded car ... I plan to purchase my wife a Lexus SUV soon and move to a bigger, more prestigious area in a year or two.

Zach's Advice

I never feared the word "no" and never listened to all the naysayers. I went for it every single time, and I always contacted the biggest names and offered my services and ideas! People always told me that what I was doing was crazy, that it wouldn't work, couldn't work, and I should just do it part-time. I never gave up, and every month it gets better and better! Do what you love and believe in it!

6. Skills Improvement/Training. There is a vast market for skills improvement, from vocabulary help to speed-reading and math skills. And I've seen some interesting digital learning products for school-aged children to adults.

Moonlight on Tom Haibeck

Tom's Moonlighting Story

I decided to make a book that I had previously written available online. At first it was like a mail-order business—people would send us checks, and we would mail them hard copies of the books. It was incredible to suddenly start getting checks from people throughout the world, but it was labor-intensive. That changed when we discovered the magic of e-books—and instant downloads of an electronic product through **clickbank.com**. My site is now ranked at the top of most search engines for the keywords *wedding+toast*. I'm selling roughly $1,000 a month through my e-books—with NO spamming or e-mail marketing at all. It's like money from heaven.

Before Moonlighting Online, I ran a PR firm in downtown Vancouver, BC on my own. Big overhead, lots of headaches. Constant deadlines, demanding clients, and the challenge of meeting payroll each month. It was tough. Life is a lot simpler now. I work out of my home and enjoy the commute from my kitchen table to my office ... I also get a lot of great feedback from my customers—they love the books and it's a great feeling to be able to help people shine as they overcome their fears about speaking at a wedding.

www.weddingtoasts.com

Tom's Advice

I hired a bright young lad who had just graduated from a computer science program, and asked him to build me a great web site and get it ranked at the top of the search engines—in exchange for a share of the e-book proceeds. He did it!

7. Entertainment/Travel/Lifestyle. This last topic is always popular, but I'd place a warning on it. If you are considering an entertainment project, I'd be extremely careful, because what people consider entertainment can change in an instant.

Moonlight on Mark Myszak

Mark's Moonlighting Story

Before using the internet to generate an income, I was playing cards for a living and had little time for much else. The main challenge was the fact that if I wasn't at a card table, there was no income. Setting up passive internet income has allowed for a more secure and predictable lifestyle. The relationships that are developed online are amazing in their diversity. So many talented people all over the world can communicate at literally the speed of light. My online business is focused on training aspiring poker players how to become consistent winners. We have over 2,000 active members and are building a team of aggressive tournament players.

www.smartholdempoker.com

Mark's Advice

My best piece of advice would be to take advantage of the internet as a communication medium. There are world-class experts in every area that are willing to assist in your success. Do not be intimidated to simply ask.

Chapter 4

How to Figure Out What Information to Sell

Coming up with your idea is the fun part. You should go through all your experience and knowledge and try to come up with a list of possible projects.

What do people always ask you about?

_____

_____

_____

Do you have special knowledge others would like to know?

_____

_____

_____

Have you experienced certain setbacks in life and overcome them?

_____

_____

_____

Moonlighting on the Internet

Have you succeeded in a career that many people fail at?

_____

_____

_____

What subjects interest you the most?

_____

_____

_____

What hobbies do you enjoy most?

_____

_____

_____

What jobs have you held?

_____

_____

_____

What skills do you have?

_____

_____

_____

Next, I'd consider asking five close friends and/or family members and jotting down their answers to those same questions.

For instance, one of my best friends has a surefire way to pick up women on AOL Instant Messenger. I'm sure guys would pay to find out his secrets. It's amazing! I've seen it done right in front of me in about five minutes.

You should brainstorm at least 10 project ideas. Trust me—it's not that hard. Carry around a small notebook with you, and you'll be amazed at all the ideas you'll come up with. Don't evaluate them. Just write them down.

I'll give you a rundown of a couple of ideas I've had recently:

1. My stepbrother has won hundreds of thousands of dollars in government bids on medical equipment. Is there an info product out there for small-business owners?

2. John (the guy I mentioned earlier) can pick up women online. Is that a member's-only site possibility?

3. While I was talking with a friend the other day about a compilation book of the greatest headlines, he said headlines and titles are not copyrightable. So why couldn't I create an e-book filled with the greatest-selling titles of all time—perfect for any self-publisher?

4. One of my friends is a whiz with FileMaker software. I bet people would love to get an online tutorial of what he knows.

The other thing that I recommend is for you to check out what is on your own computer. That's a big source of potential information products. Maybe you're a freelancer who sells to corporations. You have all sorts of forms and letters and all sorts of marketing collateral material that other people, other freelancers, would be interested in. What if you created a course for other freelancers?

> *The other thing that I recommend is for you to check out what is on your own computer. That's a big source of potential information products.*

People will usually discount something that they do well, but don't make that mistake. It could be anything. I know of a guy who sold a video on how to build a brick fence. That's all he did—sell a one-hour video. He sold that information to libraries and worked only a couple of days a week, and was making about $65,000 a year. And then he figured that other people who have products or books or videos or whatever would be interested in knowing how to sell to libraries. He turned around and created a course for others on how to sell to libraries. So don't discount what you know. Maybe you're not the world expert on something, but as long as you know more than most people about the subject, you can create some kind of information product on it.

The key is not to sell yourself short. So any desire that somebody's got, if there's a market for it, you can make it work. Test it out and see what happens. There are lots of quirky markets with hobbyists willing to pay for information. Here's one of my favorite student success stories—Nathan Morris. He started his online information business from his college dorm and his mother accused him of drug dealing because he was making so much money. Here's his story:

Moonlight on Nathan Morris

Nathan's Moonlighting Story

In high school I grew extremely interested in cars ... I had a 1992 Honda Accord, which I thought was the neatest car ever. I became active in online discussion forums regarding the car and learned a number of ways to improve the acceleration and top speed of the car. I purchased some of my first performance upgrades as I was working two and three jobs in high school, and from then on I was hooked. In late 2003, I grew tired of working all the time and having my social life interrupted by having to be at work. To make me even angrier, I was often told when I could and couldn't work, when I could vacation, and yelled at for being two minutes late. I wanted to start a business, and what ultimately happened is I took all the write-ups I had collected over the previous two years, compiled them all on an easy-to-use CD, and sold them on eBay. I got my first order for $20 and I was absolutely thrilled. Soon enough I was selling enough CDs that I decided to expand out to other car models—so out came a CD for the Honda Civic. I carried this out well into my freshman year

www.madscienceindustries.com

of college, when I would pack my backpack up every day and ride my bike over to the post office delivering three and four packages to be shipped out. I was psyched, as I was now making $800 a month roughly, and the only thing I could think of was "do something that works and find ways to do that for more and more people," a line I pulled from a Kyosaki tape I listened to often as I was driving to and from work or school. More and more CDs were made, and soon enough I was breaking into the $1,000 range per month.

Right at the peak of my success, however, I got a nasty phone call from a guy I had never met. He wasn't too happy that I was selling a CD with some of his write-ups on it. At that point, I figured that since it was available for free online, it was okay to sell it in a big compilation. Well, I learned that wasn't the case, and that U.S. copyright law would probably not side with me on the case. I decided it was best to stop selling the CDs, and I was a little crushed at this point. However, being resilient, I decided to look over some customer feedback I had gotten over the year or so I had been in business. I noticed overwhelmingly that they bought the CD for a particular piece of information that I had actually written myself. That information was how to take a Honda Prelude engine and drop it into a Honda Accord. This is a pretty common practice, as the Honda Accord engine isn't very stout, but the Prelude engine drops right into the car and gives hot rod guys a solid platform on which to build more horsepower. I quickly drafted two versions of the book and put them into a Word document. I had just about had it with going to the post office all the time, and I had come across many information marketers such as Yanik Silver who were distributing books online. Wow, what a novel thought. I could literally put together this book one time, put it online, and with some software, have it so that people would come to my web site much like a vending machine. They'd put in a $20 bill and get out a digital copy of my book. Well, at that time I was still convinced that knowing how to program was a great benefit, so I sat down, and in my spare time, I wrote up a payment and delivery system and did all kinds of technical stuff that I don't care to bore you with. After six months, I finished the software. The book was online and almost instantly bringing in sales. If you can't already see why knowing how to do all this stuff was a hindrance, I'll get into that a little more in a just a few—hold on tight.

The interesting thing is that there is already, in fact, a lot of material that is freely available online that covers the material I cover in my books on this engine swap. You don't need to come up with something no one has ever done before, so go ahead and pull that out of your head. People pay me day in and day out to get access to my book, which I have groomed over the years into what I believe is the best resource available for this particular project. This is not my only online venture anymore, but it is currently generating a high five-figure profit for me per year. Better yet, all my hobby projects are tax-deductible as long as they are done for the purpose of creating new products or in some way related to the business itself. This is a great example of turning a hobby or interest into a viable income stream.

After several years online, I still have the Ultimate Resource Guides site selling books on engine swaps to enthusiasts around the globe day in and day out. I now also provide creative marketing solutions to other businesses. In 2006, I began a new five- to six-figure venture where I create humorous Flash games for companies to use in their marketing. I regularly produce games for Atom Entertainment, owned by MTV's **addictinggames.com**. On the side, I also have a number of one-page web sites that feature games that my team and I have produced—all of which are doing well, adding what I believe will be easily over six figures to my income this year. So, from a bunch of hobbies, I've built a growing six-figure enterprise, and I am only 21 years old at the time of this writing.

I am truly blessed. I am living the dream of having a full-time income without working. I keep working, however, as I'd like to land myself deep in the seven-figures-a-year bracket by the time I'm 28—a goal I set when I was in high school. I'm driving a Lexus that I paid for and a project Honda Civic that I've probably put as much if not more into than the Lexus—it's a hobby, I guess. I'm looking at buying a first home that could make many professionals jealous, a home that will be paid for in full; and I'm working toward being able to pay off my mother's house and maybe giving her some other nice things in return for all the things she's done for me over the years. If that's not a blessed place to be sitting at 21 going on 22, I have no idea what is. Every day when I wake up, there's more money in my bank accounts than I had when I went to bed the previous day. I never have to worry about what my boss thinks or what he wants, because I, frankly, am the boss. If I want to take off for a week with friends or family, it's not a problem at all, because I don't have to apply to get off and I don't have a loss of income for doing that. I am free to do whatever I can dream to do, and THAT alone is success. Even once I hit the millions and hopefully decamillions in years to come, I don't think any of that is going to be as big of an accomplishment as having the freedom to live without a job.

Nathan's Advice

First of all—just get it done. If you have an idea, even if it flops horribly, get it up on the internet right now and start working on making money. If you do nothing, you make nothing, and if you do something, you might make something. Keep things simple—a one-page dinky little web site will almost always make more money than these monstrous 20,000-page web sites. All my big sites make a few dollars a month, and my smallest, most simple and primitive web sites make me thousands a month. I think my first million will be made with a few one-page web sites. Don't be afraid of failure; you'll learn a lot from it, and trust me failure is a certainty at some point. Accept that you'll have it, but know that you'll ALSO have a lot of wins. I've hit home runs with maybe eight of my projects out of over 50. Those eight wins were so worth the many failures. Trying ideas on the internet costs about the same as this book, down to a few pennies. It doesn't take millions, thousands, or even hundreds—most ideas can be thoroughly tested for less than $20. Finally, if there's something you don't know, don't feel like you have to learn it— in other words, don't even order an HTML how-to book. A lot of times, places like **elance.com** or your local high school kid can be great resources to get your idea online and working for you fast. This was probably my biggest pitfall. Pay attention—I knew everything there is to know about the internet and web site development. The problem with that is, instead of spending an affordable $200 for software that was prewritten, I wasted six months of time trying to write it myself. Today, there are so many dirt-cheap resources for non-techno-wizards that using the excuse of not knowing how to do this stuff is just that—an excuse.

Researching the Online Marketplace

If I were starting from scratch and I didn't have an idea, here's what I would do:

- ◆ Download a copy of the software called Good Keywords—it's free and they don't even ask you for your e-mail address. This is where you'll find it: **www.goodkeywords.com**.
- ◆ Good Keywords will give you some insight into what people are searching for, and then you can simply stand in front of that stream of traffic with what they want.
- ◆ If you've created a list of what you thought were sound keywords, you can look at what others are using in searches related to that subject.

Another resource I use frequently can be found here:

inventory.overture.com/d/searchinventory/suggestion

Figure 5-1 illustrates the keyword suggestion tool (KST) from Overture. This tool is sporadic and often down; however, it's the easiest and quickest way to check what the demand is for particular searches. For instance, maybe in our list I wrote that I had a parrot as a kid and I taught him how to talk (I had a parakeet named Marvin, but that's another story). So, if I were considering selling a parrot-related information product, I would start by typing "parrots" into the KST.

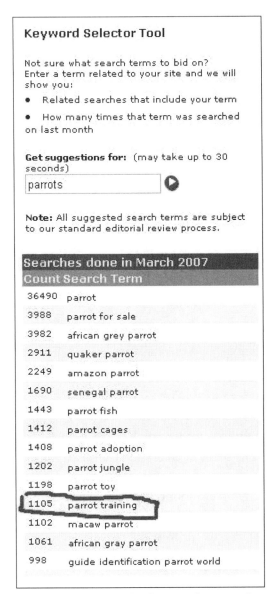

Figure 5-1. Using the keyword suggestion tool from Overture

Now, this tells me how many people have searched on parrot-related phrases last month. The one that catches my eye is "parrot training" at 1,105 searches. I can click on this phrase and get even more specific keywords related to parrot training. This tells me there is a demand for parrot training, and it falls under the "How To" category we discussed.

Our next step is to see who else is selling anything related to parrot training. A quick trip to **google.com** and typing in "parrot training" tells me there are lots of competitors. Oh-oh. That's not a good thing, right? Wrong! Take a look at Figure 5-2.

Each of the spots on the right side is a paid advertisement. That means companies are bidding certain amounts for their ads to show up on Google when people type in "parrot training." Most amateurs would stop right here, because there's too much competition. Actually, the opposite is true to a certain extent. If you see competitors, this means that there is a market for the product and people are buying it.

A friend of mine sells a book on how to teach your parrot to talk, and he does pretty well with it. And I know another guy who's done really well. He was really good at teaching his parrot how to do tricks—making the parrot ride a little unicycle or doing silly little tricks. Parrot owners loved it.

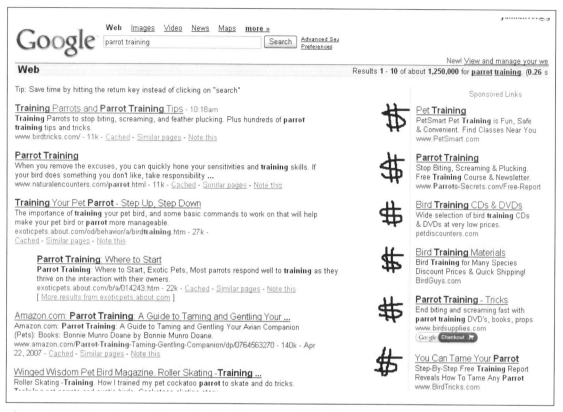

Figure 5-2. Google search results for "parrot training"

Before we move on with the parrot training example, let me show you an amateur information marketer's dream: over 20,000 searches for a "How To"-related topic on "how to tie a tie" (with the three phrases I circled in Figure 5-3). Hot dog! Seems like a perfect info product—you can grab your neighbor's digital camera and show off your Half-Windsor tying skills.

Well, a trip to **google.com** gives us a different story (Figure 5-4):

A big fat goose egg for the number of advertisers.

Either you've hit on an undiscovered goldmine (not likely), or nobody is willing to pay for this kind of information. Now, trust me, people will pay for odd information. My friend Glenn Livingston is living proof of that. He's a psychologist by training, but developed a knack for identifying unique marketplaces and figuring out what people want to spend money on.

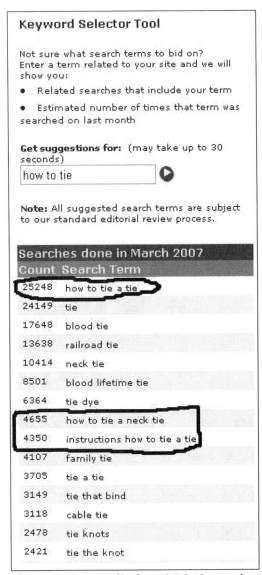

Figure 5-3. KST displays 25,248 searches for "how to tie"

Glenn is kind of an odd success story, because he used to work with some of the biggest corporations on the planet, such as Bausch & Lomb, Whirlpool, and Nabisco, and he billed them $100,000 to $500,000 per project until he decided to fire all his clients to sell a $9.99 e-book on guinea pigs. Crazy, right?

You can imagine the kind of response he got from his family, friends, and colleagues! Glenn made up his mind to move out of the corporate consulting world and focus solely on creating new businesses that would provide totally passive income … with no headaches, no client "emergencies," no ridiculous work hours, and no time away from his family. Glenn was able to start banking $2,000 a month with his guinea pig e-book. Then he quickly tested and duplicated this success in other markets, and within six months after launching his "piggy project," had worked up to $6,300 a month in passive income. But it gets better: In another six months, he was able to double the business, and approximately six more months after that, was able to DOUBLE it again!

Glenn is in 14 niches that have absolutely nothing to do with "making money on the internet." He's got sites out there making him passive income on guinea pigs, alpacas, body language, sudoku, wastewater management, pygmy goats, disability, life

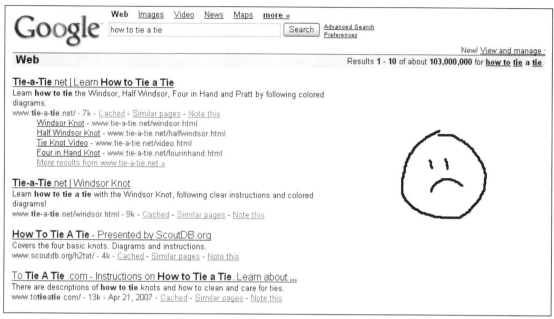

Figure 5-4. Google search results for "how to tie a tie"

coaching, radon, and a variety of other markets. Glenn spoke at my Underground™ Online Seminar II and explained his process to the audience. He's also put up a special recording explaining his methods for readers here: **www.moonlightingontheinternet.com/niche**.

Once you start recognizing marketplaces, you'll see them everywhere. My friend Michael Holland is another great example. He's got sites related to home decorating, RC cars, kids' rooms, and a bunch of others he won't let me share in public. The truth is, you don't need to be an expert on all these marketplaces either—and I'll show you how in a moment.

Okay, on with our research . . .

Head over to **amazon.com** and do a search on books for "parrot training" (in quotes), shown in Figure 5-5.

Click on the first result and check out the book's sales rank, usually displayed as shown in Figure 5-6. For this example, the book *Parrot Training: A Guide to Taming and Gentling Your Avian Companion* by Bonnie Munro Doane is ranked #26,625 on Amazon under the book category.

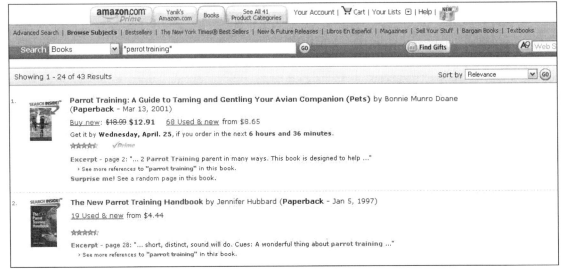

Figure 5-5. Amazon.com search results for "parrot training"

That's a good sign for identifying a good marketplace. Anything ranked from #5,000 to approximately #150,000 is pretty good and means we might have a potential product. I like to see to see a high sales rank but not to top 500 to 1,000, because usually those are either fads or overly competitive marketplaces.

The funny thing is, you might feel a little guilty when I share with you my information marketing secrets for online selling, because the price you get for the digital download is often five times what a "regular" book costs on Amazon or in the store, if you do it my way. This parrot training book is $12.91 on **amazon.com**, but the friend I mentioned to you is selling his e-book for $47 plus.

Finding Ideas When You're Clueless on What to Sell

Amazon.com is a great spot to find product ideas if you don't have a clue about which marketplace you want to go into. (Don't worry: if you are still unsure, I have plenty of other ideas to give you coming up.)

Go back to **amazon.com** and click on "Top Sellers" from the top menu.

From there, choose a product category. I like to explore "books," "magazines," and "software" when looking for information product ideas.

Product Details

Paperback: 224 pages
Publisher: Howell Book House (March 13, 2001)
Language: English
ISBN-10: 0764563270
ISBN-13: 978-0764563270
Product Dimensions: 9.2 x 6.1 x 0.6 inches
Shipping Weight: 14.1 ounces (View shipping rates and policies)
Average Customer Review: ★★★★★ based on 11 reviews. (Write a review.)
Amazon.com Sales Rank: #26,625 in Books (See Top Sellers in Books)
(Publishers and authors: improve your sales)

Would you like to **update product info** or **give feedback on images**? (We'll ask you to sign in so we can get back to you)

Figure 5-6. Book sales rank under "Product Details" heading

How about "software"? Sounds good. When I did this search today, some of the top sellers were Adobe Photoshop Lightroom and Adobe Photoshop—programs that help you with graphic work. And there were Roxio Toast, Roxio Easy Media Creator Suite 9, and Adobe Premiere Elements—programs related to digital media, moviemaking, etc.

So that tells us there is lots of interest in graphics, working with digital photos, multimedia, etc. Any info product that could help people create their own movies would probably be a winner.

You could create a hands-on tutorial using a new product I mentioned to you called Camtasia. This is so cool!

Go to **www.camtasia.com**, and you'll see this is a macro recorder. Everything you do on your computer and anything you say into a microphone (attached to your computer) can be recorded and played back. So, if Adobe Premiere Elements is a big seller, you could create a tutorial for that using Camtasia software. Pretty cool, right?

You are piggybacking on the success of another product. Are you starting to see how easy this is?

Another resource to get your brain cells going with ideas is a hidden gem called **clickbank.com** (Figure 5-7). Go there and click on "marketplace" at the top of the page, and you'll be greeted by thousands of digital products already being sold. You can either browse through categories of products or search specifically for topics.

Figure 5-7. Clickbank.com search

Just click around and you'll surely get some ideas. Now, the point here is not to copy any of the sites or ideas but to create something better and different.

> **Note: Clickbank.com** will handle all the details for selling your digital product, from taking the credit card to paying affiliates. Check the video on the companion CD to see how easy and simple this resource is for information marketers.

Chapter 6

Evaluating Your "Brilliant" Idea

We need to research the market to gauge your possible success with any product idea before you fall in love with it. My philosophy is that it's too difficult to try and create something and then have to decide, "Okay, now whom can I get to buy this?"

You need to think of it in the opposite way. Think market first and then think product. Unless you are familiar with your target market (i.e., you're one of them), I suggest you follow this section to gauge market interest.

When choosing a market, it's important to think about the following three qualifiers:

1. **Do they have money?** If your target market is welfare mothers or people with severe credit problems, you might want to reconsider. But if you're targeting doctors, you know they have a decent amount of disposable income.

2. **Are they easily reachable?** Are there easy ways to reach your target market? Do they have their own e-zines and blogs that they read? Is there a site that they already come to online that would be cost-effective to advertise on or joint venture with?

You can search through newsgroups and forums to find where your target hangs out at **groups.google.com**.

3. **Are they online?** This is important. Unless your target market is online, you can't sell them an online, digitally delivered product. I know this sounds simple, but you wouldn't believe some ideas I've seen out there that forget to make use of this critical point.

Once you've decided on a market, think about solutions you can provide. With your list of possible product ideas that made the cut, you will next hit the search engines …

Research Using Search Engines

Okay, back to the search engines …

Head back to **google.com** and check out the number of returns provided for your search term—in this case, "parrot training." Usually, the more the better, because that means there is a lot of information on that topic and people need a way to quickly and easily sort through that information.

In addition, use the search engines to find discussion boards and lists for your market. Type in "your market + discussion board" and see what comes up. Visit these discussion boards and "lurk" (look and read) for awhile to gauge your market's interest in a possible new product. For instance, if I go to a parrot discussion forum and I see a lot of questions about training, then I know I'm onto something.

> *I want to point out that while I use the search engines for research, they can also be used effectively to drive traffic to your web sites.*

I want to point out that while I use the search engines for research, they can also be used effectively to drive traffic to your web sites. I know just enough to be dangerous in that arena, so I had Andy Jenkins, whom you'll learn more about in another chapter, prepare a special report on search engine optimization just for Moonlighters. You can get your copy at **www.moonlightingontheinternet .com/SEO**.

And finally look around for the dreaded "c" word—competition. Like I mentioned, a lot of people start getting scared when they see the competition doing the same things they were planning on doing.

Evaluating Your "Brilliant" idea

Don't!

You should be glad. You don't want to be the only one trying to create a market for a digital product. Be sure to bookmark all the competitors' sites (you'll see exactly what we'll do with them later on). Remember, the only thing you need to do is create a slightly different twist, angle, or spin. You can tweak their offerings to capture the market. (Note that I did not say copy!)

The big difference is going to be your marketing.

Think about the market for business letters or sales letter templates that my site **instantsalesletters.com** competes in. There are lots of software products, offline books, and online templates (some even free) that offer something similar to what I have. But—and this is a big but—I've positioned the site in a way that is different from my competitors. Plus, another great benefit of competition is the ability to do profitable joint ventures (JVs). We'll talk more about JVs later on, but I just want to mention something that you should consider.

If I turn around right now and look behind me in three directions, I can see that I have bookcases filled with manuals, books, and tapes (in fact, I just had to buy another six-foot bookcase last week). Would you like to take one guess about which subject the majority of these resources deal with?

If you said marketing and advertising—you're absolutely right!

Think about your own life.

If you are really into a subject like gardening, do you only get one magazine on gardening? Do you only have one book in your bookcase about gardening? Do you only buy one set of gardening products?

Absolutely not!

And that's the same question you ask when it comes to your target market—especially if you can find a rabid, hungry market.

So, having these competitors gives you the ability to endorse their products and services, and they'll do the same for yours—and you both profit. Remember, your customers would probably buy from your competitors anyway, so why not profit from their inevitable purchases?

Picking a Winning Project

There is always a balancing act I have to maintain between effort expended on a project and potential return. Start with a quick and easy project first, to work out the kinks and build your confidence. Then it becomes a cookie-cutter system to do it again and again. Or, if you are feeling ambitious, you can work on more long-term projects that have a higher potential payoff. But get one or two small winners under your belt first to see how this can work.

One more thing—don't get married to your project idea. I want to test things out as quickly as possible and either see them fail or succeed. Then I know where to focus my efforts. But don't worry about product creation—we're still in the idea stage and setting up our foundation. This is critical, because if you create a product the market really, WANTS, you'll have an easier time!

Moonlight on Andre Hendricks

Andre's Moonlighting Story

I started back in 2003 with a simple web site that is still making me extra income at **acethatjob.com**. I was working full-time and set up the site because of my previous experience in the recruitment field. I figured I could use what I knew about the industry and help people get into decent jobs with the right résumé and interview training in the form of audio downloadable mp3 files or give them the option to listen online. From there, I created another site, **www.free-lance-couriers.com**, and after buying and implementing Yanik's Instant Sales Letters®, my business transformed.

Before Moonlighting, I was working 80-hour weeks. I had no time for myself and had to forgo many holidays and time with my family in South Africa due to financial constraints. My life was pretty depressing and mundane due to the fact that I kept working in circles, and the way I see it, it was like eating soup with a fork—you keep busy, but you see nothing. I knew something had to change … anything … because I was going out of my mind!

www.acethatjob.com

Today, I make a full-time six-figure income from seven online businesses. I have an e-mail list of around 5,000 addresses. We get around 15,000 visitors to the **freelance-couriers.com** web site and around 8,000 to the other sites combined. I'm moving full-time into my passion, which is marketing and sales consulting. I earn between $15,000 and

$35,000 per month, and my life has transformed from worrying all the time to actually doing what I want with my wife and my beautiful 18-month-old daughter, the freedom to do anything and go anywhere, and best of all, being able to hop on a plane to see my parents in South Africa whenever I choose. It's great! I never knew how much one could appreciate everything when one doesn't have to worry about money anymore.

Andre's Advice

Knowing what I wanted has been my biggest "aha" moment. For years, I have been searching for a way to make money, but never defined what it was I wanted out of life. I was so distracted by financial worries that I never took the time to sit down and write down what I wanted … what would make me and my family happy.

Once I realized what I wanted, I realized what I lacked to get there, so I started reading books on marketing, sales, internet marketing—the lot! I decided to be led by a few mentors like Yanik's master skill in copywriting, other mentors like Dan Kennedy, Jay Abraham … and worked on my goals piece by piece every day. Determination carried me through many depressing days, but nothing compared to visualizing what I wanted to become or have when I got there.

Chapter 7

Creating Your Information Product

I know some people get nervous at the thought of "creating" a product. Let me tell you, it's much easier than you think. Trust me. I'll show you a couple of tricks that will help you knock out your new digital product more quickly and easily than you imagined.

I break down info products into two main categories:

1. Written (e-books, PDF files, online newsletters, etc.)
2. Non-written (audio, software, video, etc.)

In addition, you can have a combination of written and non-written material with your offering.

Now, let's talk about how you get these things pumped out ...

You Write or Create It

The first way is to create it yourself. That means you stick your butt on the seat, put your hands on the keyboard, and write it yourself (if it's a written product). That's one way to do it. For some people, this is easy; others can't stand the thought of sitting at their computers and typing for hours and hours.

Well, it doesn't have to be that bad.

I can crank out reports in just a couple of nights, and a full manual wouldn't take me any more than two weeks. When you create nonfiction, you don't need to worry that much about style—just deliver tons of content and useful information. Write like you talk. People won't mind—in fact, they'll probably like it better.

> *When you create nonfiction, you don't need to worry that much about style—just deliver tons of content and useful information.*

Let me share with you a big secret ...

Your Outline Is the Key

If you spend some time creating your outline first, you'll find that writing the product is a breeze. You should think about creating "chunks" of your product and making your outline modular. So anytime you have a spare 15 minutes you can write one section. It doesn't matter where you start because you'll go back later and create the transitions.

Here's a sample outline for a project I recently did:

Outline "How to Make Instant Sales and Massive Profits with Cheap Broadcast Faxes"

I. Introduction

◆ For less than half the cost of a postcard, you can send a powerful sales message to practically any prospect across the country (and you won't have to pay for printing, either). What I'm talking about is broadcast faxing. And you won't have to wait around for your mail to be delivered or for an ad to run in a newspaper or magazine.

◆ You'll have instant results, and you'll know right away if something worked or it didn't.

◆ How it works and how to do it.

◆ Getting past the myths.

◆ Who can use fax marketing and how.

II. Direct-Response-Only Marketing

◆ Mass marketing and advertising agencies are 100 percent wrong (not based on results)—only image-conscious name-building B.S.

> ◆ Understanding direct response—the only purpose of any advertising or marketing expenditure is to make a sale in some measurable and accountable way.
>
> ### III. TESTING, TESTING, TESTING
>
> ### IV. How to Create Powerful Advertising
> ◆ *Advertising mistakes*
> - Following your competition (marketing inbreeding)
> - Not using powerful, benefit-packed headlines (headline formulas)
> - Thinking people will not read a lot of copy (copy of Merrill Lynch ad with over 6,000 words)
> - Being too boring
> - Focusing on your company, logo, problems, etc., instead of the customers
> - Not having a compelling offer and a reason to act now
> - Trying to advertise everything
> - Not tracking or testing marketing messages (include sample tracking sheets)
> - Coupon
> - Stealth fax marketing under the prospect's advertising "radar"

Now, using this outline, I go in and add "meat" to the skeleton I created. If you can write a 500- to 700-word article (that's less than two pages), you can create a manual. Just think of your information product as a series of interrelated articles.

Creating your outline first makes you think clearly about each of the topics you'll cover, and it helps put them in a logical order.

Believe me, this really helps!

Also, with a complete outline, it doesn't matter where you start writing, because everything is modular. (I'm referring to nonfiction products here. Fiction isn't something I'm familiar with, so I can't give you much advice. Plus, fiction is a much tougher sell using our model.)

Or you can use the power of a mind map …

Power of Mind Mapping

First off, here's the definition of a mind map, straight from **wikipedia.org– en.wikipedia.org/wiki/Mind_mapping**:

> A **mind map** (or mind-map) is a diagram used for linking words and ideas to a central key word or idea. It is used to visualize, classify, structure, and generate ideas, as well as an aid in study, problem solving, and decision making.
>
> It is similar to a semantic network or cognitive map but there are no formal restrictions on the kinds of links used. Most often the map involves images, words, and lines. The elements are arranged intuitively according to the importance of the concepts and they are organized into groupings, branches, or areas. In other words, a mind map is an image-centered radial diagram that represents semantic or other connections between portions of information. The uniform graphic formulation of the semantic structure of information on the method of gathering knowledge, may aid recall of existing memories.

You want to start with a central theme or idea in the middle of your page. (I've put my example in a piece of software I use, but typically my mind maps are drawn by hand with pen and paper.)

Then you create branches radiating from the center that encompass points related to your main topic. Then, under the radiating main points, you can have further sub-branches, etc.

I love mind mapping for all kinds of uses because it fits the way we think on a subject. You've most likely been taught to make a linear outline when taking notes or trying to organize your ideas. It can be frustrating, because our brains don't always output information in a perfectly ordered and structured way. Many times, one thing will trigger an idea for something else and then something else again. That's why mind maps are the perfect way to dump everything out of your head and onto paper or the computer screen. To enhance your memory of your mind map even further, you can enhance it with colors, pictures, images, different shapes, etc.

For me, mind mapping works because all I need is a paper and pen, and I can have an orderly flow for what needs to be done in minutes instead of struggling for hours.

One of the biggest ways I've been using mind maps in my business is for product development.

Mind maps are perfect for product development because of exactly what I mentioned before. If you are creating an information product and you have all these ideas swirling around inside your head, it's hard to get them out in a logical way without driving yourself crazy. But with a mind map, it's easy.

Figure 7-1 illustrates a mind map for a made-up example of an information product, "How to Be a Clown for Fun & Profit!"

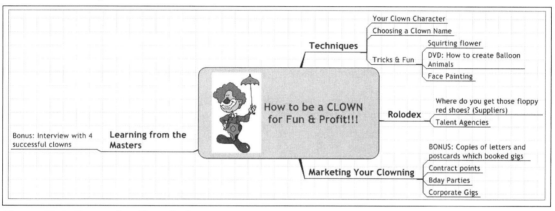

Figure 7-1. Example of a mind map

Now, I did this in literally five minutes and I have no clue about clowning. If you actually know about a subject, you can do better than this. But notice a few things. As I'm coming up with stuff, I'm thinking of what would make really exciting bonuses. Fact is, a great bonus will sell your main product. So, if the main product here is an e-book, then the bonuses I see are:

◆ Four audio CDs with interviews of successful clowns

◆ DVD or online video on how to create balloon animals that kids and adults love

◆ Copies of letters, ads, and postcards successfully used to land gigs

◆ Million-dollar Rolodex of suppliers and talent agencies

Like I said, I created this in five minutes without any knowledge of the topic, but looking at it, it's not bad at all. I bet someone interested in clowning would buy this.

Moonlight on Shawn Futterer

Shawn's Moonlighting Story

I got started in late 2005. Funny story, actually: I knew Yanik Silver from our weekend volleyball games, but I didn't exactly know what he did or who he was outside of our weekend games. One day I was discussing with him an opportunity I wanted to take advantage of by creating a web site for downloadable content. In early 2005, I had completed a professional certification in Project Management, and in doing so, I discovered a huge business in certification exam prep. I wanted a piece of the action, so I created an e-book with my experience, advice for others, and tips and tricks to pass the grueling four-hour exam. After Yanik's advice, I began to notice an upward trend in site visits and sales. Now, I have an extremely niche product—Project Management Certification Exam Prep—with lots of experienced competition in the market, so I needed a differentiator. I morphed my original e-book into additional products, so now I was able to sell similar content in multiple ways at very different price points.

Before Moonlighting Online, my financial life was rather boring. I made good money in my day job, paid all my bills, and still had a little left over for savings. But once I made the move online, I was able to create a bit more financial freedom. My web site is now paying my mortgage, car payment, and more each month. Most times, I don't even remember when it's payday at the day job! The cost to run my site was roughly $20 a month, and the only other investments I made were my own time and effort, so almost everything was profit! During the first few months, I attracted a few hundred visitors and had about a 10–15 percent sale-to-visitor ratio. Not overly impressive, but I was making money. Today, I receive 3,000–5,000 visitors a month and have a 40–50 percent sale-to-visitor ratio. Remember, I have a niche product. There are only a few hundred newly certified people each month across the globe, so I'm capturing a very good portion of them.

www.readysetpass.com

Before Moonlighting, my personal life was good. I'm married to a wonderful woman and have one child, and another is on the way. We did everything you'd expect a family to do—vacationed once or twice a year, bought a new car every few years, etc. Today, it's a very different story, and we are able to do a lot more—if we want to! Most of our family lives in Texas, and we like people to visit us, so now we are able to buy them the plane tickets to come out and see us. My wife, Stacy, wants a new Lexus. Before, I would have had to scrimp and save, but today I can go down to the dealership and drive away in that new Lexus without the expense hurting me financially. Today, I spend a small portion of my evenings ensuring that my web sites are running smoothly. They are both on autopilot, so it's not too bad. I'm enjoying the financial freedom I have. My wife shops more than ever. (She's a shopaholic—what can you do?) My son is five years old, and his college fund is worth more than I am! We're able to invest more money these days. Having extra income is great, but using that extra income in ways that allow your money to work for you is even better.

Shawn's Advice

My "ahas" have been plentiful—mostly at the receipt of advice from Yanik. After the launch of my community site, I was presented with an opportunity to partner with a global project management company. We've recently solidified our business relationship and are moving forward at a fast pace with everything. If I'm not careful, I might find myself doing this full-time!

When I'm outlining a product, I want to mind-map what will be in each section of a product, what bonuses and what kind of guarantee it'll have, and sometimes even the big idea that I'll use as the theme for the sales material. Just let yourself go and have fun with it. One idea usually triggers another, and you're off and running.

Speak Your Product

I'll give you a super-easy way to get your product written: tape-record it. If you ever do any speaking, a teleseminar, or even if you just sit down with a friend and let them interview you, you can talk about whatever your subject is and then have that tape transcribed. That transcription becomes the basis of your information product.

> *I'll give you a super-easy way to get your product written: tape-record it.*

Very nice!

Look under "secretary services" in your Yellow Pages for someone to do your transcriptions, or try **www.idictate.com**. For one cent per word, real people will transcribe any recording you give them.

Ghostwriter

Did you realize that there are tons of starving writers out there who are more than happy to write for you so they can pay their bills? Really. I used to suggest that people go to the library and get a publication called *Literary*

Marketplace or run an ad in the paper, but I have an even easier solution for you. It's a site called **elance.com**.

I've used it myself and have been happy with the results. Here's how it works: you post your project details and service providers bid on your job. You can review people's portfolios and ask them questions on a private discussion board before you hire them. Plus, the best part is that to you it's all free! The service provider gives **elance.com** a percentage of the fee that they win.

> You can hire people to do anything, from writing reports, manuals, and books for you to designing software.

You can hire people to do anything, from writing reports, manuals, and books for you to designing software. Now there's almost no excuse not to create the product, even if you have no clue about it.

Do What You Do Already

Here's a cool way to create a project right away—do what you normally do anyway, but record it. Here's what I mean: one of my colleagues, Alex Carroll, is a whiz at getting radio publicity on talk shows. He's been on over 1,100 of them selling his book on how to get out of speeding tickets. So, now he took his expertise at getting free publicity and turned it into a cool product. He recorded himself pitching to the show producers and his follow-up conversations with them leading up to his interview.

Now, understand the beauty of this: he had to do this anyway to get on the show, but now he's leveraging his activity by turning it into a hot product.

Do you see how cool this is? Something you're probably already doing anyway—just capture it somehow to turn it into your product.

I told this idea to one of my friends, and I hope he creates his product, because his expertise is building traffic to his site at super-cheap rates. He negotiates on the phone anyway; so he just recorded his conversations— Wham! Instant product!

This isn't as hard as you might first imagine. It's all in your expectations. I always expect things to be easy for me—and guess what? For the most part, they are. Keep that in mind.

Creating Your Information Product

Remember, your main goal in creating your product is to get something quick to test. Later, you can go back and update and make it better only when the market tells you they're willing to buy.

You want to get your content ready so you have something to sell, because remember, we are delivering instantly via download. You only want to see if this is going to sell or not. When I started out, I didn't have nearly as many templates on **instantsalesletters.com** as I have on my site now. I sold my product for a lower price and I didn't have as many bonuses, but I wanted to see if the darn thing was going to sell.

And if it didn't, then I'd say "NEXT!" and move on to my next project.

Personally, I like sites (projects) that can bring in a few thousand per month and take a minimum amount of time to test their market validity. Then you can create a stable of these sites, all running concurrently and all bringing in automatic revenue for you. I like to know as soon as possible if something is going to work or not. So, I'd rather spend 10–25 hours creating a product and doing a pretty good job that can be revised later if it's a winner than spend 100+ hours making a perfect product.

> *Personally, I like sites (projects) that can bring in a few thousand per month and take a minimum amount of time to test their market validity.*

For most people, their big problem is actually doing something. Coming up with ideas and thinking about the cars, boats, and houses is the easy part. The hard part is implementing.

Listen, everyone wants to wait for the perfect opportunity to do something. I say, *just do it!* Do you think my first effort at creating information products was perfect? I don't think so. In fact, I don't think any of my information products are 100 percent perfect, but there comes a time when you have to release it to the market and see what happens.

If you are still feeling lost for an idea, don't worry, because coming up I'll show you three more ways to "steal" an idea!

For a complete list of the resources Yanik uses and recommends, go to **www.moonlightingontheinternet.com/Infoguide**.

Part One

Moonlighting on the Internet Method #1

Section 2

Where to "Steal" Your Bestselling Idea

Okay, I promised you I'd share with you some of my coolest ways to "steal" an idea to use for your new digitally delivered information product ... and here they are:

1. Licensing
2. Joint Ventures
3. Public Domain

Let's talk about each of these in detail so you can see how exciting this is.

Originally, when we talked about using your own expertise or something you knew about or something that you can research, you were like, "I don't know anything." I'd probably challenge you on that.

But let's play devil's advocate and say, "Okay, you don't know anything and you don't have any expertise that somebody would pay for."

Now, I'm going to give you three other ways by which you can create your own information product without having your own expertise.

Licensing

This is one of the best shortcuts to creating an information product. To get a good grasp on licensing, think about Disney. Have you ever seen the Mickey Mouse character on a lunchbox or a toothbrush?

Most people don't realize this, but Walt Disney will license out their cute little mouse and let other manufacturers use it on their products, in exchange, obviously, for money. These manufacturers typically pay a license fee and ongoing royalty on each product sold. It's a good deal for both parties. Disney doesn't have to be in businesses they don't have expertise in, and the manufacturer gets a proven sales boost using a known character.

How does this apply to information marketing? It works the same way, but instead of licensing a character, we are licensing the content from the copyright holder.

I have a student whom I walked through this process. We approached a "real" publisher to license one of their business books. They weren't selling it online or really doing much with it.

So my student negotiated exclusive online rights for this product. And, I'm almost embarrassed to tell you, the amount he paid them for this license fee … it was only $250 up front.

This was an advance against royalties, and he pays a certain percentage of royalties, which I can't reveal, but it's pretty small. It's not 40 percent or 50 percent or 30 percent, or anything like that. It's really small.

Bam! He's got an instant downloadable product he can sell!

I'd be more than happy to give a small percentage of every sale if I didn't have to create my own product and I knew that this was a proven product.

> *I'd be more than happy to give a small percentage of every sale if I didn't have to create my own product and I knew that this was a proven product.*

Now you might be thinking, "Why would a publisher do that?" Well, the real reason is they don't have time to do it themselves. Or they've neglected a title. Or for whatever other reason. It doesn't matter—you just need to know that this is possible.

This works well for titles that didn't come out six months ago. So if something is evergreen, and you find a book that's 5 years old or 10 years old but the information is still valid, you work out a deal with the publisher. It's not that hard. And one more thing—people assume that big companies know how to market, but that's wrong. Publishers will throw a certain amount of money at it, and if it doesn't catch right away, they're on to the next project.

They have so many things going on that they can't bother to worry about it. For them, the royalty income is extra money. It's an asset that was lying dormant. Ernesto Verdugo from the Netherlands did exactly what I showed you:

Moonlight on Ernesto Verdugo

Ernesto's Story

I was a successful speaker and consultant. I was the head of training for one of the big four European airlines, but after September 11, the training department was dramatically affected and I was offered the opportunity to start on my own on a nice settlement. The start was great, but then suddenly we started suffering the roller coaster income syndrome, and we were working 28 hours a day, 10 days a week. It was exhausting. Until one day we met Tom Antion, who is a public speaker, and he shared with us what he was doing on the internet, and in those days he said, "*All you need is one idea!"* And he was right. We went to the Overture inventory tool and searched for one specific subject and bingo! 70,000 searches a month! WOW! Little competition and the potential to GROW dramatically.

The problem was, we had no idea about the topic and we didn't have the time to write the e-book. We were also unaware of eLance or anything like that, so, using our creativity, we got hold of authors who had already written books and whose books were out of print, and we offered to be their online publishers on a 50-50 deal, and they happily agreed. So within a few months we had really nice books converted into e-books, and that's how we got started!

Today, my life is completely different. I'm still a public speaker and I organize seminars, BUT now I get to say YES to whomever I want to say YES to and take only projects I'm interested in. I'm debt-free. I own real estate property in three countries, and I have a feeling of accomplishment and tranquility that I never felt in my corporate years. In 2001, I read Robert Kiyosaki's *Cashflow Quadrant* book and I guesstimated that I was going to be out of the rat race by 2015. In fact, it was on my goal list! Amazingly enough, through the internet, it took me 15 months to get my cash flow to be larger than my expenses. Without the internet, this would have never been possible. After four short years online using OPI (Other People's Ideas) as a lever, I sailed through the rough times and am living a great life with my wife and son.

www.seeingwithoutglasses.com

Ernesto's Advice

There are literally hundreds of authors out there who would love you to be their online publishing company. They have NO CLUE about how to do it, so they will happily work with you. Out of my eight information products, NONE of them were written by me. For example, in **www.seeingwithoutglasses.com**, the author is 80-plus years old, and he was thrilled to suddenly be PUBLISHED online—and that's the same with **stepbystepimmigrationcanada.com**, another one of my sites. Why not become an instant publishing company?

Here's another great success story showing that you can do this anywhere in the world. Tadahiro "Hiro" Ogawa licensed some of my products to translate and sell in Japan …

Moonlight on Tadahiro Ogawa

Hiro's Story

I started my info business about one year ago. I first bought reprint rights from Mark Joyner and simultaneously I started my own newsletter. **www.d-publishing.jp** And then I contacted Yanik and asked him to make me his Japanese licensee. I began by selling his Instant Sales Letters® in the Japanese language.

Before Moonlighting, my life was not so good. Every day I worried about my future and my next month's revenue. Today, less than one year into my business, my sales are about $300,000 per month with about 30 percent profit. Now I have a lot of time and money— yes, I still work hard, but the difference is, I do not need to work: I enjoy my work!

Hiro's Advice

Money is infinite. If we don't sell, the entire economy does not work. So I am obligated to sell something.

Note: Every once in a while, I will license one of our products to sell. If you are interested in being one of the first to hear about the next license, go here: **www.moonlightingontheinternet.com/license**.

Okay, let's move on to our next method of "stealing" …

Chapter 9

Joint Ventures

This is another nifty way of creating your own information product, if you don't think that you have your own expertise.

All you do is find somebody—it could be a best friend, it could be a colleague, it could be somebody you know—and you approach them and say, "Let's create an information product together." And most of the time they'll say, "Huh? What?" And you tell them, "Listen, you create whatever it is and I'll market it, and we'll split the profits." You can do the split any way that you want, any way they agree to, depending on how much work they do.

My good friend Jeff Walker started this way. He found a guy who had excellent content related to the stock market and partnered up with him to sell his information. Jeff is "infamous" in certain circles for mastermind product launches now, based around the methods he first used with this stock market information business when he was in a crunch to pay his taxes.

Here's another great example of a joint venture with an expert. Another friend of mine named Dean Jackson created a product called "Stop Your Divorce." It's for people (mostly men) who come home one day and their wife decides they've had it with them. So they say, "Honey, we have to talk." And the talk is that she wants a divorce. Not very good.

Moonlighting on the Internet

So what do most men do? They go on the internet and type something like "how to stop my divorce."

Trust me on this: Dean is not a psychologist or marriage therapist or anything like that, but he realized that this was a good market that he could sell an information product to.

He found an ad—believe it or not, this is the story that he told me—in *USA Today*, about this guy who is doing consultations via the phone. He called this guy and mentioned his idea to him. The way the deal works is that Dean keeps all the money when somebody buys their e-book, and the doctor gets all the money on the back end for ongoing private consultations.

Dean started off with this e-book selling for $29. Then he raised the price and found that either sales went up or stayed the same. So he basically gave himself a pay raise. Right now, I think it's around $79, which costs him absolutely zero to deliver. I don't know the numbers now but several years ago he told me he was making $30,000 a month with this web site. It's pretty amazing. So you can do it in a big way or do it in a small way. There are lots of people who have information that other people would pay for. If you don't think you have that kind of information, you can do a joint venture with them and set it up, no problem.

> There are lots of people who have information that other people would pay for. If you don't think you have that kind of information, you can do a joint venture with them and set it up.

Here's another example on a smaller scale, and it's about something that I did. One day, I saw on **cnn.com** that the amount of time that people spend in traffic had increased something like 50 percent in the last five years. My brain is always working on crazy ideas and I thought, "That might be a cool little information product. Let's give people an exercise book showing exercises that they can do while sitting in the car."

So I approached my trainer whom I work out with. His response was, "Well, that's probably a bad idea because it'll cause a lot of accidents while people are exercising in their cars." And I said, "All right, maybe that won't work."

So we fiddled around with the idea a little and we came up with a different version. What do most people do? They sit on their butts, in front of a computer, at work or wherever it is, and they don't exercise or anything like that because they don't have time to do it. So that was when the idea of "Get Fit While You Sit" was born.

I couldn't pull it off myself because I didn't have expertise as a fitness expert. I'm in pretty good shape, but in no way have I studied nutrition or do I have the knowledge to design exercises for this. So, I don't have the credentials for it, but that didn't stop me because my trainer had that expertise.

I took a different approach on this one and designed what I wanted him to develop from a marketing point of view first, based on what I thought would sell. We started with the premise and then designed the exercises around that. We came up with exercises to do in front of the TV, exercises to do at work, exercises to do on the airplane, exercises to do around the house (such as cutting the lawn), and calculated how many calories one would burn with each exercise.

> *We came up with exercises to do in front of the TV, exercises to do at work, exercises to do on the airplane, exercises to do around the house.*

Then I gave him that list and I said, "Okay, now go design these exercises." So it took him some creativity and research to figure out which exercises would work best, and he came back after doing his work on it. We could have created a simple online video workout program, but we decided to turn it into a simple e-book.

We spent an hour or two in a vacant office and I had Jeff doing these exercises with everyday objects. He's got, like, the Yellow Pages in one hand, curling them. And he's got a box of tennis balls, or something like that. I took pictures of everything, and trust me, I'm no Ansel Adams.

Then we moved our "set" to a couch in the waiting room of the gym so it looked like someone's living room. I had him do the other "watching TV" exercises there, and we were set. We put up this site in 2001, and it's been over six years, but it's made money every single month. Anywhere up to about $1,100—it's been as low as about $200, but mostly it falls in the neighborhood of $500. It's like having an uncle sending you $500 checks every month. Who wouldn't want an extra $500 a month?

Now, I want to point out some important lessons from what I described. I said, "I gave him a list of what I wanted the product to look like." And you and I know that what everybody does is they create something and then they're worried about how to sell it ... whereas the real way to do it is start off with your sales pitch. What would it take to sell this thing? What should it look like in order to be saleable? And then you create the product to fit that. Many times, I'll write the sales letter first. We'll talk in detail about the sales letter, and I'll even give you a simple fill-in-the-blank example.

Moonlight on Robert Plank

Robert's Story

My niche is web programming. I got started around 2000 trying to sell web templates. I only sold one or two. In 2001, I learned PHP and I began working as a freelancer. Again, I only got a few low-paying jobs here and there. In 2002, I did a joint venture with Gary Ambrose and Brian Garvin. I spent several months creating and debugging a script called Lightning Track for them, which was a link tracker and split tester. After the launch, we split up the money and I'd only made a few thousand dollars. After that, I went back to freelancing, but I had the idea of writing articles explaining how to make some of the scripts I'd made. Those articles eventually turned into e-books. What made the e-books so popular and so easy to write was that I had applied my own twist to teaching the material instead of doing what everyone else had done. Since then, I've written 10 e-books and 10 large web applications, plus several smaller scripts not worth mentioning. Because the info products are my own, I sell them over and over,

www.salespagetactics.com

as opposed to freelancing where I only get paid for work one time.

Today is the 20th of the month and I have already made 140 sales this month, totaling $1,834.54—that's over $600 per week. Keep in mind, this is all playing-around money on TOP of the income from my regular day job, which I love. My internet marketing business on the side only takes a couple hours out of my day after I come home from work ... Once a month, I choose one of my info products, knock the price way down to something like $10–$15, and send a mailing. This gets me an average of $1,000 in sales from about 20 minutes of work.

Before my online business took off, I had no time for anything. I was starting out in college, living in a tiny $625/month studio apartment, making $800 every month if I was lucky, which barely paid for rent, food, and school. I had no car and was always worrying about how I was going to pay the rent that month. Today, I am a college graduate. When applying for a real-world job, I stated subscriber and sales numbers, which set me apart from other applicants for that same job, who had perhaps a college education and a retail job for employment experience. I was able to state on my résumé that I had created certain info products related to my field, establishing myself as an authority on the subject. I rent a two-bedroom townhouse apartment. I have a car and am not in debt. I have enough money saved to trade my current car for a much nicer car and pay with cash, but I would rather save up for a house. I will have enough money for a down payment on a house in three years if my income stays at this level, which it definitely will, because my subscriber list is only growing larger. I am creating bigger and better products, etc. Meanwhile, many of my friends are still living with their parents, broke, or having trouble paying off student loans.

Robert's Advice

I guess from experience I've noticed my online income never really took off until I started creating partnerships—not trying to do everything. I would make a script or e-book, partner with a copywriter for a 50/50 split, and make more sales than either of us on our own.

Let's move on to our third way of "stealing" information: this one will keep you up for hours with the possibilities …

Chapter 10

Public Domain

I call it the 100-percent-legal way to "steal" millions and millions of pages and endless sources of content for any kind of information product you want to develop. It's amazing stuff!

I've been using this for years, and I finally let the cat out of the bag and started teaching it. People have gone crazy with it, because it's so exciting. You can literally take information without asking permission and without paying a dime in license fees. Now, I'm not an attorney, nor do I play one on TV, so this is not legal advice, but rather my best marketing advice from really doing it.

Okay, so what is it? Public domain is material that the public (that's you) can use (or exploit, as the case may be) any way they want. It falls into four main categories:

1. **Generic information like facts, numbers, ideas, titles, blank forms, etc.**

   Works granted or donated to the public domain (yes, in some cases copyright holders will make their work available to anyone to use).

   Just one example is P.T. Barnum's autobiography. He took his autobiography and donated it to the public. Anyone can use this, reprint it, do whatever they want to do with it. This is popular now with software applications. So many of what I lovingly call "propeller-heads" would love to put their software out there and make it available for the greater good of everyone else.

2. **Works by the government or its agents.**

   (This is an amazing archive by itself!) Nearly all federal works are public domain, and some state publications are also.

   The US government is one of the biggest sources of information out there. There's information from tons of government agencies. Maybe you want to sell to investors—well, the SEC (Securities & Exchange Commission) has a bunch of info you can use for FREE!

   A friend of mine grabbed a bunch of material from the SBA (Small Business Administration) and used that in her product. There are a lot of ways the government can help you out and create your information product for you. I'm looking at something right now on my shelf that I'm thinking about doing, and I guess it's free game for other people out there, but the U.S. Department of Interior is in charge of fish, wildlife, and so on. So you could put out directories and resources on wildlife and fishing, for example.

3. **Formerly copyrighted works that have fallen into public domain or lost their copyright due to a number of different situations.**

When you add all of this up it becomes a veritable mountain of incredible information (millions and millions of pages) sitting right under your nose—all free and all yours for the taking!

A lot of our work is going to be centered on either government publications or formerly copyrighted works. For a formerly copyrighted work, here's the information you'll need to figure out if the work is public domain:

Your Public Domain Cheat Sheet

1. Anything published in the U.S. before 1923—this goes for anything published in the U.S. or abroad and then republished in the U.S. before 1923.

2. Works first published in the US from 1923–1963 are in the public domain if they were not renewed in their 28th year. Estimates are that 85 percent of works were not renewed. Foreign works published anywhere before 1909 are in the public domain.

3. Foreign works published from 1909–1923 with copyright notices are now in the public domain.

Copyright Charts for U.S. Published Works

Published before 1923:	public domain
Published 1923–1963 and not renewed in the 28th year:	public domain
Published 1923–1963 and renewed:	95 years from date of first publication
Published 1964–1977:	95 years from date of first publication (automatic)
Created 1978 or later:	Life of author plus 70 years* (does not have to be published)

*If work is made for hire or under a pseudonym or anonymously, then copyright protection lasts 95 years from date of publication or 120 years from date of creation—whichever ends first.

Note: International copyrights are different based on the country. For full information, get a book called *The Public Domain* by Stephen Fishman, Esq.

Here's where it gets exciting: we can do anything we want with the public domain material. That means we can retitle it, we can cut and paste parts of it, we can use one chapter of it if we want, we can rework it if we want. Truly anything. And depending on how much you rework it, if you add your own foreword, a couple of illustrations, and maybe some additional comments, you could set yourself up as the co-author and re-copyright it.

Once a work falls into the public domain, anybody can use it. So if we're looking at a public domain work, such as Shakespeare's works, I could publish them and sell them. Or, if I wanted to create what's called a derivative work, I could do that, too. You've probably seen the movie *West Side Story*. That's a derivative of *Romeo and Juliet*. It's the same story, set in a more modern setting.

We can do whatever we want with a public domain work. We can use it as the basis for different works. And public domain's not limited to literary works: it encompasses photographs, videos, movies, musical works, etc.

Finding Your Public Domain Gold Mine

The first place I'd start is with a book search.

Online Book Searches

At **alibris.com**, use advanced search to search via title keyword and publication date (either before 1923 or before 1963). Figures 10-1 and 10-2 illustrate how to do this. (*Note:* See the video on this topic on the bonus companion CD-ROM.)

Now, the tough part is that you have no way of analyzing or looking at the results you get back. You don't know if those books have any good material in there without buying them. But it's not that big a deal, because it usually only costs a few dollars and a few days to get the books delivered so you can check them out yourself.

Another good resource that searches multiple used book sites is this site: **www.addall.com/used**.

Library or Used Book Store

> *Be sure to write down all the titles and authors of the books that were published before 1963 on your subject.*

Your local library is a good place to continue or start your search. You can browse through all kinds of books on your intended subject. Be sure to write down all the titles and authors of the books that were published before 1963 on your subject. I like used book stores. You never know what you'll find in there—and don't limit your search to books. Magazines and periodicals are a gold mine of material to use. Sometimes I'll go into a used book store with no topic in mind and see what strikes me. That's how I found a book on figure drawing that I'll tell you about in a moment.

Figure 10-1. Click on **alibris.com** "advanced search" option

Government Sites

In some cases, you can use government information entirely for your product. In other cases, you might use some government information as a bonus or to supplement the main information product. Here are different sites to browse while keeping your mind open. Also, don't forget that each agency has its own site with tons of information.

www.firstgov.gov: Catalog of US government publications

www.gpoaccess.gov/cgp/index.html: Federal Citizen Information Center

www.pueblo.gsa.gov: www.library.okstate.edu/govdocs/browsetopics

www.access.gpo.gov: www.gpoaccess.gov/cgp/index.html

Google's government search engine: www.google.com/unclesam

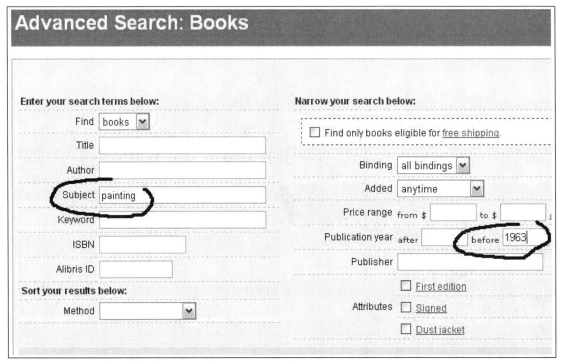

Figure 10-2. Using **alibris.com** advanced search

For more places to search for public domain information, go to: **www.moonlightingontheinternet.com/publicdomain**.

Clearing Rights of Public Domain Works

Onward. It's important to be thorough in clearing the rights to our title.

If you're working with a government publication, you're on the safe side if it's federal, since nearly everything created by the federal government is public domain. No need to go further. Now, on the state side, it depends on the document. The easiest thing to do is to contact the agency issuing the document and ask them.

Okay, with a written work for which we think the copyright has expired, it gets a little more interesting ....

Public Domain

As you remember, anything published in the U.S. before 1923 is public domain now. No need to go further. However, if your work was published between 1923 and 1963, then we need to do some digging ....

Researching 1923–1963 Works

Okay, let's talk about researching works from between 1923 and 1963, because this is mportant. The years 1923–1963 contain a bonanza of material that could be in the public domain. The most important thing we need to know is if a work was renewed in its 28th year.

> The years 1923–1963 contain a bonanza of material that could be in the public domain. The most important thing we need to know is if a work was renewed in its 28th year.

If it was not renewed in the 28th year, that material became public domain. However, if it was renewed, the copyright extension lasts 95 years. If it was renewed, it's not going to be up for grabs for a long time. But, you know, the good part is that most people didn't renew: the estimates I've seen say that 15 percent of books from this period had their copyrights renewed.

So, let's talk about how to check if a copyright was renewed. There are three ways to do this:

1. Do it yourself
2. Check with the copyright office
3. Hire a firm to do it for you

If a work was published between 1950 and 1963, the Library of Congress and the copyright office have made it easy on all of us, because you can go to **www.copyright.gov** and search (see Figure 10-3).

Once there, select what the work is—whether it's a book, a piece of music, etc. You select that button, and they have another one for serials, as well as one for documents.

Most of the time, you'll probably be working with books, so click over on the left side. As Figure 10-4 shows, they let you search by author, title, or claimant (the person, either a corporation or an individual). There's also a registration number you can do a search by, so if you have the original registration number of the copyright document and some other information, you can do a combined search.

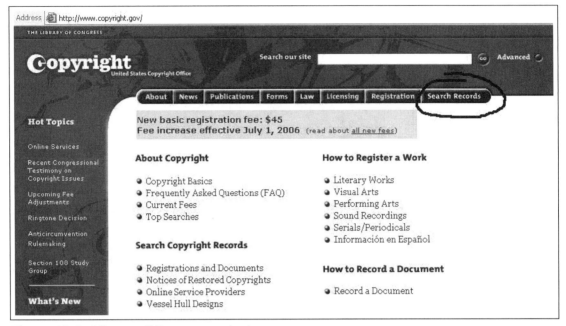

Moonlighting on the Internet

Figure 10-3. Library of Congress web site

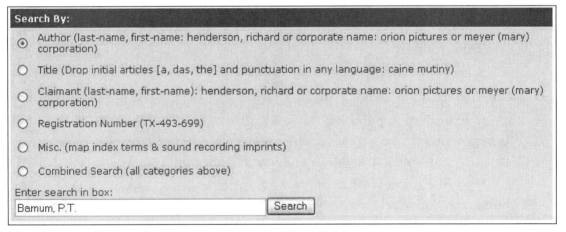

Figure 10-4. Library of Congress search by various fields

I will start by typing in the author's name (last name, first name). Now, there are two options here. There's a brief summary display and there's a full record display. Select full record display (Figure 10-5) and it'll tell you all about the original work and when it was renewed (Figure 10-6). So this

is a little different, but you can see as you're playing around with it that it'll tell you when the work was created, when the copyright was registered, and when it was renewed.

Check one or more terms, select the type of output display, and then click Submit:

☐ BARNUM, MIKE (1 item)
☐ BARNUM, ORA GEORGE, 1958- (1 item)
☐ BARNUM, PHILLIP R (3 items)
☑ BARNUM, PHINEAS T (2 items)
☑ BARNUM, PHINEAS TAYLOR, 1810-1891 (2 items)
☐ BARNUM, RHODA W., 1924- (1 item)
☐ BARNUM, RICHARD (1 item)
☐ BARNUM, RICHARD STEVEN, 1965- (1 item)
☐ BARNUM, RICHARD, 1947- (3 items)
☐ BARNUM, RIGGERS (1 item)
☐ BARNUM, ROBERT G (1 item)
☐ BARNUM, ROBERT GERALD, 1961- (1 item)

Select type of output display:
○ Brief (Summary) Display
◉ Full-Record Display
[Submit]

[More Items]

[Conduct Another Search]

Figure 10-5. Selecting the Full Record Display option

In this example, the only new material being claimed as copyrighted is the introduction, because they used the 1855 autobiography *The Life of P.T. Barnum*, which is public domain. If you find a work for which the copyright has been renewed, that means it is still in copyright and you cannot use it. You can use any facts, ideas, or titles, but you can't go out and do all the great things you want to do with it. If I'm doing a search myself, I don't feel confident unless I do the search on different criteria. So I'd start with an author search. If that didn't pull up anything, I'd move to title, and then I might even try the publisher. I try to be as thorough as possible.

1. Registration Number:	TX-836-352
Title:	Struggles and triumphs : or, Forty years' recollections of P. T. Barnum / [Phineas Taylor Barnum] ; edited and abridged with an introd. by Carl Bode.
Imprint:	New York : Penguin Books, c1981.
Description:	394 p.
Note:	Originally pub. in 1855 as The Life of P. T. Barnum, written by himself.ISBN: ISBN 0-14-039-004-9.
Claimant:	acViking Penguin, Inc.
Created:	1981
Published:	17Dec81
Registered:	7Jan82
Author on © Application:	Viking Penguin, Inc., employer for hire of introd. by Carl Bode.
Claim Limit:	NEW MATTER: "introd. by Carl Bode."
Special Codes:	1/B/D//A
Cross Reference:	acP. T. Barnum. SEE Phineas Taylor Barnum , 1810-1891.

Figure 10-6. Full Record Display results

Next, let's talk about books published between 1923 and 1949. This is a little bit harder to find, but it's still searchable online here: **www.digital.library.upenn.edu/books/cce**. At this site, volunteers have input all the copyright renewal records, but they've uploaded them as graphics. Now, you add 28 years to the date of the copyright notice on your work and start with the listings there. It will show the copyright renewals in alphabetical order.

Figure 10-7 illustrates what a listing looks like:

```
Let's neck!   © 15Dec44; AA479462.
   Processing & Books, Inc. (PWH);
   10Apr72; R527130.
```

Figure 10-7. Copyright Renewal Records

In this example, you can see that the original work was published in 1944, and the copyright was renewed in 1972. Now, the thing with these records is that you want to make sure you check years 27, 28, and 29. So, for example, in the case of a work published in 1941, you would look up entries for 1968, 1969, and 1970 to be thorough; the work could have been renewed during the 28th year after publication, and this is taken from the actual date of publication. So you want to make sure that you look up all three of those years, to be doubly sure and thorough. Plus, be sure to not only check the author's name, but also the publisher's name.

Moving on …

Let's say you don't want to do this yourself or you want to be extremely thorough. To document your public domain search, you can have the copyright office do it. However, the bad part about them is they're pretty slow, and there's really not that much benefit to having them do it. They charge you $75 an hour, and they tell you it's going to take eight to twelve weeks to do a copyright search.

So that's why I think your best option is to hire a search firm. This is, by far, the easiest, and it's going to cost you a couple of bucks. At last check, it was $90 to do a renewal search. The top company is a law firm called Thomson and Thomson; they're going to be listed in your Rolodex. They're a DC law firm, very quick turnaround, and easy to deal with—**www.thomson-thomson.com.** I've also been using a smaller firm in Virginia called Hynak & Associates—**www.hynak.com**—and they're a bit cheaper if you mention my name.

You give them the title, the author of the work, the date it was published, and so on—all the information you have on it. And they'll come back and tell you whether or not the copyright was renewed. Then you put that in your file for documentation purposes, and you're all set.

Now it's time to talk about turning our "clean as a whistle" public domain work into a product. Remember, we now have the power to do anything we want with it. We can sell it as-is, we can cut it up, we can create derivative works from it, etc. We are only limited by our imagination.

> … it's time to talk about turning our "clean as a whistle" public domain work into a product. Remember, we now have the power to do anything we want with it.

But to help get your imagination going, how about I give you a couple of examples of products created using public domain content?

We sell a "gold" package of my best-selling Instant Sales Letters® templates. And we had about 66 percent of people go for this gold package.

The gold package consists of business letter templates plus a book that I found in the public domain called *How to Write Letters That Win*. It's an awesome book, so I had someone retype it for me, and then I created it as a download. It costs $15 more for the gold package, and 66 percent of people go for it. Now when you have 300–400 people buying something each month, and 66 percent of the people pay you an extra $15, that's pretty cool. So I've been using public domain for a long time.

I'll give you another example that should get you excited. I wanted to prove that you could use public domain to create a product from scratch in a marketplace that I had absolutely no knowledge of, no ties with, no mailing list, no people I could do joint ventures with, nothing.

So I chose artists. What do they say about artists? A lot of people say, "Starving artists."

Not really a very good marketplace to go after, most may say. Remember, one of the criteria that we use is "Do they have money?" The answer here is a big fat no! Right there, I had one strike against me. The other strikes were that I had no list, and I had no expertise.

But what I did was, I found this little book in a used book store called *Anatomy and Drawing*, by an illustrator named Victor Perard. It shows all about how to draw the human figure and anatomy, legs, arms, head, whatever. The book was published in 1939, so that meant I had to investigate the title further. I sent the title and details over to my law firm, and they confirmed that the copyright was not renewed. From there, I had the work scanned so that I could turn it into a digital format. The company I use is **www.megainternetsuccess.com/pdscan**—they will scan the book for you and send you a digital file that you can manipulate. That's important, or else you won't be able to cut and paste the portion of the work you need. It'll be one big image file (like a graphic). I had done that before, and the results weren't good.

The next step was writing my sales letter for it, a simple, basic sales letter. Anybody could have written it. You can check it out at **www.figuredrawingsecrets.com.**

I renamed the book and gave it a better, more descriptive, benefit-oriented title. It's now called *Figure Drawing Secrets*, instead of *Anatomy*

and Drawing. You can see it's for sale under the original title on Amazon as a real book, and cheaper than what people pay online for my version (Figure 10-8).

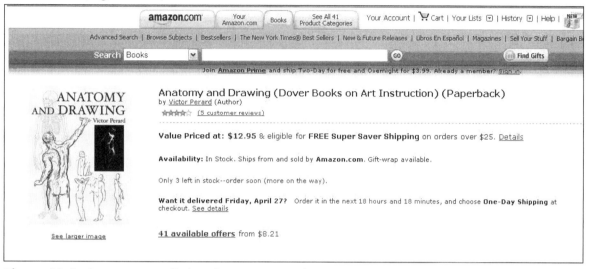

Figure 10-8. Amazon.com listing for *Anatomy and Drawing*

And then I started advertising it. Within a week, I made my first sale. We sell it for $14.95, so it's not very much (but more than the paperback version on Amazon and for a bigger profit margin). If I paid a little more attention to it, I could definitely get the sales numbers way up there. But it's just like one of those little things that runs by itself on autopilot. It's been running like this for two years now—making about $200–400 every month. It pays for a couple of dinners out and shows that you can do this with just about any marketplace. Don't worry, I'll be covering the promotion process in the next chapter.

> *It's been running like this for two years now—making about $200–400 every month. It pays for a couple of dinners out and shows that you can do this with just about any marketplace.*

One of the best parts about public domain is that you don't need to be an expert yourself in the subject matter. One of my students, Dale Gibbons from Salem, Oregon, took several public domain crochet patterns and followed my advice to bring in $4,055.05 in less than three months with his first niche site.

Another way to use public domain works is to take a generic title and make it more specific. My student Matt LeClear did this with several sales-related works he found in the public domain. He told me that he "authored" seven e-books for his audience of real estate agents. He said, "*I take old sales books and rework them to have a slant towards real estate agents. When sales die down on each new product, I simply go to my 'vault' and write a new volume! Then I release it to my opt-in list (all of whom are real estate agents). I now gross $10k–$20k in online sales a month with my eyes closed. Before I bought your kit, I was lucky if I pulled in $5k for the whole month.*"

I love public domain examples, so let me share two more from my friends.

The first one is Rebecca Fine, from Seattle, Washington. One of her friends sent her a little book by Wallace D. Wattles called *The Science of Getting Rich*. I believe it was published in 1910. And she loved this book so much that she wanted to share it with other people. It struck a place in her heart. So she said, "What I want to do is just give this book away." So she started e-mailing it to friends, and it started spreading around. She finally got tired of getting so many requests to download this book or sending the file to people that she put it up on her web site. Remember, 1910 is way before the 1923 cutoff that we talked about, so she could do whatever she wanted with it. So once she put it up on her web site, she got a little bit smarter about it and put her name and her web site on there so people could find it. All of a sudden—these are her words, not mine—she "accidentally built a nice six-figure business with this little viral e-book." By "viral," I mean people pass it along, then other people pass it along, and so forth. Following this, what she did was take the main content of his work and turned it into all kinds of derivative products. She created an audio CD with the same words in the book by recording into a microphone. Now, she has a derivative work on which she owns the copyright, even though the words she's recording are all in the public domain. I love Rebecca because she's the perfect example of creating an "internet lifestyle" business. She just e-mailed me. Here's what she said:

> As for "moonlighting," I guess you could call what I do that since I hardly "work" at all. I've been mostly traveling since that first Underground seminar and the revenues just keep going up: can't beat that! Just got back into the States (I'm in gorgeous Asheville, NC, at the moment) after spending the last seven months exploring Mexico, and will now go ahead and get that cruising sailboat this summer to take off to who-knows-where. Friends ask me if I'm going to sail AROUND the world and I always reply that I'm going to sail ABOUT the world. Maybe around, maybe now; we'll see! I'll keep going as long as it's fun. And it'll be REALLY interesting to see how I can run a bunch of online stuff via satellite connection and so on. It's all very exciting to me.

So, how easy is it to create a product?

And then she went a step further. She has what's called an e-class around the e-book, where she e-mails people lessons out of the book. Then they do homework, after which she critiques their homework based on the principles in the book. So she built this whole business around this public domain book. One of the things I love about her story is that if you go to **amazon.com** right now, there are several people selling the same book. Remember, if thousands of people use the same public domain book, it still remains public domain.

I have another example, which is pretty wild. A friend of mine named Matt Furey helps people get in better shape. He was doing a wrestling camp in Iowa when he stumbled upon this dusty manual from 1911 or so by a guy named "Farmer Burns." Farmer Burns was this great, much-publicized catch-wrestler at the time. Now, I don't know what that is, but Matt's people knew what catch-wrestling is. Matt read this material, and he thought it was some of the best material he'd ever seen. It was this correspondence course that Farmer Burns used to sell by mail. I don't remember how many lessons there were, but let's say there were 15. What Matt did was bind up all 15 lessons and photocopy it to sell for $50. Remember, it's public domain—we can do whatever we want with it.

Once people started buying it, he thought, "Hmm, this is pretty good. People are buying it. Maybe they want a more advanced version of this." Matt then created videos around each of the lessons in this Farmer Burns catch-wrestling course. You know how much he sold them for? Hope you're sitting down. He sold the videos for $599! Yep, he makes a nice six-figure income each year, from the videos of this Farmer Burns outfit. So, public domain can be big or small.

Now, let's say you didn't have the expertise to videotape yourself like Matt did. No problem—you could hire a wrestling coach or someone to do the moves.

Want even more successful examples?
Go to: **www.moonlightingontheinternet.com/success** to see even more info marketing success stories we couldn't fit in the book.

Moonlighting on the Internet Method #1

Section 3

Building Your Web Site

Chapter 11

Getting Your Site's Foundation Built

W e've covered how to come up with an idea, how to test it, and how to "steal" an idea. Now we start working on our foundation. We'll cover registering your domain.

Registering the Right Domain

Your next assignment is to register a domain. For this purpose, I suggest **www.ultimatediscountdomains.com** for a good, inexpensive option.

Dot-com is the best way to go. I prefer dot-com over dot-net or dot-org or any other domain name extensions (if you want to protect your best-selling brand, then you might consider registering all the versions). The domain I used for my project is the title of my book—**www.figuredrawingsecrets.com**. Notice there is a built-in benefit in the domain. I like to use domains that have benefits and meaning attached to them along with my top keywords. For example, **www.instantsalesletters.com**. If you heard that domain you'd know what it is, and there's a benefit to it. Also, when deciding on a domain name, don't pick something that can be easily misheard or misspelled. For example, **www.4herlove.com**—if you told me that domain name I'd wonder if it was "four," "for," or "4," or "fore" like a golf pun. Who knows? Make it easy.

There are still a lot of good domains left if you use a prefix that's descriptive, like I used "instant" in front of "sales letters." I've also used "mega" and "ultimate" when looking for domains. A good tool is **www.nameboy.com**, which lets you enter keywords and gives you suggestions for available domains.

Or here's another tip for you—there are tens of thousands of good domains that expire for one reason or another. You can buy expired domains or names that others are selling at auction. Some of the bigger resources for this are **www.sedo.com** and **www.godaddy.com** (look under "domains" and find the option for bidding on auctions).

Possible names: _____

Possible names: _____

Possible names: _____

Possible names: _____

Possible names: _____

> Even though registering a domain seems like a simple process, there are more considerations than I can cover in this book. I've set up a special audio for you that covers all the factors involved and more. You can listen by going to **www.moonlightingontheinternet.com/domains**.

Okay, now the next part of our foundation is domain hosting.

Domain Hosting

When my friends launched their first sites way back in the "dark ages" of 1997, they were paying almost $150 a month in hosting and data transfer charges. Today, it's cheaper than ever to find a good host and get going for a few bucks a month.

Now, don't forget that I'm a total computer dunce, so I've asked my "techie" guy, Paul Galloway, to jump in here and help out with some guidelines. Paul is also the author of *Internet Marketer's Little Black Book*, which is full of tons of resources—**www.theinternetmarketerslittleblackbook.com**.

Here's what Paul had to say about the subject of web sites and web hosting:

What It Takes to Get Your Own Web Site

Okay, so you've got a great idea and you want to get online with it ASAP— what's required?

If you've never done it before, it can seem like a daunting, nigh-impossible task. In reality, it's relatively simple and everything but the web design can be done in about an hour.

The first thing you need to do is register your domain name, which is your web "address." For instance, if you're selling cookie recipes, you might try to register "cookierecipes.com." If it's something simple like that, chances are someone else has already registered it, so you have to try variations like "besthomemadecookierecipes.com" or "downhome-cookierecipes.com," etc.—just try to make it relate to whatever your site is about.

> The first thing you need to do is register your domain name, which is your web "address."

There are several places you can go to register a domain name ("domain registrars"). A couple popular ones are **ultimatediscountdomains.com** and **000domains.com**—and it will usually cost $8.95–13.95 to register a domain for one year.

When you register a domain, you'll be given all kinds of upgrade options, such as hosting, mail forwarding, etc., but I usually stick with the domain registration and do my hosting elsewhere (see the web hosting discussion elsewhere in this book).

Once you have your domain registered, you'll need to get a web hosting account. Before you choose a web hosting solution, be sure to review the section in this book where I discuss the various things to look for in web hosting. You can get hosting for less than $15/month (much less in some cases).

Now, once you have a domain name and a web hosting account, you have to connect them. This involves changing a setting at your registrar (where you registered the domain). When you get a web hosting account, your "welcome" e-mail will usually include "Domain Name Server" or "DNS" information. This will consist of two values similar to these:

- NS1.YOURWEBSERVER.COM
- NS2.YOURWEBSERVER.COM

Log in to your domain registrar account and poke around until you find the "nameserver" settings screen. Enter these two values for your name servers and you're done!

Usually within a few minutes (but it can sometimes take a full day), your site will be "live"—there won't be anything there to speak of, but it will be accessible to anyone on the internet. Now it's just a matter of you putting your desired content there!

The "how" of web site design is beyond the scope of this book. But getting started can be as simple as creating a document in Microsoft Word, clicking "File ➔ Save As," and saving it as a "Web Page, Filtered" page. Save it as "index.html" (this is the default name most web servers look for) and upload it to your site.

> *Microsoft Word is only good for the most basic web pages, so if you're going to do anything more complex than a half-dozen simple pages, I'd encourage you to get a web design application ....*

Microsoft Word is only good for the most basic web pages, so if you're going to do anything more complex than a half-dozen simple pages, I'd encourage you to get a web design application such as Dreamweaver or FrontPage. There are even some pretty good free web design applications at **nvu.com** and **freeserifsoftware.com**.

I've mentioned "uploading" files to your site, but how is this accomplished?

When you get your web hosting "welcome" e-mail, it will usually include FTP information. FTP stands for "File Transfer Protocol," and is usually what is used to copy files from your local machine to a remote server (your web hosting server). If you have a professional web design application like those mentioned above, it may have FTP functions built in. If not, you'll need to get an FTP program such as WS_FTP or CuteFTP. There are several free FTP programs available, too—just go to **download.com** and search for them.

Regardless of what you're using for FTP, you'll need to configure it using the FTP settings specified by your web hosting company.

So, in summary, here are the steps to setting up your own web site:

1. Register your domain name.

2. Get your web hosting account.

3. Point your domain to your web hosting account.

4. Create your content (web pages).

5. Upload your content to your web hosting account.

Again, everything except the web content creation can be done in an hour or two, so you can get started right away.

What to Look for in Web Hosting

One of the most critical decisions an online business owner will make is the selection of a web hosting company. The wrong choice here can result in lost revenue, lost customer goodwill, and a lot of wasted time. And you'll probably lose some hair, too. Do you get the gist of what I'm saying here? Good!

BEFORE you start looking at web hosting companies, you need to decide what software you'll be running on your server.

For instance, if you're going to have a membership site, you need to do some shopping around for a membership site management application.

Or if you're going to have an online e-commerce store, you will need to decide which shopping cart and/or content management system to use.

Only AFTER you've selected the software to use should you start looking at web hosting options. The reason for this is because software is usually designed to run on a specific kind of server (either Unix/Linux or Microsoft). Some of the bigger software companies offer versions for both platforms, but this is an exception to the rule.

> *Only AFTER you've selected the software to use should you start looking at web hosting options.*

If you have software that can work on either platform, I usually recommend a Unix/Linux server platform—there's more software available for that platform than for Windows, and this is especially true for open-source (free) software.

Okay, now let's talk about your web hosting choices.

Account features are good to review (and I will review some in a moment), but there are so many companies offering nearly the same features that it's almost a non-issue. Almost. Price isn't a determining factor either—server space is very cheap these days.

But the really important things are RELIABILITY and SUPPORT.

You need to be sure they have redundant connections to the internet "backbone" and that they are *up* 99.99 percent of the time (nobody can guarantee 100 percent uptime, but some get very close). And if there are problems, you don't want to jump through the hoops of a ticket system. Trust me on this, you'll want to pick up the phone and talk to a real live person ASAP!

I'm not going to recommend any hosting companies here, because like stocks, past performance doesn't guarantee future results. The best thing is to visit the web hosting forums and see what people are saying. One good forum is "Web Hosting Talk": **www.webhostingtalk.com**.

Once you find a couple of hosting companies that look reliable and have verified that they have live support, compare the account features.

Here are a few things to consider:

Bandwidth. This is how much data your account can transfer each month. These days, most accounts have more bandwidth than they need, but that's not always the case. If you're going to have an active multimedia-intensive site (with lots of video and audio files), you will want as much bandwidth as you can get. If someone downloads a 20MB audio or video file from your site, that counts as 20MB of bandwidth. If you're mostly serving web pages, bandwidth shouldn't be a factor unless/until you start getting a LOT of site visitors (thousands every day).

Disk Space. This is how much hard drive space you can use on your server. It used to be that 10MB (megabytes) was plenty for most sites. But now a single audio file can take 10–20+ MB by itself, and video files require even more space. So bigger is better. It's fairly common to see drive space of 50–100GB (that's gigabytes with a G—a gigabyte is 1,000 times more than a megabyte) or more these days. A 50GB account could hold 2,000 20MB audio files with room to spare.

CGI Scripts. Sometimes this is referred to as cgi-bin access. If you are on a Unix/Linux platform, make sure you have this. It's required for most CGI scripts (programs) designed for these systems. This is a standard feature in most accounts, but make sure it's available.

PHP. Software written in PHP is usually associated with Unix/Linux web servers, but some Windows servers can run it, too. If any of your desired server software is written in PHP, make sure your account includes this. This is a standard feature in virtually all Unix/Linux hosting, and is getting more common with Windows.

MySQL. This is the database system most PHP programs use. If you have PHP, you'll probably also have MySQL. But check to make sure, especially if you're using a Windows server (which may only have the MSSQL database). Make sure you can have multiple databases (usually this is standard).

Cron. This is a Unix/Linux scheduling program that is required by some software. It allows you to schedule the automatic execution of a program at regular intervals. Highly recommended and standard on most accounts.

Backup. Make sure your hosting company offers daily data backups of your account.

Domains. Make sure your hosting account allows you to have multiple domains. As your business grows, you'll undoubtedly have additional web sites you want to set up.

Fantastico. If you're using a Unix/Linux web server, I highly recommend you get an account that includes the Fantastico add-on—this will allow you to install many powerful web applications with the click of a button.

For most small businesses, "shared hosting" (where the same web server is used for several clients) offers you plenty of bandwidth and disk space, and it's a good place to start. You can always upgrade to a dedicated server later. Make sure your web hosting company offers both options, as the upgrade will be simpler if it's done without switching hosting companies.

> I've negotiated a special deal with one of the top hosting companies for "Moonies" on a budget who are just getting started. Check out **www.moonlightingontheinternet.com/hosting**.

Putting E-Mail Robots to Work for You

And next on our hit list is a tool that is indispensable—it's called an autoresponder, and you'll wonder how you ever got along without it.

What the heck is an e-mail autoresponder?

"E-mail autoresponders" work like a fax-on-demand system. Maybe you've seen the systems where you call from your fax machine, dial a certain code, and you get a document in your fax machine? Well, an e-mail autoresponder works the same way. If you send an e-mail to an autoresponder address, you'll get back a prewritten message. Until recently, you could only do a one-time autoresponder with one message coming back, but now you can set up a whole sequence of autoresponder messages going out on any day you choose. For example:

Message #1 might go out immediately.

Message #2 goes out two days later.

Message #3 goes out on day five.

Day eight comes another message, etc.

Do you see the beauty of this whole thing yet?

The best part about it is that everything gets done automatically for you because it's triggered when prospects submit their e-mail addresses. So that means you can set up your system once, and it keeps working like a tireless money-making robot, making sure no prospect slips through the cracks. Because the majority of your customers WILL NOT buy on the first visit to your site, it's critical that you have an automated way to follow up with them several times to entice them back to your site to make a purchase. Sequential autoresponders give you that AUTOMATED follow-up without the headache of having to do it yourself manually. Plus, with the service I recommend, you can automatically take buyers out of the prospect sequence so they don't keep getting bothered.

There are two recommendations for autoresponders: the first one is **aweber.com**. This is the best autoresponder service, because that's all they do. They work hard to ensure high e-mail deliverability and are always adding features (and this is the service I use). The other option is to use an "all-in-one" solution that includes a shopping cart, affiliate module (we'll talk more about this), tracking, etc. A good solution for this can be found here: **www.moonlightingontheinternet.com/cart** (you can try it for a 30-day test run).

Here are a few of the best ways to put a series of autoresponders to work for your site:

◆ Follow up with prospects who download an excerpt from your product or sign up for a trial service.

◆ Encourage them to come back to your site for more information or to make their first (or repeat) purchase.

◆ Send out additional testimonials about your product.

◆ Make special offers (that appear to be time-sensitive).

◆ Send articles demonstrating your expertise in the subject matter they are interested in.

◆ Provide an "evergreen" newsletter to prospects to maintain contact.

◆ Automatically follow up with buyers to sell them even more and make sure they stay happy!

Think about how nice it will be to automatically and consistently follow up with customers to increase sales!

You should be adding a subscribe box on your main site so you can start capturing e-mail addresses and names of interested prospects rather than letting them slip through the cracks. Here's an example of one from the figure drawing site (Figure 11-1).

This illustration shows that I'm giving away a preview of the e-book. It's probably one of the easiest ways to get people to give you their e-mail address and allow you to start building a list. This is important, because I can literally wake up any morning with an idea, or if I want to promote somebody else's product to my artist list, I can make money on demand!

Taking Money

Next we need to think about how to take money … ka-ching! There are two main ways to do so:

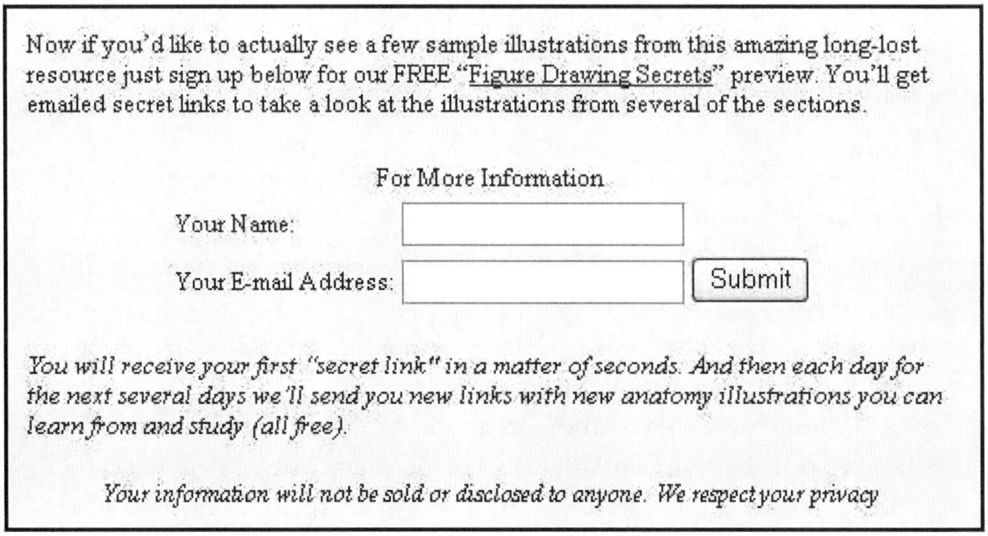

Now if you'd like to actually see a few sample illustrations from this amazing long-lost resource just sign up below for our FREE "Figure Drawing Secrets" preview. You'll get emailed secret links to take a look at the illustrations from several of the sections.

For More Information

Your Name: [   ]

Your E-mail Address: [   ] [Submit]

You will receive your first "secret link" in a matter of seconds. And then each day for the next several days we'll send you new links with new anatomy illustrations you can learn from and study (all free).

Your information will not be sold or disclosed to anyone. We respect your privacy

Figure 11-1. Example of a subscribe box

1. You get set up with your own merchant account and start accepting MasterCard, Visa, American Express, and Discover.
2. You get a third party to do it for you.

There are pros and cons to each. If you want the absolute simplest solution to accept credit cards and get going without worrying about much else, I suggest **www.getclickbank.com**. We talked about them before. Clickbank will allow you to sell your digital product while it takes care of most of the details for you. They will cut you a check every two weeks for the products sold and cut your affiliates a check, as well. That's the good part. The bad part is, you obviously pay more than if you had your own merchant account. It's about $50 to get set up, and then they charge you $1 plus 7.5 percent of the product cost for them to handle everything.

A second way that costs you less and lets you accept credit cards is taking payment via PayPal. They've really made big strides since eBay purchased them, and they're worth considering as an option.

And finally, there's your own merchant account. You will pay about 2.5 percent in fees to accept credit cards, but you have to handle customer support and deal with affiliates (which we'll cover shortly). If you are serious about the business, set yourself up with a merchant account—**www.sure-firemarketing.com/creditcard**—but if you want to just dip your toe in the water, go with **clickbank.com**. As of now, another limitation of Clickbank is that you can only sell digitally delivered products.

Shopping Cart

If you want total control of everything and plan to go full-time, use the "all-in-one" resource I recommend at **www.moonlightingontheinternet.com/cart**. You'll have all the bells and whistles to run a complete e-business.

Moonlight on Bernadette Doyle

Bernadette's Story

Before Moonlighting, there was lots of travel working for clients on-site and overnight stays. **www.clientmagnets.com** Sounds glamorous, but it isn't. Having a baby then would have been—if you'll pardon the pun—inconceivable. In January 2005, I launched my first online product, and today I've built my list to 7,500. I can work from home and I don't have to leave my eight-month-old baby. These days, I work 25 hours a week, yet I make more money than when I was working 75 hours a week. In fact, last week I made £11,838.82 in seven days!

Bernadette's Advice

I was told that if I cultivate a loyal following of clients and prospects, I could really produce cash on demand—and it's true, and it can be for you, too.

All right, let's get into some more exciting stuff and decide what our package looks like by . . .

Chapter 12

Creating Your HOT Offer

With your product idea, you should be thinking about how you're going to package your information.

Will it be an e-book?

A members-only site?

A set of audio interviews?

An online newsletter?

Or maybe a combination of all of the above?

Remember, there are no correct answers and you can set the rules. Go back over our list of information products selling right now on the web and think about how you're going to package yours.

My **instantsalesletters.com** site is really a combination of tools/templates, e-books, and a private membership site. When people buy, they register their own password, and that gives them unlimited access to our member site. Now, inside the site they'll find the sales letter templates (these are HTML pages, so people can copy and paste them into their word processing programs). They also have access to several e-books (downloadable PDF files), as well as an Excel spreadsheet that helps them figure their profit and loss on a mailing.

Here's is what my original offer looked like:

> $29.95 gets them lifetime access to our site with the 34 fill-in-the-blank sales letter templates for four different business types. Plus they get two bonuses: bonus #1 is an e-book on direct mail secrets and bonus #2 is an Excel spreadsheet. Both bonuses are worth more than double the cost of membership. Everything will be backed by a 100 percent money-back guarantee for one full year.

Not a bad deal, but after I found out that the market was interested, I increased the number of templates, bonuses, etc. (and of course the price) to make the product more appealing.

So think about your offer ...

How Can You Make Your Offer as Irresistible as Possible?

Your job is to create such powerful offers that anyone reading them would say to themselves, "My goodness, I'd have to be a complete idiot not to take them up on this deal!"

Your job is to create such powerful offers that anyone reading them would say to themselves, "My goodness, I'd have to be a complete idiot not to take them up on this deal!" Your goal is to provide a dollar of value in exchange for a dime. In effect, you are selling money at a discount. This makes it easier to get a high number of people to say "yes" to your proposition. And bonuses can help sway customers to buy.

Many times, I might even take something out that I was originally going to put into the product to use it as a bonus. Bonuses really do sell! Here are a few bonus ideas for you:

◆ Software. Check out what's available as "freeware" from **download.com**.

◆ E-books. There are tons of e-books that come with free redistribution rights. Do a search for free e-books.

◆ Articles. You'll notice that a lot of people give away their articles for extra publicity. You can compile these into an excellent free bonus.

◆ Your own tools. I love to give away stuff I've already created for my own use, because it doesn't take me any time and it is highly valued. For instance, with the Instant Sales Letters package, I give people my own spreadsheet that I use for direct mail profit and loss. I've also given away copies of letters and templates I've used for my own business.

◆ Other public domain material

◆ Licensed products/reports/software, etc.

◆ Free reports

◆ Free spreadsheets

◆ Free audio

◆ Free video

◆ Free consultation

◆ Free critiques

◆ Free membership

◆ Other people's products or services

◆ Discount coupons toward a service or product

◆ Free reprint/resale rights

Keep adding value and more bonuses until you come up with an offer that makes your prospect feel guilty for not ordering. We'll cover this when we talk about copywriting and EXACTLY how to achieve this.

Okay, let's look at a real example of a compelling offer …

The Real-World Offer for *Anatomy and Drawing*

Here's the offer I created for the *Anatomy and Drawing* public domain material I told you about:

1. First, I changed the title to something more compelling—*Figure Drawing Secrets*.

2. Next, I took the chapter on head and neck illustrations and pulled it out as a bonus. From my research I found that drawing faces is one of the most important things to artists. That's one of the real hot buttons. So, this is one of the easiest ways to create a bonus.

3. Third, I started looking at government information for potential bonuses. With a quick search, I found information at **www.firstgov.gov** that lists information for art grants. What an awesome bonus! People

love free money, and it's a proven bestseller. Maybe you've seen Matthew Lesko, the guy on TV with all the question marks on his suit selling his "FREE Money from the Government" deal. That infomercial has been around for awhile, so that means it's a good seller. That's a perfect idea for a bonus.

4. Finally, I went to **www.download.com** and did an advanced search using the criterion "free license" along with different keywords such as "art," "drawing," and "graphics." I found a couple of potential software products. Then I checked them out to see if they were any good. Some are a total waste, and that will make customers furious at you.

It's important to read the restrictions on the distribution of the software. Typically, "freeware" software can be given away any way you want—however, you definitely need to read the terms. For instance, the software I wanted to include takes people's photos and turns them into cool screensavers along with transitions. I figured that "artsy" people probably have some images they'd like to create as cool screensavers. I read the restrictions, and I was a little concerned because it wasn't clear if I could give it away or not. To get clarification, I e-mailed a polite note to the person behind the site and asked and for permission. I also made it a point to include my regular e-mail address and not my **surefiremarketing.com** account, because some software people are not very commercial. Here's what it said:

> Hello,
>
> My name is Yanik Silver and I'mrepublishing a book on anatomy drawing for art students. (The site is not yet up.)
>
> I found your program the other day from **download.com** and I'd love to include your product as a free bonus to anyone that gets our e-book. As per your licenseagreement, I am emailing to request permission.
>
> I can direct people to the **download.com** site here:
>
> http://download.com.com/3000-2407-10127107.html?tag=lst-0-17 so they will always get the latest version.
>
> I really appreciate the opportunity to help get the word out about this fabulous program.

Please let me know if this is okay with you.

Thank you,

Yanik Silver

yanxxxxxx@comcast.net

301-770-0423

I got the OK from the developer, and that was how I was able to give out another bonus.

Moonlight on Stacey Parks

Stacey's Story

I got started at the beginning of 2005 by writing an info product, *The Insider's Guide to Film Distribution*. I had started hearing about internet marketing ... and then began reading everything I could on marketing info products—including your newsletters and web sites. So I sat down finally and wrote my info product, went into credit card debt, and hired someone to build a site for me—which took a little leap of faith—and started selling my product!

Before Moonlighting, I had more free time at night, that's for sure! But, hey, I also didn't have the extra money I have today or the financial freedom to help my family ... I had a lot more debt that I've since paid off ... I wouldn't be debt-free if it weren't for this side business, and I certainly wouldn't be a homeowner! Today, I've grown from one info product to three;

www.filmspecific.com

I have separate sales sites for each and have recently started a membership site per the inspiration from your Underground Series II DVDs ... I cater to a niche of independent filmmakers seeking distribution, and they are CHEAP! But despite the odds and everyone telling me I could never get indie filmmakers to reach in their pockets and pay for information, I've had a profit of almost six figures so far. I work full-time for BBC Worldwide, so this is totally a moonlighting gig ... and now the momentum has started to pick up, and I'm clearing at least a few thousand every month with one part-time employee working for me. We have a nice new home, I'm debt-free, and I help my family when I can and when they need it. I'm really happy with the financial freedom I have ... and it's all from making just a few thousand extra bucks per month.

Stacey's Advice

I looked at what was out there and thought, if they can do it, it's certainly worth a try! What's there to lose but a few hundred bucks on your credit card to get started?

Moving on—let's discuss pricing.

How to Price Your Information Product

The next piece we need to consider is pricing for the product. The worst thing people can do is underprice their products. You can sell digital information (delivered totally online) products for $14.95 to $99-plus all day long.

One of my friends, John Harricharan, put his work of fiction called *Power Pause* at **powerpause.com** and is selling it for huge margins. His e-book, only about 120 pages long, covers a fantastic three-minute exercise to get whatever you want in life: health, wealth, happiness. I love his book. Anyway, he started selling it at $29 and only one person bought it. Then he raised the price to $39, and maybe two or three people bought it. Then he made it $49, and a couple more people bought it. At $69, a couple more people bought it. Finally, he went all the way up to $97 and he got a flood of orders. In his first year selling this e-book, he made six figures practically without trying, as a side project. He's a real published author, published by some major book houses.

> *If your information will easily help someone make an extra $5,000, you could sell the info product for $100 or $200 easy, right?*

The big thing to consider is, how much value are you providing to people? If your information will easily help someone make an extra $5,000, you could sell the info product for $100 or $200 easy, right? But if your market is a little more hobby-related, such as needlepoint or crochet, then it's a whole lot harder to get a couple of hundred dollars for something. If you have a digital product, I'd probably price it around $14.95 to $19.95. But these are only guidelines. The best thing is to test price points. Also, the more obscure and specialized the information is, the more you can price it for. To broaden your prospective, here's one of my Underground™ Millionaire MasterMind members, Lance Allen. He sells everything from downloadable e-books to higher-priced workshops on a very interesting topic.

Moonlight on Lance Allen

Lance's Story

I had gotten a reputation on a local online message board for having a lot of success with women, and guys kept coming to me for advice. Finally, in February of 2004, the moderator came to me and told me I should run a workshop. He also introduced me to Dan Kennedy's and Yanik Silver's material later that year. I was making some money on the side and still had my full-time job. I didn't get into active online marketing until late 2005—I'm not sure what the heck took me so long!

Before Moonlighting, I basically had two full-time jobs—my full-time gig at a tech company and my hours-for-dollars gig coaching guys personally. It was an exciting life for awhile, but with all the work, it got old quick. Most importantly for me, at 33 years old, I still felt like I was a failure in business. I spent most of my time in college writing long business plans. I'd worked at Netscape and many of the other hot companies in the big web boom. I'd even started my own dot-com with some friends and raised millions of dollars, only to watch the market and the company go south. I'd worked hard all my life and tried a lot of things, but I still felt far away from any real financial success. What was worse, before I met Yanik, I thought I would have to go find business partners and investors for another shot at wealth. I didn't realize I could build my part-time hobby into a global business all on my own without having to answer to anyone.

In the middle of 2005, I made the move to PickUp101 full-time, and we were just starting to think about products and online marketing. I was working my tail off, and over the course of the year, we made enough to cover expenses and basically pay me a modest salary. What I really did that year was lay the foundation for an online business that launched in December of 2005. In 2006, we had well over 10 times the growth, bringing in over $2 million in revenue. Now, in April 2007, we have coaches all over the world and a huge fan base that gets our e-mails every day and can't wait to get our next product. We'd always had great products and workshops, but before we got online, not many guys were getting exposed to the material.

www.pickup101.com

Today I eat a lot better, I travel better, and I have much better vacations. It's fun to go to the best restaurants whenever I want and to go shopping without ever looking at prices. Honestly, as great as the lifestyle improvements are, the satisfaction of knowing that I'm truly in control of my work and my finances is much more gratifying to me. Another huge benefit is meeting happy customers. Guys come up to me all the time and thank me for introducing them to the material we sell. They're basically just thanking me for doing my job—that never happened to me in tech.

Moonlighting on the Internet

Don't shoot for the moon right away and start some huge business when you haven't proved yourself. Instead ask yourself, "How can I make a little money RIGHT NOW?" to prove you're on the right track and give yourself some confidence. If you can just make a little bit at first, then you'll have a much better perspective on how to make more later. I used to spend a lot of time discussing big business strategy; now I just follow the money.

Brainstorm an irresistible offer. Make your offer so appealing that anybody would have to be crazy to not take you up on it. Think about the ultimate end benefit of what your prospect would want and make sure your offer has all the elements they need to get to the finish line.

Main Product: _____

Format: _____ (e-book, membership site, audio, etc.)

Bonus Idea: _____

Format: _____ (e-book, membership site, audio, etc.)

Bonus Idea: _____

Format: _____ (e-book, membership site, audio, etc.)

Bonus Idea: _____

Format: _____ (e-book, membership site, audio, etc.)

Bonus Idea: _____

Format: _____ (e-book, membership site, audio, etc.)

Bonus Idea: _____

Format: _____ (e-book, membership site, audio, etc.)

Moonlight on Joe Dean

Joe's Story

Before Moonlighting, I spent years putting on live, large-scale themed adventures (hired actors, commissioned costumes, sets, fog machines ... all kinds of cool stuff). It took so much time from my family, though. I have three sons now and am grateful for every minute I get to be with them, thanks to the opportunities that the internet has provided.

Only in my dreams would I have ever imagined my current career and lifestyle. As a professional treasure hunt and theme adventure designer (yes, that actually is a legitimate profession), I've developed hundreds of themed events for corporations and private parties over the past 25 years. The exorbitant amount of hours I was spending on them was thrilling and consuming when I was single. Once I became a father, my heart wanted to pursue a new "treasure" ... raising my children.

Through the internet and with $32 in 2001, I launched a web site to share my expertise with those wanting to plan a treasure hunt for their parties and corporate functions. As the popularity of the site grew, so did my inventory of new themes and types of party downloads offered on the site.

www.questexperiences.com

Six years later, I have an amazing FULL-TIME residual income selling the products that I created years ago and relying on the marketing that I put in place at that time. Although I occasionally release a new product, it feels great to know that I only do it when I feel inspired to do so. Having the residual income has allowed me to be with my kids every day while simultaneously pursuing my childhood dreams of designing and building a large-scale entertainment facility. I rely heavily on the inspiration and "boost" I get from the customer comments I receive, giving me the confidence to go after my bigger dreams. I may not be a millionaire in the bank, but I feel like the richest man in the world.

Chapter 13

Setting Up Your Site

Okay, now we are ready to get your web site built. And just in case you are thinking, "Oh no … I don't have any technical expertise to build a site," don't worry.

I'm a total computer dunce. That's the honest truth. I could not put up a web site if I needed to. If it were going to save my life, I could not put up a web site. So you don't need to. I've made a whole lot of money selling information without putting up my own web sites. There are lots of people who can put up a site for you, from college kids to high school kids, or you can hire someone on these freelance sites we already talked about—**elance.com** or **rentacoder.com**.

But you can also learn HTML pretty easily to put up a simple site. You don't need to have any kind of fancy site, anything real flashy or using all the latest technology. What you really want on your web site is the sales letter. Your web site will look more like direct mail. A lot of people might call it junk mail, something that they're familiar with. But that is the kind of stuff that will sell, because people come to your web site and they read the sales copy, the words, and make a purchase based on doing that. That's why the other Moonlighters and I are making money while we sleep. Your site has to be like your 24/7 salesperson.

To tell you the truth, my wife thinks our sites are UGLY—but it doesn't matter. I've tried prettier, and prettier usually doesn't increase our sales.

> *To tell you the truth, my wife thinks our sites are UGLY—but it doesn't matter. I've tried prettier, and prettier usually doesn't increase our sales.*

Most of our sites are just one long sales letter with nothing but words. And people are always asking me, "Oh, do people really read all of that?" And the answer is, "No, people don't read all of that if they're not interested in it."

So if I'm not an artist who wants to learn how to draw people better, I'm not going to read all of that. If I'm not a small business owner who wants to learn how to create better direct mail or web copy or e-mails, I'm not going to read anything on the sales letter site.

Here's a snapshot of my **getfitwhileyousit.com** site (Figure 13-1)—you'll notice it's a simple letter enhanced with a few graphics.

You want to target people who are interested. And I don't want everyone reading it.

But if you are interested, then you'll read every word. A lot of people think that short copy is the way to go, because people don't have a long attention span, and so on. On the web, it's certainly true that more people skim than read. But you want to create your site in such a way that if they skim, they see the bold text, they might see text highlighted in yellow, bigger subheads, so they get enough of the picture that they can actually make a buying decision. Sometimes, they'll read all the way through.

But you've got to answer people's objections, you've got to explain the offer, you've got to make it good, you've got to provide some bonuses, talk about your guarantee.

So it comes down to formulas (unless you want to get good at copywriting). And I'm going give you a simple fill-in-the-blank template that starts on page 114 as an easy shortcut.

Figure 13-1. Getfitwhileyousit.com snapshot

"[Hot Testimonial]"
Well-known person

Stop Putting Up with [Annoying Task] ...

"Here's How You Can Quickly and Easily Get [Benefit] Guaranteed to [Outcome They Want] ... Without [Annoying Problem]!"

Dear Friend,

How much is [product/service] worth to your business?

Suppose you could [take an easy step] and [get the compelling benefit they're looking for].

Imagine ... [help them picture the ideal situation].

Sounds too good to be true?

Well, it isn't if you have the right [tools, resources, etc].

Think about it. A [magic bullet] is the most powerful [employee, skill] [you could ever hire/learn, etc]. [Explain why it's so wonderful]. Simply put, [reiterate how great the magic bullet is].

But Creating That [Magic Bullet] Is the Hard Part ...

It could take you years and can cost you a small fortune to figure out just the right combinations that make some [magic bullets] work— while others fall flat on their faces.

But instead of knocking yourself out trying to come up with the right [what they're looking for], you can now have it inside a new [product] called:

"[Name of Info Product]"

At last! Every [benefit they wanted] is here.

But don't take my word for it, here's what customers from all over the country are saying about this unique [your info category] system:

["Testimonial"]

["Testimonial"]

["Testimonial"]

I know you're probably still skeptical and a bit on the conservative side, but think about this—if you keep doing the same things over and over again—you'll only succeed in getting the same results. That's why I want to let you try out my proven [product]—completely and totally risk-free! (I'll tell you about my unique guarantee in a moment)

Which of These Powerful Secrets Could You Use to [Benefit]?

[Bullet]

[Bullet]

[Bullet]

[Bullet]

[Bullet]

[Bullet]

[Bullet]

[Bullet], plus lots more

Okay, So What's the Cost for This Incredible Resource?

Well, realize that this [whatever your product is] could easily sell for [hundreds/thousands] of dollars. In fact, if you asked a top [expert], like me, to produce [your product] for you, you'd be charged in the neighborhood of $x,xxx to $xx,xxx, not including [some additional charge].

I currently charge a minimum of $x,xxx.xx for [job/service, etc]. So at bare bones minimum you're getting thousands and thousands of dollars' worth of [whatever it is] at your disposal.

But I'm not going to charge you anywhere near that amount or even my minimum project price. In fact, your total investment for [restate what they're getting] is only [$xxx.xx].

So what's the catch? Why am I practically giving this resource away?

Well, it's simple. [Explain reason why].

[#] FREE Bonuses for Ordering by Midnight [Deadline Date]

Free Bonus Gift #1: [Explain Bonus and give value]

Free Bonus Gift #2: [Explain Bonus and give value]

Free Bonus Gift #3: [Explain Bonus and give value]

Together these [#] free bonuses are worth more than [double/triple, etc.] your investment in the [Info Product Name]—but they're all yours absolutely free when you order by midnight [deadline date].

100 percent Risk-Free Guarantee:

Your success in using [product] is completely guaranteed. In fact, here's my 100 percent Better-Than-Risk-Free-Take-It-to-the-Bank Guarantee:

I personally guarantee that if you [state guarantee].

If after a full 12 months, you honestly believe that I haven't delivered on this promise, then let me know and I'll issue you a prompt and courteous refund. Plus, the free bonus gifts are yours to keep regardless, just for your trouble.

Is that fair or what?

That means you can try out all the [material] at my risk, while you see if they work for you or not. And if they don't produce, I honestly want you to ask for your money back. And I'll let you keep the free bonus gifts as my way of thanking you for giving the [your product] a try.

There is no risk whatsoever on your part. The burden to deliver is entirely on me. If you don't produce immediate profits using these instant sales letters, then I'm the loser, not you.

Look at it this way—$x,xxx is really a painless drop in the bucket compared to the money you're going to waste on ineffective [whatever they're currently doing] this year. That's why . . .

You Really Can't Afford Not to Invest in These [Your Product]!

It's easy to get started right away. Just [order instructions: click here/call/fax/mail, etc].

Get ready to [big benefit they want].

Sincerely,

[Your Name]

P.S. Just think! You'll never again suffer through the pain and hassle of [big pain or hardship they're having].

Let me cover a couple key parts of the template for you, starting with . . .

Chapter 14

Headlines That Sell

Your headline's job is to immediately get your prospects' attention and stop them dead in their tracks. On the web, you only have an instant once people hit your site before they decide if they'll leave or stay. It's what they see immediately (the headline) that will have the most impact on your sales.

My headline on **instantsalesletters.com** is "In only 2½ minutes you can quickly and easily create a sales letter guaranteed to sell your product or service … without writing."

Does that pretty much grab your attention if you're interested in selling your product or service? I think so. There is always something going on inside your visitors' heads, and you need to do two things:

1. Break their preoccupation.
2. Enter the conversation that's already going on inside their heads.

Let me explain.

To break someone's preoccupation, you need a strong attention-getting headline that says, "Hey, this is for you!"

Here's what Robert Collier, one of the greatest direct mail copywriters of all time, said about writing sales letters:

> The reader of this letter wants certain things. The desire for him is, consciously or unconsciously, the dominant idea in his mind all the time. You want him to do a certain definite thing for you. How can you tie this up to the thing he wants, in such a way that the doing of it will bring him a step nearer to his goal?

Think about that statement for a moment. It's pretty profound and doesn't apply to sales letters. On the same note, how about these words of advice from John Caples: *"If you have a good headline, you have a good ad. Any competent writer can write the copy. If you have a poor headline, you are licked before you start. Your copy will not be read ... Spend hours writing headlines—or days if necessary."*

John Caples says that he's seen one ad pull 19½ times better than another one simply by changing the headline.

I don't think these masters would have placed such a great importance on headlines if they didn't matter. In fact, John Caples says that he's seen one ad pull 19½ times better than another one simply by changing the headline. I believe it. In my own tests, the best I got was about 2½ times, but that's still pretty darn good. So, for spending the same amount, you can more than double your response—not too bad.

Now, when coming up with powerful headlines, you want to be able to answer the questions nearly everyone has on their minds whenever they read your ad. Here are the questions you need to zero in on:

◆ So what?

◆ Who cares?

◆ What's in it for me?

◆ Why are you bothering me?

If you have good answers to these four critical questions, then you're well on your way to success. I usually write 75–100 headlines to find the right one. I know this sounds crazy, but it's time well spent!

Here are a few of my proven headlines from our sites:

Introducing the amazing new workout program that's the laziest way to get in shape—works almost any place, anytime, anywhere … even while watching TV!

At Last! You Can Draw People and Figures Perfectly in Any Position … Without a Model!

In Only 2½ Minutes You Can Quickly and Easily Create a Sales Letter Guaranteed to Sell Your Product or Service … Without Writing!

Answers to Almost Any House Plant Question (Who Else Wants the Happiest and Healthiest House Plants in the Entire Neighborhood?)

It's easier than you think if you have proven headlines that you can model and adapt for your purpose. I've put 100 top headlines for you inside the online resource section at **www.moonlightingontheinternet.com/headlines**.

Bullet Points

Bullet points are critical to your site's success, because having one compelling bullet point that a prospect really wants to know about can sway the sale in your favor. Remember, people don't want to read the book you're selling—they only want the "secrets" and information inside.

> *Bullet points are critical to your site's success, because having one compelling bullet point that a prospect really wants to know about can sway the sale in your favor.*

That's why bullets are so critical. You need benefit-driven and curiosity-arousing bullets that will make your prospects whip out their wallets and order. Really, bullets are like mini-headlines, so use the same powerful words to build desire and stress benefits or state how they can avoid pain. This is good! Now, we're cooking! We're getting into desire now. Each one of our bullets is like a little fan that keeps stoking the flames of your prospect's desire.

Bullets help people read on the computer because they can scan the bulleted points. So leave lots of space in between your bullets to break up the copy and make it look easy to read. And to help you out, here are some simple bullet formulas you can plug into your site (the underlined areas are the fill-in-the-blank spots):

- <u>Six</u> of the top-selling products on the ___ and why.
- How to turn $xxx into $x,xxx in less than <u>14</u> days with _____.
- How a _____ got # new customers in <u>nine</u> days.
- The amazing secret of getting <u>new customers</u> for your <u>business.</u>
- How to <u>revive a dead car battery</u> without <u>jumper cables.</u>
- Stop ____ without expensive _____.
- Quick and easy _____.
- Five simple ways to _____.
- The secret of _____.

Moonlight on James Jordan

James's Story

I got started online in 2002. I wrote a book on bodybuilding mainly for skinny guys to gain muscle and decided to market it online for cost reasons.

Before Moonlighting, I lived in a hellish apartment, as I had lost everything in a tough real estate market where I live. I didn't even have enough money to buy a $20 e-book by Ken Evoy. It was a huge risk and investment for me to get Yanik's $1,500 Ultimate At-Home Internet copywriting course, but I did, and since using the material, one of my sales letters has sold over 35,000 copies of a $37 to $67 e-book.

I receive around 1,500 to 2,800 unique visitors per day and sell an average of $200 per day net. I have a list of over 25,000 active subscribers. This may not seem impressive, and really it's not, except for the fact that I haven't done a thing to keep this business going since 2004. Basically, it has sustained itself with nothing more than the initial investment in time back in 2003. I am sure that if I actively pursued it, I could make an extra $10,000 to $30,000 a month with it. Today, I have a nice home worth over $500,000 in a high-end area, and a mortgage that is nearly paid off. I am debt-free and own my vehicles, and have even been fortunate enough to provide an excellent education and lifestyle for my two kids and wife. My little internet business was the stepping stone for me to now be a 50 percent owner of 157 acres of land with massive cash flow and profit potential, which I am currently developing ... all because I took the

www.gainmuscleandlosefat.com

time to learn how to write a sales letter and put up a web site.

James's Advice

When I discovered it is not the amount of traffic but the quality of targeted traffic that matters, I took the very same book and changed its name from *The Detailed Physique*, a fitness book targeting the general fitness market, to *Underground Mass Secrets*, targeting skinny males aged 18–35 who wanted to gain muscle and strength. Literally overnight, when I did this and put up a professional sales letter, my sales went from $200 a week In November 2002 to over $2,000 a wekk by May 2003.

Want more successful examples?

Go to **www.moonlightingontheinternet.com/success** to see more info marketing success stories we couldn't fit in the book.

Part Two

Moonlighting on the Internet Method #2: eBay

Developed by Sydney Johnson

> Facts about eBay that are worth paying attention to:
> - ◆ $7–8 billion is run through eBay's platform every quarter.
> - ◆ Every hour, eBay registers 3,000–4,000 new users.
> - ◆ The eBay site gets more searches than Google.

To tell you the truth, I've always known eBay was a huge business with a huge number of transactions, but I mainly thought it was just about people selling off junk they didn't want or raiding garage sales and reselling that stuff.

Boy, was I wrong!

Here are some interesting facts that might make you stand up and pay attention to eBay as another proven moonlighting method.

Moonlighting Online

According to a new survey conducted in 2005 for eBay by ACNielsen International Research, a leading research firm, more than 724,000 Americans report that eBay is their primary or secondary source of income. In addition to these professional eBay sellers, another 1.5 million individuals say they supplement their income by selling on eBay.

Whoa!

That's pretty exciting. But the problem is: whom to believe? There's no doubt you've seen at least a half-dozen offers on TV, on the radio, online, etc., about "eBay secrets." I've checked out many of them, and unfortunately, most are completely worthless or so basic that they could have stolen the tutorials straight from eBay. Or if they have good information in there, it's not about how to create a truly leveraged business on the side. It's usually about how to sell "one-off" items—which means you are always reinventing the wheel! Dumb. That's one of the reasons I asked Sydney Johnson to contribute to this part—namely, because she understands that you want to create auctions that you can keep relisting over and over. You want to be able to do the work once and keep getting paid for it.

Sydney has been successfully selling on eBay since the winter of 1996 and has not been just talking about it like many other "Johnny-come-latelys" to the eBay auction craze!

I've known Sydney for several years now, and if you want to get her all riled up, just start mentioning some of the bogus "eBay secrets" peddlers out there. She's totally blunt and a real firecracker of a lady. Sydney's the real deal who sells on eBay day-in and day-out with her automated systems. Pay attention, because she's successfully worked with thousands of students over the years to create a system for profiting from eBay in your spare time …

And for more information on Sydney, see her bio at the end of chapter 19.

Chapter 15

The eBay Machine

O ne thing I'd like to talk to you about are the advantages of having your own auction business—a surefire way to make extra money and have fun at the same time! Selling on eBay and other auctions has to be one of the best ways to make good, solid cash every month. And thousands of people, right now, right this minute, are doing it successfully.

There are over 212 million registered users on eBay, and the site receives billions of visits. People spend more time on eBay, according to eBay's web site, than any other online site, making it the most popular shopping destination on the internet, which means that people come looking for exactly what you're selling. And you don't need to spend hundreds or thousands of dollars in advertising to get a customer to your door. The cherry on the icing—you have about zero risk.

So this is really awesome stuff. Having been dubbed the "auction queen" myself, I know what I'm talking about! I happen to be, in fact, one of the original sellers on eBay. I've been selling on eBay since 1996, and have been interviewed by *USA Today, The Times Online, Investor Business Daily*, and numerous other media outlets.

So what led me to all this success? Well, it all started with eBay in the winter of 1996. And you know how life throws you curveballs? I stumbled on this site by accident. According to eBay, there are currently 1.2 million people earning a full-time or part-time living on the site. Not sure where that number came from, but back in 1996, things weren't quite like that. And many people don't even realize how different it was. There was a relative handful of us, most of us knew each other, and we all bought each other's stuff. Moreover, people sold silly, stupid things, such as smelly socks and "nonsense" stuff.

At the time, eBay was nothing like the monolithic organization it is today. Everybody asks me, "Was it easier or was it harder back then?" Well, I'd say it was a bit of both. Anything I put up, I sold. So that part was easy. But there was no help. There was nobody to teach me. There was no software, there was no support of any kind—so that made it definitely harder.

That first year I quit teaching because I decided, "I have to get out of this classroom." So I did all of these other things to make a living somehow. I tried it all, from real estate to multi-level marketing, all the usual stuff. In the meantime, I kept selling on eBay.

And one day, just like that, I woke up and the thought struck me, "Duh! What am I doing? Why don't I try making a full-time business out of eBay?"

I'm not entirely sure, but I may have been the first person to try and do that. To let everything go and focus on eBay. So that's how long I've been around on eBay. It was just fun at first. It was entertainment, more like a game. Nobody took it that seriously in those days, including Pierre Omidyar, who built his business and is presently rolling in dough, thanks to eBay. I would think to myself, "Gee, that seems so obvious. Why didn't I think of that?" Everything's obvious after the fact, right? As they say, hindsight is 20/20.

> *I would think to myself, "Gee, that seems so obvious. Why didn't I think of that?" Everything's obvious after the fact, right? As they say, hindsight is 20/20.*

Anyway, I got hooked into this, I said, "Okay, I'm going to be serious about this," I went ahead and never looked back. I remember like it was yesterday: the very first item I auctioned—just one item—made me $1,073.86 in profits! How could I forget those numbers?

If you've ever sold anything on eBay, you know that feeling you have when you first start, when you're logging in, looking at your auction every 30 seconds. "Has anybody bid, I wonder?" you keep asking yourself. And when I logged into my account in those first weeks, I couldn't believe these numbers. I was hooked from that moment on.

I've sold all kinds of things, most of them not very interesting items. I've sold everything from leather goods to kitchen products to business courses. I love that part of it. I even sold ready-made web sites, as well as zillions of books.

I also came across a couple of really interesting opportunities. Let me tell you about them …

> *I've sold all kinds of things, most of them not very interesting items. I've sold everything from leather goods to kitchen products to business courses.*

One guy I knew was cleaning out the attic in his house, which happens to be located in my neighborhood, and he found 19 years' worth of *Life* magazine, which was defunct for a while but is now back in circulation.

"If you'd just take this crap," he told me, "and get it out of here, that'd be great." Of course, I replied, "You betcha!"

I ended up selling all those magazines one by one for over $3,000, and he just *gave* them to me! That was amazing.

I remember another time when I went to a storage auction and bought its entire contents for $10! One of the items was a snowmobile that had never been used.

Another time, I happened to be at somebody's house, and my friend said, "If you'll take this stuff out of our backyard, you can just have it." Did you ever see one of those old pedal cars? They were made out of metal and kids would sit in them and pedal. They were a precursor to Hot Wheels. They were all rusted out and horrible. And I thought, "What am I going to do with this stuff?" But my motto is "Don't turn anything down." Each one of these cars sold for $500 or $600.

The things people buy shocks me. The legend, and I don't know if it's true, is that Pierre Omidyar started the eBay site because his girlfriend, who is now his wife, was a Pez collector. Go figure. Why would anybody want a bunch of Pez holders? I don't know. I don't know why they would want old rusted-out pedal toys, either. I am constantly surprised by what folks want to buy. But if they want it, I'll sell it to them.

Moonlight on Andrew Lock

Andrew's Moonlighting Story

Working for someone else made me miserable. I was constantly frustrated with the incompetence of management as well as the unreasonable demands they placed on me.

So, I decided to start an online business and chose to go the eBay route because it was a ready-made business that was (and still is) inexpensive to start and simple to operate. That was back in 2001 and was probably the best decision I ever made, as not only do I love what I do, I now have autopilot income! Imagine PayPal deposits 24/7 while you sleep. It's truly exciting and it has enabled me to make the choices I want to make rather than being a slave to a traditional business. My lifestyle has been transformed!

www.andrewlock.com

Andrew's Advice

I knew that the single biggest challenge with online businesses is getting sufficient traffic to a web site. I discovered that eBay is the largest e-commerce web site online, with a large percent of all U.S. internet visitors using it at least once a month. Since that's where the most buyers can be found in one place online, it made logical sense to put my offer in front of those buyers. I encourage everyone to tap into the enormous power of eBay!

Chapter 16

Finding the Right Products and Setting Up Business

Once I have my antennae up and my eyes and ears open, I can find all kinds of stuff. Stuff everywhere. The funny thing is that people write to me all the time saying, "I can't find anything to sell."

Well, once you start assuming there's stuff everywhere, look around. You start seeing goodies everywhere. They're all over the place.

Think about it. There are billions of products on this planet, and people think, "Well, I've got to have hundreds of different items to sell on eBay." But the truth is: No, you don't. I never had more than half a dozen, maybe a dozen items to sell at one time.

Now, when I say "products," I'm actually referring to product lines. For instance, I sold a lot of leather goods. I consider leather goods to be only one kind of product. So, if anybody tells me they can't find half a dozen different products or product lines to sell, I don't have any sympathy for that. They're tripping over goodies everywhere, and they can't see it. Even what people think is "trash" can be valuable merchandise!

Most sellers on eBay, in fact, start by following a pattern. They start selling things around their house, stuff they don't want anymore, which is a perfectly logical thing to do. This is a great way to experiment and learn the game with no risk.

And then they may start feeling more brave and going to a few garage and yard sales, finding things for $5 and putting them up for sale.

For instance, I have a student who recently bought some guy's lifetime collection of sports cards for around $10. He put them up for sale on eBay, and he's already sold some of them for $400 and $500. One never knows.

But see, the thing about this is that you read all this silly advice on the internet that may say, "Go to garage sales to make your fortune on eBay." That's good. That's a great way to *practice* and to *learn* and even have fun, but one should keep in mind that it is NOT a business plan. Sellers need a genuine business plan if they want to earn more than a few dollars here and there, because you can go to garage sales all day long and maybe come home with 50 things or nothing at all … it could be totally hit or miss.

The most important thing is that you have to decide whether you want to have an eBay business or an eBay hobby. If you want an eBay hobby, go to garage sales. If you like that and it's fun, that's cool—but it's not a business. Just keep in mind that someone's trash could be valuable merchandise to you. It could bring you a lot of money.

The idea is to start off small; dip your toes in the water. The beauty of the whole thing is that it costs NOTHING to sell on eBay. You can sign up for an account, fill out the information, and *voila*! You've got a business.

Figure 16-1 illustrates how you can list something for sale on eBay for as low as 20 cents. Give me a break! How can anything be any cheaper than that?

I have a friend who was telling me about some guy he met. The guy's grandparents came here from Poland, and he's working hard. He's got this plan to go back to Poland and start building bowling alleys and miniature golf courses. He said the people of Poland love America, and he knows he could get rich by doing that.

Insertion Fees	
Starting or Reserve Price	Insertion Fee
$0.01 - $0.99	$0.20

Figure 16-1. The eBay insertion fee

And I thought to myself, "Oh my gosh, imagine me trying to go to Poland and build a miniature golf course?" It boggles my mind. The risk is so high, and so is the investment capital that would be needed.

The eBay Experience: Getting Your Business Straight and Making Money Without Risk

So here we are in this wonderful internet business atmosphere, and here's this incredible opportunity that costs almost nothing. 20 cents. Big deal. If somebody can't afford to risk 20 cents, they sure don't need to be trying to build a business. So I always tell my students: You risk 20 cents and it doesn't work, so what? The important thing is that you've learned something. Move on, try something else, and keep experimenting.

I have to tell you, there's one thing that gives real marketers a tremendous advantage. And that is that the marketing on eBay is incredibly amateurish. Anybody who knows anything about internet marketing can outdo all of those people who are trying to sell products there. They have no back-end, they have no upselling—they're so amateurish!

Most people see eBay as a site where you can put up your widgets, collect your money, and then sell the next widget. They don't see beyond that. That said, it's true that you can go ahead and start selling on eBay. It's as easy as that—but if you want to have a real business, I strongly advise everyone to go through all the steps to set it up properly: to form a legal entity such as a corporation, get a business license, the whole nine yards. And there is one other thing that you need if you're serious about doing this. You MUST get a state sales tax ID number, because most legitimate wholesalers will not deal with people who don't have one.

So the easiest way to make money on eBay is to first and foremost find a good wholesaler or supplier, one you can count on. Work out a listing that works well for you, and keep it flowing, keep it moving. That's the simplest way.

> *You MUST get a state sales tax ID number, because most legitimate wholesalers will not deal with people who don't have one.*

I know that here in my home state of Georgia, if wholesalers sell to a retailer, they can lose their right to do business in the state. So they have to be careful. And lots of legitimate wholesalers say, "Go away!" They won't even let you look at their catalogs and other information without that tax ID.

There's nothing to it. Getting a tax ID is usually free (although a few states do charge for the license). All you have to do is to find the right governmental agency and fill out a boring government form. Dealing with the governmental bureaucracy can sometimes be a drag, but it's more than worth it to get the proper documentation. For a complete list of agencies by state, go to **www.moonlightingontheinternet.com/agencies**.

After you get that done, it's smooth sailing. You can set the whole thing up and start selling in one day. That's what I did, when I decided I wanted to take this seriously. And in five days, I had sold my item for over $1,000. It was an old business course that I didn't want anymore. That's how simple it can be.

Most people have things they don't want anymore. All they have to do is look on eBay, and they can tell pretty quickly if there's any kind of market for it. Take a chance. List it for 20 cents and see what happens.

On eBay, you have options concerning the length of your auction: 3 days, 5 days, 7 days, or 10 days (Figure 16-2). I don't recommend the 3-day option. The 7-day option is best. Sometimes, I go for the 10-day option. You can put something up, and in a week you've got it sold.

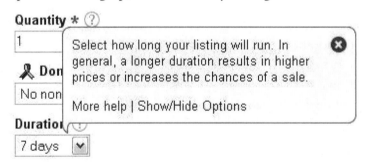

Figure 16-2. Length of auction options

People have to understand what eBay is. Most think that eBay is an auction site, but that's not what eBay really is. It's a giant traffic machine, period. That's what it does. That's what it's giving its customers. That's why people come there.

Millions of people come to eBay every day. And not only are there tons of buyers, but these customers very kindly target themselves. That is, they segment themselves into the correct markets, and you, the seller, don't have to do a thing to make this happen.

Let's say you wanted to buy a new digital camera. In that case, you're not going to be hanging out in the jewelry department. You're looking where the digital cameras are. So this means you're a targeted buyer.

There's one other thing about eBay buyers—most of the time, when people go on the internet, they're looking for information. But if somebody comes to eBay, they know this is not an information site. eBay is a SALES site, so the expectations are different.

With eBay you have:

1. Huge numbers of customers
2. Very targeted customers
3. Customers who come with a "buying" mindset

Therefore, what eBay sells is access to this lucrative traffic, and sellers have access to a pool of buyers.

So, you may still be asking yourself, "Where can I find some products?" I have already mentioned wholesalers and suppliers. In the classes I teach, probably half the time is spent discussing this issue of finding products. Most people don't believe me when I say that's the easiest part. I promise you, it is. But nobody believes that, because there's so much competition. People who don't understand eBay very well are intimidated by that.

> *In the classes I teach, probably half the time is spent discussing this issue of finding products. Most people don't believe me when I say that's the easiest part.*

Why People Buy on eBay

Basically, everybody has to understand that there are two reasons why people buy on eBay.

#1: The merchandise is so unique, rare, valuable, and hard to find that passionate, avid collectors flock to it. You can make really good money in this market, but you have the problem of locating inventory. Unless you're a part of that specialized market already, that can be a problem.

Besides the above, this market requires specialized knowledge. Go take a look at some of the coin listings on eBay, and you'll see what I mean.

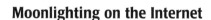
Figure 16-3 gives an example. You'll see listing titles such as "1882 S BU/GEM MS64/65 Morgan Silver Dollar PROOFLIKE." Only folks serious about coin collecting can understand what that means!

Figure 16-3. Coin listing on eBay

#2: People want consumer items at a bargain price. This would be the easiest way for the average person to make money for two reasons: (1) it's easy to find inventory and (2) specialized knowledge isn't a requirement for communicating with your potential customers.

Product Sourcing—Drop-Shipping, Wholesale, or Closeout?

Once you decide you want to sell out of the consumer market, there are three main categories to consider for these kinds of products:

1. Drop-shipping
2. Wholesale
3. Closeout or liquidation

There are advantages and disadvantages to each. Everybody I talk to says, "Oh, I want to do drop-shipping." Don't we all? It's great because you don't buy the product until it's already sold, so there's no risk and you never have to package and ship anything. Different companies give you access to a whole array of drop-ship products, and their inventories are regularly updated (Figure 16-4).

Figure 16-4. Drop-ship option

But I have to tell you I have not had much luck with it, and I don't know many people who have. The reason for this is that when you go to a drop-shipper, what they're doing for you is providing a service, and that is handling the shipping for you. This means that they're going to charge more. They MUST charge more, because instead of sending an entire box of widgets, somebody has to locate a single widget and carry it to the shipping department. That costs extra, and suppliers pass that extra cost on to you, the eBay seller. This almost always makes a drop-shipped product too expensive to successfully compete with similar products on eBay.

The other end of the spectrum is the closeout business (Figure 16-5). And boy, are there bargains to be had! You can often buy really popular goods for 5 cents and 10 cents on the dollar. Ooh, that sounds great, doesn't it?

Name Brand Closeouts, Apparel, & Jewelry –

Figure 16-5. Closeout dealers are quite easy to find

But the problem with that is that closeout dealers usually will only accept big orders. Big, B-I-G orders! Their minimum order might cost $2,000 and involve 500 units of whatever you're buying. Most folks don't want 500 widgets sitting in their basement, for obvious reasons.

Another problem is that your merchandise is sight-unseen, and it's not returnable. So dealing with a closeout dealer can be a bit frightening. We all know that the higher the risk, the higher the potential profits. For people who don't mind risk, this is a terrific option. For most people, however, this much risk is unacceptable.

I personally think that wholesalers are the best option. Wholesalers are the "in-between." That's what I've done in my business, for the most part—

Moonlighting on the Internet

deal with wholesalers. They're safer than closeout deals and more economically feasible than drop-shipping.

Do keep in mind, however, that suppliers don't fit into neat little categories. A single supplier might deal in both regular wholesaling and either drop-shipping or closeout.

> *I buy products in wholesale lots and have them sent straight to the fulfillment house, and they handle all the shipping for me in a professional manner.*

Another issue is shipping and handling. Everybody wants to get out of the shipping business. I know I do. When you're more skilled and more profitable, you can do what I do now and use a fulfillment house. I buy products in wholesale lots and have them sent straight to the fulfillment house, and they handle all the shipping for me in a professional manner.

But you can't start off that way. You've got to start off doing some shipping. And that's the way it is. Like any other business, you have to pay your dues, and that's part of the price.

Product sourcing is a long, involved subject, but there are wholesalers all over the place.

As far as product choice is concerned, I wouldn't necessarily suggest that people find a product they are personally interested in. One of the biggest mistakes that folks can make is believing that because THEY like something, everybody else will too! The way I see it is, you have to be an opportunist first. Find something—anything—that will sell. Once cash flow is no longer an issue and you are skilled at selling on eBay, then you become more selective. Personally, if it's not immoral or illegal, I will sell whatever people want to buy.

136 ✦

Chapter 17

"The Flood"

I teach my students a method I've nicknamed "The Flood." Here are the steps you need to take to pursue "The Flood" method when selecting products to sell:

#1. Get on wholesalers' information lists. Get yourself on the information lists of dozens—even hundreds—of wholesalers. How to locate these wholesalers is an involved subject, but it's the critical first step. And once you start looking through their printed catalogs, online catalog sites, brochures, etc., you will begin to find some products that look interesting to you.

#2. Do objective market research. Do your homework—your market research. The first step is discovering whether there is any demand for this product you have selected. This is the part where it's easy to make a fatal mistake, because many people fall for what I call "backward marketing." What most people do is see something and fall in love with it. "Oh, I know everybody's going to love this!" And they rush out looking for buyers. It's an emotional response that has led to much pain and defeat in this business.

To succeed, we need to be able to step back and look at what we're doing in an objective and unemotional way. For our own sakes, we can't become emotionally invested in certain merchandise. I'm sure you've heard what Marlon Sanders said: "Find out where the demand is and throw yourself in front of it." That's the best advice I've ever heard as far as market research is concerned.

#3. Scope out the competition. Seek out the competition and assess whether we can successfully compete in this niche market. Only if what you discover seems to give you a green light should you consider a product.

When people get in trouble, it's because they haven't done their homework! There are no exceptions to this rule.

A great example: one of my e-zine readers sent me an e-mail that disclosed, "I bought 100 DVDs for $10.99 each. I listed them on eBay for $10.99 and I didn't get a single bid. So then I go and look at the competition, and they're selling the same thing for $6.99 and $7.99 or even less (see Figure 17-1). What do I do?" DVDs are a cutthroat business. You don't buy first and then ask these questions! You do it the other way around. People don't get in trouble if they'll do that.

	THE MATRIX REVOLUTIONS *Keanu Reeves*Moss*2 DVDs*SEALED	℗	4	**$4.25** $4.95
	HARRY POTTER AND THE PRISONER OF AZKABAN *2 DVDs*SEALED	℗	10	**$3.75** $4.95
	▨ Star Trek - The Complete First Season (2004, DVD)		-	**$0.99** $3.99

Figure 17-1. The competition for discount DVDs is fierce on eBay

Some of the items I started selling successfully were regular stuff, such as briefcases, kitchen stuff, sheets, pillowcases, comforters, clocks, tools, car parts, software, posters, and toys. Nothing exciting. These are common things that people want, I've discovered. I have also sold things that are considered seasonal (see Figure 17-2). Recently, for example, I bought a mass of vintage clothing, which I love. So I now have a large selection of coats in my spare bedroom. However, I'm not going to put them up for sale until around October. If I list them in April or June, they're not going to get many bids.

Figure 17-2. Some items for sale on eBay are seasonal items

It's crucial to wait for the right time to put up something for sale. I had a student recently who said she'd acquired a collection of *Lord of the Rings* goodies. She asked if she should wait or put it up for sale immediately. I said, "No, they're going to bring out that three-volume set of the *Lord of the Rings*. The collector's edition will be out around Christmas." So I told her, "Wait until then. Don't do it now. Hold onto it, and the *LotR* mania will fire up once again." That was how she'd be able to cash in.

This, of course, means you'd have to buy certain items off-season and hold on to them. Every year, I purchase tons of Halloween stuff after Halloween at a great discount—sometimes for next to nothing. The stores just think, "Get this stuff outta here!" And about two to three weeks before the next Halloween, I'll start selling it at really nice prices. If you have room to store merchandise, that's great.

The Three-Part Formula

I have a three-part formula for eBay success. Let me tell you about it:

1. Find something to sell (as I described above).

2. Once you have a selection of products, do your supply and demand homework. There are some good tools that make eBay research easy. I know you believe in tools like I do.

3. Find out how to write listings that will work. This is the hardest part, believe it or not.

When you think about this from the buyer's perspective, what do they see? They see:

1. What you're selling

2. What you say about it

3. And there isn't anything else. If you surf eBay and look at what sellers are saying, you'll find that many of the listings on eBay are pathetic, to say the least.

> *It is important to understand the value of testing. It's the whole secret to eBay.*

It is important to understand the value of testing. It's the whole secret to eBay. Let's pretend you're going to sell some of my leather goods on eBay. Naturally, you want a good listing for these leather goods so you will maximize your profits. So how can you be sure you're putting up the best possible listing?

What I usually do is experiment with that listing again, keeping track of my results, until I get a listing that's doing well. Then I let it ride—turn it into an income stream, forget about it, and go on to the next one.

Let's use my first auctions on eBay as an example. I listed 100 briefcases at a time. But after some experimentation, I discovered that I would make more money per item if I sold 50 at a time. I'm not sure why it worked that way—something about the perception of scarcity, I suppose. But the point is that I made more money from two auctions of 50 products each, such as the one shown in Figure 17-3, than from one auction of 100 products. If I hadn't experimented, I would never have discovered that fascinating fact.

Figure 17-3. Briefcases can be a popular product on eBay

Pretty soon I had a "selling machine" going. As soon as the auction ended, I relisted it. In the early days of eBay, I had to do this myself, but today there is software that will auto-relist merchandise for you, which makes this easy.

I always recommend that newcomers begin by selling inexpensive items. The profit doesn't matter at first, because the point is to learn the business first. Let's be clear about this: you WILL make mistakes! That's the way life is. We don't start out being skilled at anything, and eBay selling is no exception. You want to make your mistakes on $5 items, not $500 items, so that it doesn't hurt you financially.

Once you have this first stream of income, you add another and another to raise your profits. Then, once you learn the business, you can sell more expensive—and therefore more profitable—items.

I have another part to my success formula. I figured out a way to build e-mail lists off eBay without breaking their rules. This is an exciting and vital thing to do. As a rule, it's important to focus on repeat business; otherwise, every sale is a "first sale," which is always the hardest to make.

In all the years that I have been on eBay—and I've bought a lot, too—I got a catalog from a seller one time. One other time, I got an e-mail from a seller informing me of a sale (and I never heard from the seller again after that first time). That is a crime. And you see people on eBay with 100,000 feedback points—positive feedback, as illustrated by Figure 17-4—yet you never hear from them again. I always ask myself, what is the matter with these people? One thing is certain: they are losing money.

For example, I love earrings, and I've bought dozens of pairs on eBay. I buy from some of the same sellers repeatedly, but I've never heard from a single one of them. They could e-mail me and offer more merchandise, and I'd probably buy from them again—but for some reason, they don't bother, so they're losing business they could have had if they contacted me.

Seller: jewelryauctionstv (40300

Feedback: **98.7% Positive**

Member: since Nov-23-02 in United

Figure 17-4. Positive feedback can boost business

This is what I mean about how unsophisticated most eBay sellers are.

I use a lot of tactics that many marketers would recognize. For instance, let's pretend you bought a pair of earrings from me for your wife. All sellers can send e-mails to buyers, so my first e-mail to you would say something like, "Thank you so much for buying these earrings, and here's your cost." That's standard eBay procedure.

But what I would add is, "You bought these beautiful garnet earrings, but did you know we also have a garnet bracelet and necklace that go perfectly with them?" (Figure 17-5). The fact is, when you've got that credit card or that PayPal account handy and you're ready to pay for your purchase, that's prime time for a seller like me to offer you additional merchandise.

 Stunning 13.5CT 48 Round Garnet 18k Gold Bracelet B046

Figure 17-5. Offering additional merchandise matching the item purchased can be a great business move for an eBay seller

In my course, I speak about upselling, and I mention that in my experience, it has added 50 percent more to my profits. What confuses me, however, is that nobody on eBay does that. Nobody! I never see those tactics used anywhere on eBay. Many sellers seem to live in a fog, and I don't understand why.

"The Flood"

This gives people who understand back-end selling a huge advantage!

Some sellers on eBay think it is better to sell large numbers of items and make only a small profit on each. Others prefer to sell a high-end item one time. In my case—and I talk about this in my course—I've done it both ways. One nice thing about the high-end items is that they're easier to deal with in terms of profit and manageability. Rather than selling 100 items, you sell one. However, if you're going to sell something expensive, for the most part, it's going to be something that's rare, and you're going to have a problem with supply. Each auction then becomes more critical. Let me explain.

> *One nice thing about the high-end items is that they're much easier to deal with in terms of profit and manageability. Rather than selling 100 items, you sell one.*

For example, I've sold a large number of first edition books. Some weeks, I would find five or six, and they would sell for $200 or $300 each. Boy, that was great! Other weeks, however, I didn't find any. So that became a problem. Then, too, in a lot of these specialized categories you have to have a lot of insider knowledge, which is not the case with traditional consumer items.

Here's another example: I was looking at some baseball card auctions the other day, and I didn't even understand the titles (see Figure 17-6). "RC BGS ..." What does that mean? If you're in the sports card business, you will know. If you're an outsider, however, you've got some studying to do.

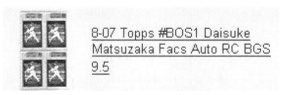

8-07 Topps #BOS1 Daisuke Matsuzaka Facs Auto RC BGS 9.5

Figure 17-6. Headings can sometimes be difficult to understand

If you have a particular hobby or love, you might find a profitable niche in a collectibles category. However, if you don't have a hobby and can't find something rare to make a whole lot of money on, you should find something else to sell and keep selling it—lots of it, over and over, for as long as there is a demand. It is important to repeat business. You will have one stream of income, and some of these types of sales will last for years.

For example, those briefcases I mentioned earlier—that was about 10 years ago, and I don't sell them anymore, but people are STILL selling them on eBay. So, if I had kept that up, that product line would have produced revenue all those years.

After you test the product, tweak the settings and make sure you're getting the maximum amount of bid, you let it ride and keep listing it. There's nothing to it. It's a purely technical thing. In fact, there is eBay management software that will auto-relist your items, if you choose to enable that feature.

Beating the Competition

You may be asking yourself at this point, "What about the competition? What if there are a thousand other sellers selling the same item?" Well, my answer would be that there are tons of ways to get around competition. Like I said before, eBay sellers are so unsophisticated.

One of the best ways to beat out the competition is to offer bonus items. I used to offer digital products as bonuses with physical products, but now that's against eBay rules. That's foolish, I think, but it's eBay's game and their rules must be respected.

Marlon Sanders loves a story I told him about my early days on eBay. In those days, I didn't know anything—and I mean nothing! I had a theory that if I liked something, the entire world would, too. That was foolish, but I didn't realize it at the time.

One of the products I thought would be a smash hit was the stove-top grill (see Figure 17-7 below). It went on the stove, and the bottom was filled with water. When it heated up, the steam and heat would grill a steak.

Because I didn't know that market research was a necessity, much less how to carry it out, it came as a shock to me that there were other people selling my grills. I had invested a considerable amount of my capital, and I certainly wanted to avoid a price war. You don't want to be in a price-only game where people are buying based only on price. A price war usually escalates, with frightened sellers offering lower and lower prices until no one makes any money.

Figure 17-7. The stove-top grill

So, I found out that some knives were being offered by a wholesaler for only 33 cents each. This same knife was selling on the internet for $8.95 and $9.95 (Figure 17-8). So I added that knife as a bonus to my stove-top grill. I explained to buyers that they were getting a $9–10 knife for free. Result: I stomped the competition. My sales were much better than anybody else's, and I made more money than all the rest combined.

Figure 17-8. The handy-dandy kitchen knife—perfect as a bonus with any grill purchase!

But you know something fascinating? The other sellers never did copy me! That amazed me. If my sales suddenly fell off, I would look around to figure out what was happening, but none of them did. I couldn't believe it was so simple. It was all about knowing Marketing 101.

The moral of our story is that you don't want to choose merchandise that 500 other people are also selling. There are lots of categories with only a handful of sellers to worry about. And if you know any marketing at all, you're smarter than they are—in terms of marketing knowledge, that is. I don't mean to be condescending, but it's true.

Figure 17-9. A low-carb recipe book is a great extra to offer with the purchase of kitchen-related items

You can put together information products to add to your physical goods, as long as you avoid calling them "bonuses" (to adhere to eBay rules). It's a great reason to make contact with your buyer so you can sell more products. For instance, to go with the stove-top grill, I could have put together a book of low-carb recipes (Figure 17-9), some of which used the grill. I'm sure that this tactic would have worked wonderfully. By doing so, I could have earned a higher perception of value in the mind of the buyer, who would most probably be thinking, "Ooh, look at all these recipes! The other sellers aren't offering these!"

The beauty of the whole thing is that it would cost me maybe $1 to print that report and send it off with my item. In the end, I would have made $5, while only spending $1. What could be more worth it?

When you're doing your research you want to make sure there aren't too many competitors, but a few competitors shouldn't scare you off, especially if the item is selling.

To explain things more clearly, let me tell you what I did one time:

I happen to be a frustrated web designer. It is a fact that I love designing web sites, so I decided I would start selling ready-made web sites because there was a good market for that product.

Before I did anything, I spent a week doing my homework and checking all the sellers who were potential competition. In the end, I could only find one guy who was doing what I wanted to do and making a lot of money doing it.

The next thing I did was print out many of his listings. I laid them out on my desk and kept going over them. I compiled lists such as, "He's offering this and I can't, but I can do better than he is doing with this issue," and I studied the market in the process.

I started selling my web sites, and within two weeks, I was making $3,000 to $4,000 every week with little effort! The amazing part is that I was taking away his business. His sales were dropping and dropping. I was following what happened with him, of course; I was paying attention to what he was doing. But he never changed anything. He never looked around.

If you were making $5,000 a week regularly and all of a sudden you dropped to $2,000, I know darn well you'd be saying, "What's going on here?"

> *If you were making $5,000 a week regularly and all of a sudden you dropped to $2,000, I know darn well you'd be saying, "What's going on here?"*

My competitor never adapted. For instance, one of the things he was doing that I made a big deal of was offering a domain name. The domain name was a part of the site package, of course. All his offers were for .net and .org and .biz domains. I made a big deal in my listing about the popularity of the .com extension. I asked, "When you think of the internet, what do YOU think of?" Of course, we think or say "dot-com." Hence, all the domains I sold were .com.

If he had been paying attention, he could have looked at my listing and started selling .com domains, like I was doing. But he never did. Does that make any sense? Not to me.

This is also a great example of how you can avoid competition—by watching what they're doing and doing something better.

Another example: I don't know Flash and have no interest in learning it. In fact, I don't want to go to a web site and watch a Flash presentation, but I know that a lot of people do. My competitor was using Flash, however, and I figured that some potential buyers would be impressed. I knew I couldn't compete with that, so I turned that into a positive. I let all potential buyers know that search engines can't spider Flash and that if they went for Flash, there would be no search engine traffic. People were buying these sites to make money and that was important to them, so I was able to negate his advantage.

Let's look at another scenario:

You've got your item. You've checked out the marketplace and it looks like the item is selling. How do you decide to list it?

The first thing you have to decide is what keywords you want to use. I  used to have a watch store, and I sold hundreds of logo watches (see Figure 17-10 below for an image of the product). Some of them had images of sports figures on the faces; some had dogs; some had angels.

So, let's take the ones that had images of famous paintings on them, such as Van Gogh or Da Vinci paintings. Do I list those in the jewelry category, or do I put them in the art category, where paintings are normally sold?

Figure 17-10. Customized watches

Using the Right Keywords

The best place to start is to figure out your keywords and put those into eBay, then look at some of the auctions that are doing well and see where others are placing their items for auction.

You MUST get the headline for your listing right. If you don't, your customers are never going to find you and what you're selling.

Most buyers on eBay search by keywords, so it's obvious that you need to have the correct keywords. And what is "correct"? It's whatever your customers are using to search, because that's all eBay is—a giant search engine. One of my watches displayed the Michelangelo painting, "The Creation of Adam," so I put the name of the painting in my title, and folks who were interested in that kind of stuff found—and bought—my watches.

Or let's take the business courses I sold. Do you list them in the "business books" category, or do you put them in "nonfiction books"?

After you list your treasures, you must test. You have to figure out what's working and what isn't. The majority of sellers put up a headline or title and a listing and leave it at that. If a seller wants to maximize his profits, he'd better do some testing!

Moonlight on Alex Jeffreys

Alex's Moonlighting Story

I was working a nine-to-five job that I hated, and even though the rest of my life seemed great, it always seemed tainted since I didn't have the income I wanted. That **www.easyprofitauctions.com** led me to try a bunch of things online and eventually discover eBay. I never would have thought that you could make a living selling off-road motor bikes and other physical products by auctioning them on eBay. The truth is, I did better than make a living: I made a killing!

Things are much different for me now. I work from home with my wife, and we recently had our first baby. So, it's a blessing to spend so much time with my family. I bought my first house for $250,000 and I have land to build another $250,000 house next year, so I can sell them both and move into a $1 million house. That's the plan. No flashy cars at the moment, just a standard automobile for the wife. I don't need a ride, since I do most of my work at home and use hers when I need to go to the gym or the local pub to meet up with friends. But when I do get one, it will be a 100 percent Porsche 911 GT3 RS.

Alex's Advice

Take your time. I'm classed as an eBay expert, but I feel there is still so much more to learn, which is why my favorite quote is "The road to success is always under construction."

You may be asking yourself, "How do I test?" The place to start is with your title or headline. I take two headlines with keywords in them and test those two against each other. I'll list them both in the same place, the same way, and allow about 10 minutes to elapse so they're not next to each other.

Additionally, I use counters on my auctions (Figure 17-11). You can get counters on your auctions from the sales page on eBay. It is important to use hidden counters.

A counter is a research tool, that's all—and nobody but you should know how many people have looked at your auction.

So you test these two titles, and you see which one does better. I'll often also test a third one, and I'll keep on testing until I'm satisfied that it's as good as it's going to get. Once I've got a good headline going, I'll start testing other pieces of my auction.

Figure 17-11. Using an auction counter

The great thing is that it does not cost an extra 20 cents to test the same item in a different category! So you could theoretically post the same auction, if you had multiple items, in different categories. It may work well that way. In fact, I did have my watches listed in both the jewelry and art categories. This way, you can find people who have different interests but would still be interested in your product.

Ultimately, it's trial and error and seeing what other people are doing. Some people say, "It's so much trouble to test." Well, yeah, it's trouble all right. But do you want a stream of income that will roll on without effort on your part, or don't you? That's the difference between making maybe $200 a month and making $2,000 a month.

Chapter 18

Your Listing

Getting the Headline Right

So how important is that headline in your listing? It's so important that I cannot stress it enough. I don't care if you're selling $20 gold pieces for 25 cents and you are the Shakespeare of advertising; if nobody sees your listing, it doesn't make a difference. You have to have a title or headline that will get people to click on your auction, period!

It's all about nouns, nouns, nouns (see Figure 18-1 for an example). Do not include adjectives in your title at all.

NEW PANASONIC LUMIX DMC-FX01 6MP CAMERA+2GB~4BONUS PINK
BRAND NEW! 2GB SD CARD+ BAG+ Cleaning Kit, FAST SHIP!

Figure 18-1. The headline should consist of only nouns

And don't insert silly expressions or words, such as "L@@k" or "Can't live without this," as seen in Figure 18-2. That's amateur hour!

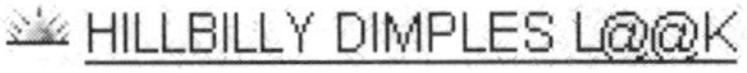

⛅ HILLBILLY DIMPLES L@@K

Figure 18-2. Example of a bad headline

The fact is, you only have a limited number of characters to write a headline. Although eBay has started allowing people to include subheads for $50, the problem is that you can run those costs up. It happened to me, and it's happened to many people. "Gee, I thought I was making a lot of money, and then I started adding up the costs and eBay is eating up most of it." You've got to keep that overhead down. Always keep this in mind.

Here's an example of a bad title and headline, one of my favorite ones (a listing for an opera CD): "Albert Einstein would have bought it." It? What is "it"? What is being sold?

So, what about the best titles and headlines? The best titles, when you get keywords, are often to be seen in the electronics section.

What a lot of people do—and I'm no exception—is that they'll find something they want to buy, and they'll do their research, then go to eBay to see what price they can find for that particular item.

So, let's say you're looking for a DVD player, and you want the Sony Model 239 or some other model. If there is a seller with a title that is specific and clear, and it refers to exactly the type of product you want, aren't you going to click on that title and look at the details of the auction? Figure 18-3 gives an example of a great title.

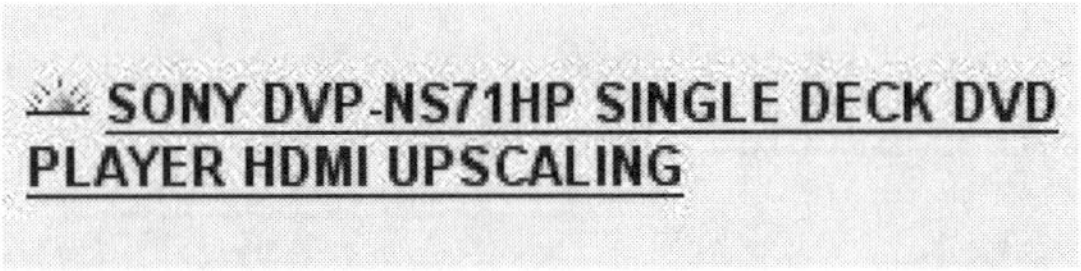

⛅ SONY DVP-NS71HP SINGLE DECK DVD PLAYER HDMI UPSCALING

Figure 18-3. The title must be specific

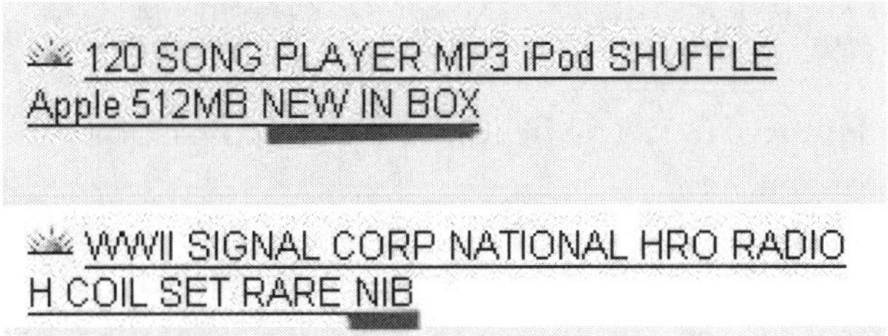

⛅ 120 SONG PLAYER MP3 iPod SHUFFLE Apple 512MB NEW IN BOX

⛅ WWII SIGNAL CORP NATIONAL HRO RADIO H COIL SET RARE NIB

Figure 18-4. People like to know they are purchasing new, unused products

Your Listing

Because this is so important, I have my students write headlines. I encourage them to think, "What do we like about this title? What do we not like?" and single out the most important elements.

If you can add a phrase like "New in box, NIB" in the title (Figure 18-4), that's great, because people don't want to buy old electronics. Once I saw somebody selling mattress covers that were not new, and that gives me—as well as a lot of other people—the creeps.

You want to let people know what you're selling. You can add something like "This is 80 percent off the retail price" (Figure 18-5). Those kinds of things attract buyers. Also, including some kind of special offer or bonus (whatever you want to call it, as long as you don't break eBay rules) would be a huge plus (Figure 18-6).

Exclusive! New NAHC MadDog Ultimate Backpack 80% OFF
Don't miss your chance! Free Shipping with Buy It Now!

Figure 18-5. Making a special offer is always a good idea

AX2 BLUETOOTH SANYO KATANA HANDSFREE + FREE BONUS

Figure 18-6. Sellers can't use the term "bonus" to attract buyers, but many other options are available, such as providing information packets or special offers

Keep in mind, don't waste your time with adjectives in the title. In the listing, they may be appropriate, but not in the title. Think of eBay as a search engine, because that's all it is. When you go to Google, you type in the words you want. People go to eBay and type in the words for the products they want. They won't add adjectives to a search, such as "wonderful painting." That wouldn't make sense. If you use these words in your headline, you're wasting your limited space.

Let's move on. After you've got your title done, what's the key to writing a powerful listing?

First, of course, you want it to look great. However, the most powerful tool that I've found for a listing is to personalize it. You don't want it to sound too corporate. People relate to a listing that's well-written.

For example, I once sold a bunch of Torso Tracks. If you remember, a few years ago, Suzanne Somers advertised the Torso Track on TV. The machine was supposed to make your stomach flat. I was doing okay with it. It was a drop-ship item—I would make about $30 on each item sold, and it didn't take me any time. So it was nice. But I changed my listing one day; I was experimenting with it.

I think you all know how many people buy that stuff in this burst of, "Oh, I'm going to get in shape," and then three months later it's sitting there covered with dust.

So what I asked was, "Are you going to buy this and have it covered with clothes in a month? Are you going to buy this and use it as a storage rack?"

I told a story, and it went something like this: "Every evening, I like to watch reruns of *Law & Order*, and I use my Torso Track. Is it my all-time favorite thing to do? No. But it's not terrible, and I've gotten into a routine, and now it's not hard to do." And that was the truth.

People ate that up. My sales went up, up, up.

Personalizing Your Listing

Another example: I had a student in one of my classes who had never sold anything on eBay. He bought some stuff, but it never sold. One time, he wanted to sell this motorcycle that I'd never heard. It's called a Ducati. Apparently, there are only about 50 that ever made it to the United States.

My student was from Ireland, and he showed me a Ducati listed on eBay. He said, "This Ducati's in better shape than mine, and it's worth about $12,000. I'll be happy if I can get $6,000 for mine."

So we discussed personalizing it. For this purpose, he wrote this incredible listing. He went on and on about how he got it from Ireland and how a traffic cop stopped him one day while he was out testing it and he didn't have a license. He went ahead and sold that thing for $8,600 (Figures 18-7 and 18-8), even though he'd been hoping and praying that he might get $6,000.

He went on and on about how he got it from Ireland and how a traffic cop stopped him one day while he was out testing it and he didn't have a license. He went ahead and sold that thing for $8,600.

He had people all over the world contact him. He got phone calls: "If the deal falls through, I want it." There was an incredible mania that he fueled. My student could

1976 Other Ducati : Ducati 900 SS

Bidder or seller of this item? Sign in for your status

Bidding has ended for this item. (aeprog is the winner)

Seller's item photo
⬇ Go to larger picture

Winning bid: **US $8,666.00 (Reserve met)**

Figure 18-7. A great winning bid

The night I collected the bike, I met the owner in Dublin (half way to my destination of Blackrock County Louth). **On my way through town a Dublin City cop on a bike** (CB750) pulled me over. I told him that I was taking the bike for a test ride. **He proceeded to give out to me for thinking about purchasing such a piece of junk.** He told me to go see Paddy Maddock and buy a BMW. If anyone knows the Irish bike scene, you should get a chuckle out of that. Well, **at least the cop didn't give me a ticket for no insurance, no tax, no license, and no registration. Only in Ireland could that happen!**

Figure 18-8. A personalized listing that produced fantastic results

have started a motorcycle business with the names he acquired through that one auction, although he wasn't interested in that.

The guy who was trying to sell the nice Ducati got a high bid of $9,210 and his reserve was $12,000, so he didn't sell it because the price never reached his reserve (Figure 18-9). He did this twice; he never paid the slightest attention to my student's auction, and it would have been easy to follow. How many Ducatis were there on eBay? Two.

He could have checked what my student's motorcycle had sold for, but instead he did the same old thing. His listing text was about three lines long—something along the lines of "This is a Ducati," and then he laid out a long list of conditions.

Then there are sellers who make it so hard for people to buy! I read a listing recently in which the seller stated, "If you want to bid on this item,

1978 Ducati : Supersport : 900 SS

Bidder or seller of this item? Sign in for your status

Bidding has ended for this item

Seller's item photo
↓ Go to larger picture

Current bid: **US $9,210.00 (Reserve not met)**

                 Get low monthly payments

Ended: Jun-26-04 14:26:22 PDT

Figure 18-9. A competitor whose reserve was not met

send me an e-mail and get permission to do so." Oh, give me a break! Now, how many people are going to do that?

Anyway, this shows us that personalizing your auction is one of the best things you can do.

When I sold my Torso Tracks, I personalized it by saying, "I watched *Law & Order* reruns and got on this thing. It's not that awesome, but it's okay. It's having an effect." And people appreciated my candor. I wasn't lying and saying, "Using my Torso Track is the best time of day for me. I can hardly wait to get on it and start exercising!" Instead, I told the truth, and it paid off.

Once you find the perfect words, you can keep running that same auc-

> *Once you find the perfect words, you can keep running that same auction with the same personalization.*

tion with the same personalization And that's what I did—over and over. It didn't matter how long I ran it, because I had a supplier for it. This happened to be one of the rare drop-ship auctions that paid off.

Drop-shipping has worked occasionally for me, but only on more expensive items. Everybody wants to sell a drop-ship item, but you can't drop-ship a $5 book and make money with your auction. However, for me it worked reasonably well with exercise equipment. I made $500 to $1,000 a month. That's not a huge amount of money, but it took me only 30 seconds to place that listing and make it work for me.

Your Listing

Besides what I have discussed, there are lots of other things you need to be aware of regarding your listing. One of these is that you want to demonstrate value. In addition, you must include pictures—good pictures—if possible; eBay allows you to upload one picture for free, but a fee applies for additional or supersized pictures. Finally, you have to learn some basic HTML, which is not that hard because a lot of the auction software will do it for you. All you have to do when you have this software is know how to type.

In the early days of eBay, everything was one long black-and-white paragraph, but that doesn't slide by anymore. Today, you have to make sure that your listing looks at least decent. Not pretty, necessarily, but certainly decent. The more professional you look, the more people are going to take you seriously. On the one hand, I'm saying personalize it, and on the other hand, I insist that your listing must look professional. You can be friendly and human while looking good.

What I teach everybody to do is keep that overhead down and not incur avoidable expenses, such as fees for extra pictures. What I do is upload my pictures to my own site, and then I can include as many as I want with no eBay fees. Therefore, you don't need to have extra pages on your web site for pictures. You need somewhere to upload pictures. Most folks get free space with their web hosting accounts, and they can use that for pictures until they get going.

As far as your listing is concerned, make sure you spell things correctly. This is one of those times when you ought to use the spell-check feature on your preferred editor. In addition, all the HTML writers have spell-check. One of the disadvantages of selling unique items is that you're always writing new listings, so it's important to make sure that each one looks good.

However, if you're selling jewelry, or some other item, again and again, all you have to do is perfect your listing and then let it run. I like to help people think of their eBay sales as a stream of income. Once you get it going, it will run on its own. That's when you can start to work on the next one, and then the next one, and so forth. Hence, it's worth the time and the trouble to get a good listing going, and that includes uploading good pictures.

> *I like to help people think of their eBay sales as a stream of income. Once you get it going, it will run on its own.*

I love earrings. So let's say I'm selling diamond earrings and sales are going well. If I want to start selling sapphire earrings, all I have to do is change the picture and a sentence or two of description, and my listing is ready. That's all there is to it. This indicates there may be an advantage to specializing in a certain area, at least in the beginning. That way, you can focus your efforts on a chosen item and create the perfect listing.

To Specialize or Not to Specialize

I had an e-mail from a student today. He said he could only think of one thing he wanted to sell, but his goal was to sell five kinds of things so he could concentrate on a different one each day.

Now, keep in mind that he's never done an auction. He asked, "Can you recommend four other things I can sell?" I tactfully said, "That is a bad way to go about this. If you've got one thing you want to sell right now, focus on the one thing and don't worry about it. When you get that going, then start looking for number two." To go out there and look for five things because you want to sell jewelry on Monday and books on Tuesday … that's nonsense.

Most people at this point may be wanting to ask me, "Hey, I only have about 5 hours, maybe 10 hours at the most, a week. Where do you suggest that I focus my attention?"

Step one, as I mentioned above, is to get on the mailing lists of as many suppliers as you can so that you start receiving e-mails with product pricing and information.

Step two is to do your homework and spend some time on eBay. It's like with me and my earring fetish—if I see a lot of earrings I would like to sell, I check them out and see what my competition is doing. That's how you start in this eBay business.

Step three is to pick out one product or product line you'd like to begin with. You've found a supplier, you've done your homework about supply and demand, and then you start working on that first listing.

The only way you can go wrong is to rush into it without thought or consideration. I sometimes have students who tell me, "In a month, I have to be making $5,000 a month from this business." Forget it. If that's how you think, don't bother starting this business. You cannot force it to happen. You've got to work through these steps.

I was speaking with a woman one day and explaining some of these things to her. She said, "That sounds like a lot of work," and I replied, "Think about this. If I created a business for you and it was making $10,000 a month, and then I said, 'Okay, Suzie, here it is, it's all yours,' and I just gave it to you, what would happen to it?" It would fall apart, because she wouldn't know how to keep it going.

If my students are not in too big a hurry, I tell them to start accumulating products. This is why I call it "The Flood." The goal is to obtain a flood of product information from legitimate suppliers.

I tell students the truth, which is, "If you get literature from 50 suppliers, most of it is going to be unusable. Maybe they want a $2,000 minimum order, or you have to buy 500 items, or whatever. But you're going to stumble over a few gold nuggets."

It's like the forty-niners panning for gold—most of it was gravel, but they got some nuggets. All it takes is a couple of nuggets, and you can make a lot of money at this game.

> *This is why I call it "The Flood." The goal is to obtain a flood of product information from legitimate suppliers.*

People tell me all the time, "I don't know about eBay. There's so much competition!" That's not the case. Yeah, there are a lot of people on that site, but most of them don't have a clue. They don't do their homework. They have no idea about marketing tactics. They wouldn't test something if their life depended on it. Therefore, if you're willing to do those things, you can easily make money on eBay on a regular basis.

Even if you only have 5 or 10 hours a week to spare, you can easily make $400 or $500 a month in profits! And once you get it going, you can do better than that. You can get yourself a couple of income streams. It's the way everything is: when you start, that's the hardest time. But once you get it rolling, it isn't so difficult. Something that used to take you two weeks may now take two days or one day.

Getting People to Bid

So, let's say you have your auction running. Obviously, you want to get more people bidding on your product, because that drives up the price. There aren't any "works every time" tactics in marketing, but the best tactics I have found to attract people are the following:

1. If your choice is between a "reserve" auction and a "no reserve," go with the "no reserve" (Figure 18-10).

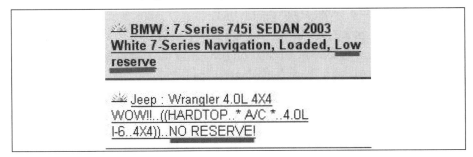

Figure 18-10. A "no reserve" auction

A reserve is a minimum price. You can start something at $10 and set a reserve of $50. If the bidding does not reach $50, you are not under any obligation to sell.

2. If your choice is between a low starting price with a reserve and a high price without it, go with the low price. Figure 18-11 gives an example of both a low price and no reserve.

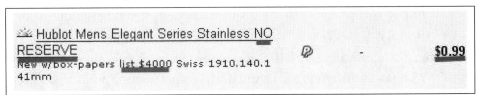

Figure 18-11. Low price and no reserve

The lower you can start your bidding, the more bids you're going to get. It almost always works, and the way it works amazes me. I've seen this countless times: There are two identical items for sale. One of them has 30 bids and the price has reached $60; the seller began the auction at 99 cents. The other item was listed at $50, and it has one bid. Obviously, the second auction is a better deal, yet buyers continue to bid on the first one, even though the price is higher.

There's some kind of psychology to a lot of bids and a low starting bid that turns people on. If there's any demand at all, you're going to do better almost every time. Buyers get e-mails that say, "You're no longer the high bidder." In this sense, eBay's "helping" them out. Of course, they're really doing it to keep buyers in the game so they'll bid again. After all, eBay wants to make money. They get a percentage of every sale. It's called a final value fee (Figure 18-12). You pay a listing fee for auctioning an item, and you pay the final value fee if it sells.

Final Value Fees	
Closing Price	**Final Value Fee**
Item not sold	**No Fee**
$0.01 - $25.00	**5.25%** of the closing value
$25.01 - $1,000.00	**5.25%** of the initial $25.00 ($1.31), **plus 3.25%** of the remaining closing value balance ($25.01 to $1,000.00)
Equal to or Over $1000.01	**5.25%** of the initial $25.00 ($1.31), **plus 3.25%** of the initial $25.01 - $1,000.00 ($31.69), **plus 1.50%** of the remaining closing value balance ($1000.01 - closing value)

Figure 18-12. Final value fees

Now, as the seller, you may be feeling a little scared. Let's say you have something that is pretty valuable, something worth around $500 or $1,000. It could be a hockey card, such as a rookie Wayne Gretzky card valued at $500. As a seller, you might not like the idea of listing it at 99 cents without a reserve, risking the possibility that someone might take it for $5—and you would be right. In this case, I wouldn't do that. You can cancel auctions, but it's not good to make a habit out of that; "Gee, it rained on my Wayne Gretzky card and I have to remove the auction" isn't a good business practice. If I were you, what I would suggest in this instance is to start low, but have a reserve.

However, there are some things that are common items. Do you remember when the Xbox first came out and it was so popular? There was actually a guy on eBay starting those at 99 cents! I showed his auction to my students and said, "How come there's no reserve? Isn't the seller taking a terrible chance?" Actually, he wasn't. He knew where the price was going to go.

> *When I sell something repeatedly, after a while I know where the price is going to go—within a small range, of course.*

When I sell something repeatedly, after a while I know where the price is going to go—within a small range, of course. In many ways, this could also be a part of your testing, finding out whether to set a reserve price or not. The issue about the Wayne Gretzky card is that it's a rare item, not a consumer item. You don't own 50 Wayne Gretzky cards, and you're not doing a Dutch auction.

Many of us remember that when we were kids, we had a wealth of items that eventually would become very valuable, but we never realized it. It may be enough to make us weep. Today, I see things selling on eBay and I think, "My grandmother had one of those!"

The eBay Auction: How Long Must It Be and When Do I Start?

I normally go for the 7-day auction. Three days isn't long enough, and the 10-day auction has an extra charge. Surprise! It's an excuse for eBay to make extra cash. It's not much money, but when you multiply that by a million, eBay's doing all right. I don't want to pay eBay any more than I have to.

Some people ask me if I have found a magic day to start my auctions. I have found that Sunday night has been good for me. The best way to find out, of course, is by testing. For example, I had a student who was selling kites and ballet stuff for little girls aged five to seven. Generally, buyers for this merchandise are young mothers, and they're most active in the mornings—I guess the kids are at school and they have a bit of free time. In my case, I have had zero luck on Friday night and very little luck on Saturday, but Sunday night is a great night for ending your auctions. You've got to test the market and find out what works best for you.

There are other things you need to know about when setting up the bids. For example, there is something called a "Dutch auction." A Dutch auction is when you sell more than one item at a time. There might be five of them or 500 of them; it doesn't make difference. Actually, this is how I sold my leather goods. However, if you are selling Wayne Gretzky cards, basketball cards, hockey cards, or baseball cards, you probably wouldn't want a Dutch auction, especially if you're dealing with valuable items. The reason for this is that you don't get as much money if you sell too many of them at the same time. When there's a perception of scarcity, you can charge more.

What that Dutch auction does is let multiple people purchase the same item at a particular price. It can be confusing. If you have 10 cards for sale, and 50 people bid on them, how do you know who wins? The lowest winning bid sets the price for everybody. You might have somebody bidding $500 on an item, but the 10th person bids $50, so everybody pays $50. Sellers do get upset about that, but if you want to do Dutch auctions, you have to accept those rules.

> *What that Dutch auction does is let multiple people purchase the same item at a particular price.*

Feature It!

There are lots of ways to spend money on eBay as a seller. For example, you can feature your item. Probably the most primo real estate on the internet is the "Front Page Featured" area on eBay. This refers to the featured listings on the front page of the eBay site. Naturally, these draw a great deal of attention because they're in such a popular location. There are always six items on the front page, and they're randomized so that no one item remains in that spot for long. However, there is a link from those six auctions to the rest of the featured items list, which gets lots of traffic (Figure 18-13).

If you pay the extra money for this prime spot, eBay tells you, "Your item will probably be on the front page of eBay, although it's not guaranteed." This sounds cool, and eBay charges you $39.95 for that wonderful location.

You can also choose "Featured in Category" (shown in Figure 18-14), which costs $19.95 and means that your goodies will appear at the top of the page in their category. That's like buying a prime listing on a search engine.

The problem with this is that results from such listings depend on what merchandise you're selling. In every case, however, featured items sell better than regular items.

Figure 18-13. Featured items list

Figure 18-14. "Featured in Category"

One of my tricks with featured items is using them to drive traffic to my other items. I used to do cross-stitch, for example. I'm so busy now that I don't do it anymore, but at the time, I had enough stock to open my own store. I created about 30 auctions and paid the $19.95 to feature my best offer.

It was a lead generator. It was advertising for all my cross-stitch auctions, and I personalized it. I said, "I love this stuff, but I don't have time anymore and I wanted to find a good home for it." Is that corny or what? But it worked: it drove lots of traffic to my other auctions, which was what I intended.

Buy It Now

Figure 18-15. The "Buy It Now" button —a cool eBay feature

Another cool feature is the "Buy It Now" button (Figure 18-15).

With Buy It Now, or BIN, the buyer can purchase the item immediately, rather than waiting for the auction to end. So, in effect, you're operating as a store. This option is popular, and you frequently see listings where the opening bid is $20 but there's a Buy It Now set at $30. So, if somebody decides, "Hey, I want this thing and I want it now. I'm going to buy it," they can buy it right this second. They click on the listing, make their bid, and it disappears. And that's the end of that.

This is an option that you, as the seller, can include, and it's one that you should experiment with.

After the Sale

Okay, so now you've got all this great information. You've put up your product. You have excitedly checked the status every 30 seconds. A week has gone by, and you've actually sold the item. You're ecstatic. What do you do now? How do you take payment?

What you do at this point depends on how you've set up your system. eBay naturally encourages you to use PayPal, as they own the company. If you do, when the buyer agrees to purchase your product, he or she receives an invoice from PayPal that gives your contact information and tells the buyer how much money is owed. You, as the seller, receive the buyer's information.

Next, once the buyer has paid, it's your responsibility to ship the merchandise to the buyer. It's in your best interest to make this shipment quick and trouble-free. PayPal will help with that by providing address information and allowing sellers to print shipping labels (Figure 18-16).

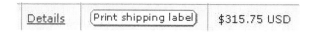

Figure 18-16. PayPal offers a "Print shipping label" feature

After the transaction, you have the option of leaving feedback for the buyer, and the buyer has the same opportunity to evaluate you (Figure 18-17). Some sellers leave feedback as soon as they receive payment; others wait. It's entirely up to you to choose your time.

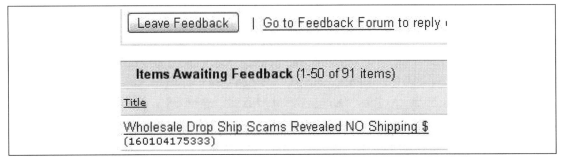

Figure 18-17. Option to leave feedback for the buyer after transaction is complete

Auction Management Software

When you're doing your first few auctions on eBay, you should do all the work yourself to learn the steps and see how the process works. If you've only got five auctions running, management is no big deal.

However, once your business is rocking and rolling, you're going to need management software. There are two kinds of management systems:

1. A service that runs online
2. Software that you buy and install on your own computer

eBay has its own system that you can use. One of its services, Turbo Lister (Figure 18-18), is free and allows the seller to "mass upload," which means listing dozens or even hundreds of items simultaneously. It's downloaded and installed on the seller's own computer.

eBay also has a paid service called Selling Manager PRO that has more features and is used online, rather than being downloaded (Figure 18-19).

I can't tell somebody what kind of software to use, because it depends on their budget, what they want to do, and whether they're willing to run the software "in house" or operate online. To get an idea of the tools you can use to run your eBay business and the pros and cons of each, go to **www.moonlightingontheinternet.com/auctiontools**.

Figure 18-18. eBay's Turbo Lister is free to use

But let's assume for a moment that we are using the eBay software. You just sold your Wayne Gretzky card, and an e-mail will immediately be sent to the winning buyer. It will say whatever YOU want it to say. I always start off with, "Thank you for buying my merchandise [name whatever you sold]. Congratulations, etc. Here is the total amount that you owe."

You want to be in charge of what is said. You don't want to use a "canned" e-mail, because if you've got a niche, you want to sell them something else. You now have this great hockey card. Maybe in the future, you will have some other card you wish to sell. If you already have a second card—perhaps a Mario Lemieux card—you will want to tell the buyer about it in your e-mail: "What a bargain! If you buy it in the next 48 hours, you can have it for only …"

Then the buyer will pay you—hopefully, he or she won't be one of those malingering buyers—and the whole transaction will be managed by your software.

Figure 18.19. Selling Manager PRO is a paid service offered by eBay

Keeping the Buyers Interested

Here is where the biggest eBay error occurs. About 99 percent of eBay sellers want to get this part finished. Not me. I want to stay in touch with those buyers! After they've paid me, I'll say, "Thank you for buying [whatever I've sold]. We hope you enjoy it. We'll let you know when we're shipping this out and we'll give you the tracking number. And, by the way, do you know about ..." Here's another chance to sell them whatever.

Then I send out a third e-mail: "Your Wayne Gretzky card has been mailed. Here's the tracking number. And did you know my eBay store sells [whatever]?"

That's the way to move your profits from adequate to awesome!

Another tip: I always put an insert into every package I send. We no longer do our own shipping. Instead, we use a fulfillment house, and now my fulfillment house adds the inserts. The insert offers the customer something else to buy, and it's always a special kind of deal.

I also discovered—the hard way—to use colored paper. I use yellowish-green or shocking pink or a similar dramatic color. The text will say, "Visit my online store" or "We have a sale through Christmas on …" In this insert, you can say whatever you want to attract more business from those buyers. It's free advertising.

If you've ever done any mail order, you know the biggest expense is the mailing costs. So back to this eBay sale—here's somebody who's already paid the shipping for me to advertise to them. Sellers miss this awesome opportunity, and it's really a shame.

If you take all of the things you learn in internet marketing and bring them into eBay and say, "How can I transfer this idea to eBay?" your profits will increase. And, more importantly, other sellers on eBay won't realize what you're doing—a big plus.

Generally, your eBay business is exposed. When you have competition, you can study what they're doing. You can see their products, their pictures, their copy, and all the details of their offers. But when you contact buyers off eBay, nobody knows it but you and the customer. Your best ideas won't be pirated by others. If you're sending inserts to your customers, nobody knows that but you. The only caveat I put on a back-end offer is to make sure it makes sense. If you sell a Wayne Gretzky card and you send an offer for a shopping cart system, that doesn't make sense. However, if you are selling a domain name or something related to web sites and you insert a shopping cart system offer, that makes sense. If I'm selling jewelry, I could be sending buyers a catalog with my new sapphire earrings.

> *Generally, your eBay business is exposed. When you have competition, you can study what they're doing.*

Dealing with Non-Paying Buyers

There is such a thing as a "non-responsive buyer": if you do enough business on eBay, you're certain to run into some of those people. Why someone bids on an item and then ignores the transaction is a mystery to me, but it's a fact of life. Figure 18-20 illustrates what it looks like when an item remains "unsold." Some sellers go ballistic and make all kinds of threats, but I see it as a cost of doing business on eBay. I don't mean I like buyers

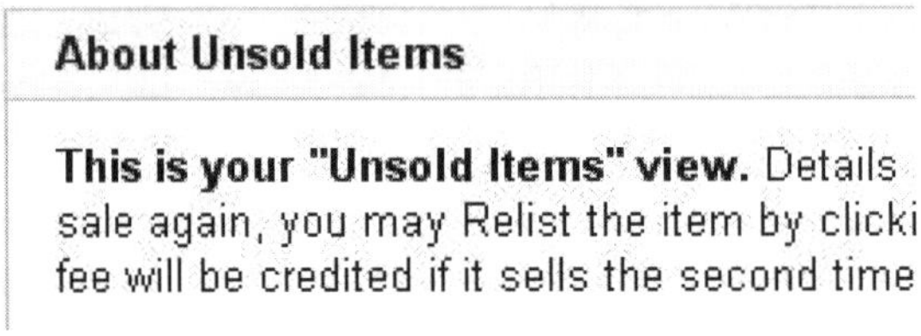

About Unsold Items

This is your "Unsold Items" view. Details
sale again, you may Relist the item by clicki
fee will be credited if it sells the second time

Figure 18-20. Sometimes buyers bid on an item
only to ignore the transaction later

who don't live up to their commitments—I'm saying that being indignant
and spending a lot of time on this issue is a waste of energy.

When this happens, you don't want to give them the chance to do the
same thing back to you and send you threats. Let it go and move on.

There are two remedies at your disposal in this case. One is what is
known as the Second Chance Offer (Figure 18-21). There are rules about
how this works, but the bottom line is that you can offer your merchandise
to the second person on the list of bidders.

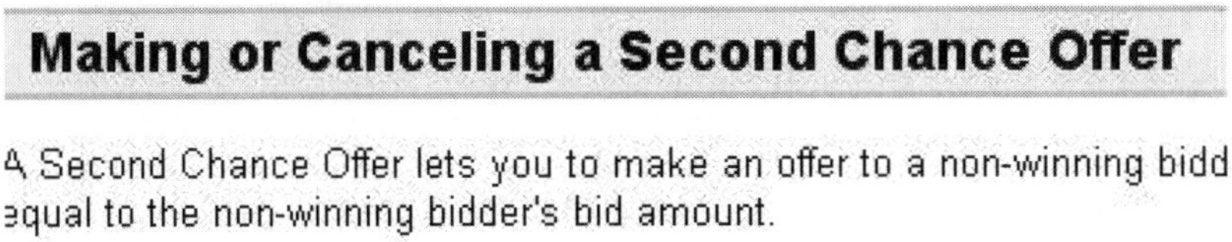

Making or Canceling a Second Chance Offer

A Second Chance Offer lets you to make an offer to a non-winning bidd
equal to the non-winning bidder's bid amount.

Figure 18-21. A Second Chance Offer

Second, eBay has instituted a system that requires immediate payment
(Figure 18-22). With this option, the item doesn't disappear for sale until
it's paid for, which is cool. The wild threats and negative feedback are coun-
terproductive. Handle the non-paying bidder in a professional manner and
move on with your business.

Feedback

At this point, I should discuss the importance of feedback. "Feedback" is a
voting system available to past customers. It can be very important, although
a lot of people don't pay attention to feedback. I don't personally pay attention to it unless what I'm buying is fairly expensive.

Requiring Immediate Payment

If you've set a Buy It Now price for your item, you can
you're selling a time-sensitive item (for example, conc
must include any related costs, so your buyer knows

How it works

1. A buyer who clicks the Buy It Now button in yo
2. Until the buyer completes payment, the item **re**
   buyer to complete their PayPal payment official

Figure 18-22. A new eBay system where immediate payment is required

Take some time to look at an eBay auction, and in the upper-right corner you will see the ID of the buyer and the number of feedback points he or she has. You will also see the percentage of positive feedback.

If you're selling high-ticket items, you want to pay attention to your feedback. However, sellers of high-ticket items usually have a lot less feedback than somebody who's selling 50 items worth $5.

Now you can reply to negative feedback on eBay. For a long time, this option wasn't available. If someone blasts you, you now have a way to respond to the criticism.

> *If you're selling high-ticket items, you want to pay attention to your feedback. However, sellers of high-ticket items usually have a lot less feedback than somebody who's selling 50 items worth $5.*

A secret for getting good feedback quickly is asking for it. You have to keep giving good customer service. If you're not responsive to people, you're going to get bad feedback—and you should. However, if you're giving good service, you're responsive to your customers, and you ask them for feedback, a lot of them will respond in a favorable way. A lot of them won't. You've got to keep asking. I send an e-mail about a week or two after they've gotten their merchandise. It says something like, "Hope you are enjoying your widget, and hope there are no problems. I gave you feedback, how about some in return?" And a lot of people will respond to that.

One other thing that you should know about is the notion of "over-delivery." If you send something along in the box that you didn't mention in the listing—something that doesn't cost you much—you will wow your customers. For instance, you can send a coupon for an online e-book. It doesn't have to be anything much. People are impressed by extra service, and they're going to remember you. More than likely, they'll also give you positive feedback.

Accepting Payments

Accepting payments is not a hard thing to do. As I mentioned, the payment method of choice on eBay is PayPal (Figure 18-23).

Join PayPal Today
Now Over
100 million accounts

> Sign Up Now!

Figure 18-23. The eBay payment method of choice is PayPal

There are some people who don't use PayPal, but the majority do, and it is the easiest way to accept payments. You will be limiting yourself as a seller if you don't have a PayPal account, because there are many buyers who won't consider any other kind of payment.

All you have to do is sign up for a PayPal account. There's nothing to it. The account is free, and some of your transactions cost nothing, although if you do much volume, PayPal will automatically upgrade you to a business account and start charging you a percentage.

Moonlight on Stephen Shulenski

Stephen's Moonlighting Story

In 2003, after being forced into bankruptcy and no job, I decided to create a product around all the tricks and secrets I learned while working for several national portrait studios and sell it on eBay.

www.maverickphotographer.com

The eBay sales of that one product on the Pet Photography Business averaged about $1,000. Keep in mind that since then I have added other products.

I am also happy to report that I've gotten married and moved to the Great Barrier Reef in Australia, where my wife and I live life on our terms.

Stephen's Advice

I decided to take full responsibility for all my mistakes and successes and stop blaming other people and things for my life situation. If I can do it, so can you!

Most people like PayPal. I recently bought something where the person would not take PayPal; I had to get a money order and mail it to the seller. I hated that, but I wanted the item badly enough, so I did it. Generally, however, I won't buy from people like that.

The big lesson is to make it easy for the buyer, and PayPal is the preferred way. I do offer people choices elsewhere, but on eBay, almost everybody uses PayPal. When you get off eBay, most folks prefer credit cards.

The great thing about PayPal is that when you sign up for a PayPal account as a seller, you can accept credit cards through PayPal. It's like having the best of both worlds.

The system has gotten more sophisticated. A lot of people rant about PayPal and all the problems they've had. I've been a PayPal user almost from the beginning; I had one problem, and that was dealt with quickly and efficiently. Maybe I've been lucky. Other people may be exaggerating their complaints. Who knows?

Managing Customer Orders

Now that you have your eBay business going, you may ask yourself, "What kind of time do you think I should allow for managing customer orders, dealing with shipping, and so on?"

make payments

- After you won the auction, an email with checkout procedure will be sent to yo All payments must go through our checkout.
- We accept the following payment methods: PayPal, Visa, Master Card, mone personal check (e-check and personal checks will be held up to 7 business
- We accept credit card payment for US orders only. We do not accept non-US
- Payments are expected within 7 days after the last winning auction is closed.

Figure 18-25. Set a time frame within which buyers must make a payment

In answer to this question, I'll tell you one thing that I think is important. I think you should set a contact time. I always do. For example, say, "I need to hear from you within three business days." Sometimes it drags a little beyond that, but the longer it takes to get a response, the less likely you are to get your money.

Some sellers give more time than I do. So pressure your buyers in a nice way and insist on payment "right now." After you receive your money, send out the shipment as quickly as you can.

That's one advantage to having a digital "extra"—you can send them something digitally right away, and they're going to be pleased because they received something from you within seconds.

When I order something, I want it to be fixed and delivered minutes later. We all do. It's tough to wait sometimes. So getting that merchandise out promptly is really important. I repeat—REALLY important. When you get payment, you should mail the package that same day or the next day, if possible.

Shipping is going to take some time. I'm not going to lie about that. My main way of shipping has always been Priority Mail, because you get all those boxes for free, which you don't get with UPS. Getting your shipping materials free is a big money saver, obviously. The U.S. Post Office has benefited from eBay, and they've made it easy to ship. You can even order labels and print them online, and a mail carrier will pick up the packages at your house.

That is a good deal. You can probably get one of your kids or someone else to stuff the boxes for you. I've had a lot of people work for me, especially mothers with small children at home who couldn't afford day care, so they couldn't go to work. The merchandise was delivered to their houses, and they would mail it out for me. It's not hard to find people like that.

Chapter 19

What Makes a
Successful Seller?

So here's a big question: What do successful auction sellers do differently from unsuccessful ones? I'm asked this question a lot, and I believe there are two things that make all the difference:

1. Successful sellers learn from what's going on. I hear so many people say, "I tried once, and it didn't work." That is foolish. Or, "I expected this auction would be a huge success, and it wasn't." Or, "I only made $X, and I expected more." Study what's going on. Scope out your competition. Don't give up and wander off complaining. Sit there until you figure out what's going on and try again.

2. The second thing successful auction sellers do is test. "I sold this and made $20, and that's great. That was good. Now, how can I make $25? What can I do differently?" I experiment with my auctions until they're as good as I think they're going to get.

The key, as I keep stressing, is to turn these one-time sales on eBay into long-term customers. In fact, that's where it helps to know some internet marketing. You keep in frequent contact with your customers, and you offer them goodies. You can have a Labor Day sale, and then you can have a Halloween sale, and then you can have a Christmas sale. You're selling jewelry and you tell them, "Just because you're my good customer, I wanted to send you this interesting article on how to clean diamonds without damaging them."

Keeping in touch is the number one thing, so they remember who you are—and offering them other items and information is the classic way to do it. And it works.

If someone's bought something from me, I take that as permission to contact them again in my business model. We always give them the choice to opt out, of course, but if they don't leave, they're going to hear from me for a long time.

I want to give you something that I stumbled onto as an example of this:

> I really messed up in my early days on eBay. I was trying to keep track of everything on a spreadsheet.

I really messed up in my early days on eBay. I was trying to keep track of everything on a spreadsheet. I was making so much money, and I was adding more and more auctions. I was on a roll. I was auctioning constantly. I was making $2,000 a week, then $3,000, $4,000, $5,000, even $6,000 a week.

But I was managing all of this activity on a spreadsheet, and it started to get away from me, to spin out of control. Not only did I have hundreds of current auctions, but as anybody who's sold on eBay knows, all auctions don't clear up in a few days. Some people drag out the process.

I was spending all day, every day trying to cope. I was sleeping three to four hours a night, trying to keep up with the record-keeping. It was awful. I finally got so blown out that I was getting negative feedback everywhere. I was sending people the wrong items, and I thought this one person paid when he hadn't and vice versa. It became a disaster.

I finally straightened it all out, but I got a lot of negative feedback along the way. I had no malicious intent; I simply expanded too quickly for the system I had in place.

So I shut down my business for a few weeks and thought, "What am I going to do with this?"

I decided I was going to sell first edition books, because I love books.

What Makes a Successful Seller?

Back then, there were no research tools, so the only way I could find out about the prices of books on eBay was to go through the completed auctions and make my own lists. It took time, because back then we could access six months' worth of eBay data instead of the current 30–60 days' worth.

I put all this information in a notebook, which I carried with me to flea markets and other such places, looking for books. I'd find a first edition of *Black Beauty*, for example, sell it on eBay, and turn a profit.

Over a period of a few months, I accidentally created a list of 250–300 avid, frothing-at-the-mouth book collectors. So, one day I decided to send them an e-mail and I told them, "I have X book (don't remember the title), and it's for sale until Friday night at midnight Eastern time. And the minimum I will take is $200."

To my shock, that was the most profitable auction I'd had up until that time! I, in effect, became my own auction site. Nobody knew what I was doing, because the e-mails were sent behind the scenes, which made it even better!

Think about the psychology of my offer. If you're drooling over the book I have, and you're willing to pay $300 for it, but you see it on eBay for sale for $98, how much are you going to bid? $98.50, right?

But that's not true if you don't know what everybody else is bidding. Instead, you're going to offer me the $300 that you really think it's worth. I had no trust issues with these people, because they'd all done business with me before. If I said, "This book is in perfect condition, except that the corner on page 14 is bent," they were likely to believe me.

It was wonderful. I was making more money with fewer auctions, all by accident. I didn't know much about marketing. That shows what can happen when we fool around, experiment, and try new things. All I knew was that I loved doing business this way, and I became determined to figure out how to put together deals like that on purpose. Anybody can do that. There's nothing hard about it.

> *I was making more money with fewer auctions, all by accident. I didn't know much about marketing.*

More Cool Secrets to Success on eBay

I'll let you in on some more secrets. There is something I've never seen anybody else do, but it's worked wonderfully for me!

People have a perception of value, and *you need to let them know how valuable YOUR product is.* Don't assume they will figure it out for themselves. I have a classic example that I teach in my class. Here it is:

I once noticed a guy on eBay selling a Seiko watch for $16.99 (Figure 19-1).

Nice Men's Lorus/Seiko S/S Dress Watch LR260
Item # 2626617154
Jewelry & Watches:Watches:Wristwatches

urrent **US $16.99**   Starting bid   **US $16.99**

Figure 19-1. It is important to tell a buyer when they're getting a good deal. Not doing so would be missing a golden opportunity, as is the case with this seller selling a men's Seiko watch.

When I'm doing market research, I will go to a shopping comparison site such as **epinions.com** and find out the retail price. I found a web site where that watch was listed at a retail price of $139. Here was someone selling the same watch for $16.99, yet he didn't point out what a bargain his merchandise was. That's missing a golden opportunity. He should have been making a huge deal out of the fact that his watch was 88 percent off the retail price!

Furthermore, he should have proved it to potential buyers. What I would do is take a picture of that watch with its full price on the other web site and include it in my auction (Figure 19-2). Prove it. Give them the URL and include that huge savings in your auction title. Of course, I'd find the highest price I could on the internet, rather than the lowest, and show that to the buyers.

Figure 19-2. Full Seiko watch price should be displayed so buyers can compare prices

If somebody's selling it for $89, I still want to use the $139, because it looks much better to show the bigger price difference. It makes my product look like an even greater bargain. The most important thing is to show them the ACTUAL PROOF. It's not enough to say, "Retail price: $189." But if you show them the screen shot, it will give you credibility.

Some sellers amaze me. They'll say, "I'm selling this for $10. Retail: $3,000." A typical example is shown in Figure 19-3. Oh, come on! Give me a break! Does anybody really believe that? Where's the proof?

$29000 26 CT RUBY DIAMOND NECKLACE 14K $.01

Figure 19-3. A listing that's hard to swallow!

The way I see it, these sellers look shady. That's not the way to do it. Some of these claims are so outrageous, you can't believe it.

Have fun selling on eBay! And don't forget—TEST, TEST, TEST, and then get one of those mini money machines going!

For a complete list of the resources Sydney uses and recommends, go to **www.moonlightingontheinternet.com/auction**.

About Sydney

Sydney Johnson, the AUCTION QUEEN, was one of the original sellers on eBay and has been selling on eBay since the winter of 1996. She is the originator and teacher of the famous Auction Genius Course, a powerful 16-hour multimedia internet seminar that teaches everything necessary to build a powerful and lucrative online auction business and includes software and numerous other aids.

Currently, Sydney has her own online auction blog and publishes an e-zine, *Auction Gold,* which has a circulation of 25,000+ readers. She is the auction consultant for WorldWide Brands and a regular contributing editor for the *Entrepreneur* magazine E-Biz radio show. She has also been on the eBay radio show.

Personal information: Sydney was a schoolteacher for almost 25 years before she ran screaming out the door to become her own boss. She tried all the usual ways of making a living "from home"—real estate, commodities trading, buying tax liens, multiple level marketing, mail order—until she discovered the internet and fell instantly in love. She began selling on eBay a few months after it opened and has been having a great time ever since.

She lives in a suburb of Atlanta and has two children, one of whom is her business partner. She considers herself the luckiest person alive!

Part Three

Moonlighting on the Internet Method #3: Affiliate Marketing

Developed by Rosalind Gardner

This Moonlighting method is the flip side of what I talked about as my "top secret" weapon for driving gobs of traffic to my sites—*affiliate marketing*. But in this scenario, you are the affiliate.

That means you promote other people's products and cash the checks! You don't have to worry about creating a product, customer support, making sure the payments go through, dealing with shipping/fulfillment, tech stuff, admin, etc.

It's a simple proposition—you send a merchant a prospect, and if that person buys (or completes an action like filling out a form), you get paid.

Sound good?

This is one of the best ways to start part-time online and see where it takes you. In this part, you'll hear from one of my favorite online friends, Rosalind Gardner.

She has created numerous autopilot businesses selling exclusively as an affiliate. Her last public number was over $412,000 in commissions selling other people's stuff online. She now earns more than that selling everything from "hard" products to services. What's more, she often earns more than the business owners whose products she promotes, all without creating or selling her own product.

Ros is an amazing success story in affiliate marketing, but more importantly, she knows how to enjoy her life. Every time I speak to her, she's either planning for or returned from some exotic vacation, or she's off enjoying the Canadian outdoors by cross-country skiing, hiking, walking, and snowshoeing … all while her affiliate sites keep making her money.

She's modest about her accomplishments, and I'm always prodding her to teach more, but she simply enjoys her lifestyle.

For more about Ros, see the bio at the end of chapter 21.

The World of Affiliate Programs

When it comes to creating your own business, it seems like everybody gets hung up on the business details—you know, "I don't know how to create a product," or "Who will deal with the customers?" or "How can I process the credit cards?" Stuff like that.

If you find yourself thinking, "I wish I could start my own online biz, but _____," I say, "Forget about it."

The fact is, there *is* a method that is so easy you won't believe it—*and* it doesn't require you to deal with any of those details. Unbelievable, right?

Well, believe it! I am referring to affiliate marketing. It is a dream come true, and I should know, because I wasn't always an internet business-woman. I'll explain what it is first and then share my story.

What Exactly Is Affiliate Marketing?

A working definition of "affiliate marketing" is commission selling for online merchants. The merchant gives you, the affiliate, a link to put on your web site that is coded with a number assigned specifically to you. So, if a person clicks on your link, visits the merchant's site, and makes a purchase, you get a percentage of the sale and a commission check.

Sometimes folks get put off by the idea of selling, but online is different, as the sale happens on the merchant's site and you are paid for the referral—or perhaps I should say, the click that leads to the sale. There are other models, but let's keep it simple for now.

Let me give you an example: everyone's familiar with eBay. Did you know eBay has an affiliate program? You can earn a commission every time anyone registers as an active eBay member through your affiliate link. So, if you tell one of your friends, "Hey, go sign up for eBay," and you give him your ID number, you'll get paid. As long as the users become active within a specified time, eBay is going to pay you up to $22 for every new user you send to them, plus you'll get 40 to 65 percent of eBay revenue on successful transactions.

Other big companies participate in affiliate marketing, too. Companies such as Dell, Sony, Eddie Bauer, and Gap are some examples, if you're interested in selling electronics or clothes online. Speaking of clothes, Payless Shoe Source and Fog Dog Sports have affiliate programs. Barnes & Noble has a program, and everyone has probably heard of the Amazon.com affiliate program. And then there's Best Buy, which sells everything from computers to software. I don't know whether everybody's heard of Hammacher Schlemmer (Figure 20-1), but they sell some fabulous stuff, if you want to put together a unique online gift store. That would be one of the merchants I would apply to as an affiliate.

> *I don't know whether everybody's heard of Hammacher Schlemmer, but they sell some fabulous stuff, if you want to put together a unique online gift store.*

There's obviously no shortage of merchants you can affiliate with. So, why would these other people pay you to market their stuff? Why don't they do it themselves?

The answer is that having an affiliate program amounts to free advertising for the merchant. Think about it: if a merchant has no affiliates, then the money they make is based only on their marketing efforts. They have to advertise; they have to get word about their site out there. However, if they have thousands of affiliates, those affiliates are spreading the word all over the internet, which amounts to free advertising for the merchant. All the merchant has to do is pay the promised commission on sales.

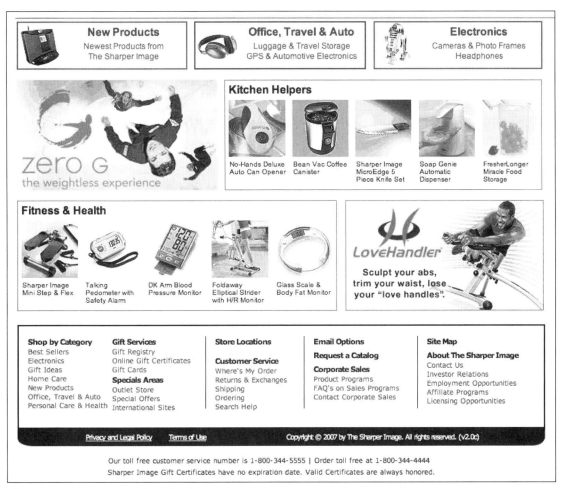

Figure 20-1. Hammacher Schlemmer

Many Ways of Getting Paid

You're probably wondering if most merchants pay you only after they have made a sale to someone you referred to them. There are many ways of getting paid with affiliate marketing.

There are pay-per-click programs, meaning if you send X number of visitors to a merchant's site, they may pay you 5 cents per click for each visitor. There's also pay-per-lead or pay-per-action. So, if you send a visitor to the merchant's site and they fill out a form, you may get paid $2 for the lead.

☾ Moonlighting on the Internet

A good example is the case of a credit card application. Say a person applies online by filling out a form at the merchant site, and they are approved for the credit card—if they got there through your link, you get paid.

I find being an affiliate for some credit card companies worthwhile, as some of them have payouts as high as $25 and even $40 per successful application. Remember, visitors don't need to buy anything, fill out a form and get approved for a credit card—then YOU get paid.

Moonlight on Brian Mckay

Brian's Moonlighting Story

I saw a story in the *New York Times* talking about the high cost of drugs for seniors. There was a picture of the storefront where this man was offering medicine from Canada at Canadian prices, which I thought was a great idea.

It was then that I remembered Paul Hartunian's story about the Brooklyn Bridge. "Selling the Brooklyn Bridge" may be an expression to indicate gullibility, but Paul actually did it! The part that stuck out in my mind was that he saw a news program about repairs to the Brooklyn Bridge and how old parts were being replaced, and in the camera shot he noticed the name on one of the trucks in the story and called to buy the wood being taken from the Brooklyn Bridge. The rest is history.

Anyway, that inspired me to call up the pharmacy guy and hop on a plane to meet him. I became his second franchisee in the country, and I then started my own site and went independent with **USCanadian pharmacy.com**. This was about six years ago.

This business is easy and sells itself. I also have residual income, in that most people keep coming back every three months. The other great feature is that there is no inventory on my end. I merely relay the order to Canada, and they do the rest.

www.uscanadianpharmacy.com

We hit a peak of $1 million a year in sales. Our profit margins are 16 percent. I spend ½ hour a month working on the business. I receive a commission check monthly, so there is no billing. It runs by itself.

Brian's Advice

Don't wait, get into gear and do it. You can listen to a million reasons why you should not do something. Action creates energy to propel ideas forward. This can be a lot of fun and rewarding. Get out there now.

How I Got Started

Some background is useful. You should know that I had a real J-O-B once and got into affiliate marketing purely by luck.

Believe it or not, my first product was for a dating service!

I got into dating services because I was a single air traffic controller, and air traffic controllers get quite a bit of time off. I think, at the time, we were working 34 hours a week. So I'd have four or five days off at a time.

So when I was off, I was hanging around in chat rooms. The internet was new, it was exciting, and it was a great way to meet people. On the other hand, it could also be dangerous, because you never knew whom you were dealing with.

By then, I had built a small web site which I used for seed exchanges—for flowers and that sort of thing. I was into gardening and had the most glorious garden in northern British Columbia, where it's cold and difficult to garden. And I've got to tell you, I was amazed by the number of people I connected with and with whom I exchanged seeds.

So, I had already realized that you could get in touch with anyone, anywhere, who was interested in the same thing that you were interested in—as long as they were on the internet.

Anyway, one day, I was surfing the internet and I saw this banner ad reading "Webmasters make money." I clicked on it—I'm always interested in making money—and when I got there, it was for the One and Only dating service network. They were offering the opportunity to affiliate with them, and every time somebody would buy a dating service membership through your link, you'd be paid a percentage.

With my experience of chat rooms and understanding of how they worked, I figured that a dating service was better than a chat room because it offered much more to singles than a chat room ever could. It made sense. The dating service gave singles a more targeted approach to find the people they were looking for without wasting their time, which was something that I saw great value in, so that made it easy to promote. I could talk about it from a first-person perspective.

By the way, I think that's an important part of affiliate marketing, to be able to recommend the product yourself. You don't need to buy every product you promote, but I think you should have a good understanding of the product. It's all too common to see people who are trying to market the internet's latest and greatest way to make a fast buck—maybe they were told they could make a lot of money with it, but they still don't know anything about the product. They're recommending software they've never used, or an e-book they've never read. I personally think it amounts to lying when someone endorses an e-book that they haven't read.

> *You don't need to buy every product you promote, but I think you should have a fairly good understanding of the product.*

Okay, off my soapbox and back to the online dating thing. It made sense to me from both a personal and a business perspective. So, I became an affiliate. My first check was for $10.99 (which was 50 percent of $22 or $21.95 or whatever it was that they were charging at the time). I was so excited, especially considering that I live in Canada and the American dollar was worth a whole lot more to us than it is now. The conversion rate now is around $1.01 Canadian to the U.S. dollar, so there's not the bonus there was a couple of years ago if you lived in Canada. That check for $10.99 validated affiliate marketing for me. It meant I could put a small site online. I could put my link up. Somebody would buy through that link, and I'd get paid for it.

As soon as I got that check in hand, I went full bore. Every month I challenged myself to earn more, do more, and be better. It meant that I could start small and see my income grow each month. I could also see that affiliate marketing had the potential to generate a huge amount of money, and boy, was I right. As long as I had an internet connection, my business would keep ticking along. Even then, you didn't need an internet connection all the time, but I'll tell you about that later.

Right about this time, things were starting to change. Remember, I had been an air traffic controller for 20 years. If you've read the news for the past few years, you know that being an air traffic controller is synonymous with stress! The company I worked for changed the contract so that the schedules were inhuman. For example, I'd be working until about two in the afternoon, and then about eight or nine hours later, they expected me to be back to work a midnight shift. *Try doing that!* I found my health deteriorating because my shifts weren't allowing me any recreational time—and I don't know about you, but I'm *all* about recreational time.

I was getting sicker and sicker and not sleeping well. Fortunately, I had already established my affiliate business. As things started to go south with my full-time job, I started gearing up as an affiliate, thinking—knowing, actually—that I could make this business my way out. Not only that, but it would afford me a lifestyle that was brilliant. I could work at home and go where I wanted and do what I wanted. It wasn't that I didn't love my job—I enjoyed it. It was fun. But it wasn't worth my life. With all of my attention on affiliate marketing, I couldn't believe how quickly my business grew!

A Business for the Lazy

The cool thing is that my business continues running on autopilot for the most part at this point. Merchants call me up, and sometimes I don't know what's going on because it's been so long since I've looked at that particular site. It's kind of funny in that way. But all the same, it's so consistent. The site is up, the links are up, the pay-per-click advertising campaign is in place, and it runs like clockwork, month after month. And generally speaking, it either remains the same or it grows a little bit.

This is an exciting way to make money if you have limited time. You take proactive actions, do them once, and get paid, *over and over again!* It doesn't get any better than that!

You know, I decided to focus on affiliate programs instead of creating my own product for the simple reason that I'm lazy. I didn't even think about developing my own product. I saw that banner ad, "Webmasters make money," and it was so easy to put up a little site, put up a link, and that was it, you're done with it.

I compare that to *The Super Affiliate Handbook,* my only product, and that whole process of writing it, which took months and months: putting it together, getting a cover designed for it, having it distributed through ClickBank, trying to get affiliates to sign up, and on and on—that was grunt work, plain and simple.

And then let's not forget dealing with customer service issues. If for some reason the site is down and somebody can't get their book, they may get upset, and I have to deal with that. The beauty of affiliate marketing is that you don't have *any of that*. All you have to do is put that link up on your site; visitors click the link, buy a product, and the merchant handles storing the inventory, shipping the inventory, and order processing. How cool is that?

Chapter 21

Finding an Affiliate Program and Working It

If you're wondering where to find all these programs and how to pick one once you find them, I'll tell you how I do it.

I generally use what are called "affiliate networks." The first affiliate network is Commission Junction (Figure 21-1). You can find them at **cj.com**. They have a whole host of merchants. Merchants join Commission Junction because they want to expose their products to the tens of thousands of CJ affiliates, so it's a win-win situation all around. The merchant pays a fee, but they get additional exposure. And the affiliate has access to thousands of merchants. I think they've got close to 2,000 merchants at CJ now.

After you create a free account, you'll be able to browse the CJ categories. The CJ interface is categorized, so you can choose from all sorts of categories such as jewelry, art, automotive, and books.

You can affiliate with clothing merchants and manufacturers. There are commerce merchants—we were talking about that before—who have credit card programs. There's entertainment, memorabilia, and anything and everything related to family. You could start a baby site, a teen site, or even a wedding site. Furthermore, many affiliates are doing well in the betting and gaming industry. There are also sports and fitness programs and

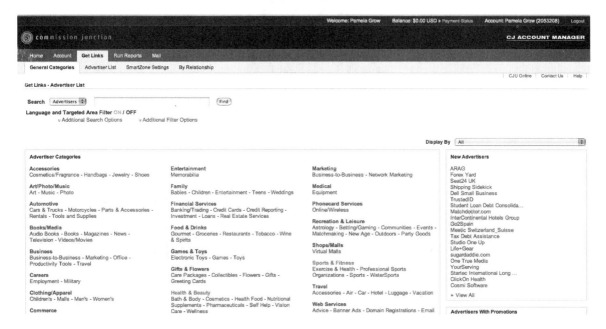

Figure 21-1. Commission Junction

travel, health, and beauty programs. Basically, there are programs on any topic you can think of. It's a beautiful place to go in terms of finding affiliate programs.

Keep in mind that there are a lot of affiliate networks; Commission Junction is the first one that I would recommend. There are affiliate networks that specialize in niche categories, such as betting, casino gambling, and that sort of thing, or financial products. For a complete list of affiliate networks and their categories, go to **www.moonlightingontheinternet.com/networks**.

Moonlight on Brian Stephenson

Brian's Moonlighting Story

I got started learning about internet marketing back in 1999. At that time, I was a 19-year-old college sophomore. A friend of mine and I had tried implementing several offline business ideas, but none panned out. A major reason was that between attending class, studying, and working our regular jobs to pay for school, we had no time to work the business. In addition, we were broke. Seriously—like rolling pennies for gas broke.

Then I came across a web site selling a "How to Make Money on the Internet" course. I used one of the many credit cards I had at that time to invest in the course. The course was incredible, and I tried to implement what I could, but never saw real results. I struggled online for a few more years and finally got a break after about 3½ years. At that time, I had subscribed to about every internet guru's newsletter and was literally getting 25 to 30 e-mails a day from about every online marketer. I read each e-mail, and my online knowledge increased exponentially. Finally, I decided to implement what I was learning and threw up a site that sold an old manual as an e-book via the ClickBank account I had created three years earlier.

Jobsearchbootcamp.com was my first attempt at info marketing that began to put an extra $30–$50 a quarter in my pocket. Pathetic, I know, but that little money made me a believer.

Fast forward to today: my online sites generate about $1,200 a month in income, with some months yielding highs of over $3,500. I drive traffic mostly through pay-per-click search engines and am also implementing a search engine optimization strategy to ramp things up. The best part about it is that because this is all affiliate marketing, there are no customer service headaches, no quotas, and no employees.

www.stephensonandcompany.com/medifast

Brian's Advice

The big "aha" moment for me was when I got the advice from someone who had already done it. If I had to do it all over again, I would not hesitate to get close to the source. I would have saved the money and paid to join someone's apprentice or coaching program. The problem I had was that I tried to figure everything out myself. Terrible idea. The best thing to do is to find one person to model your business after, invest in nothing else but that person, and avoid all distractions. Lastly, NEVER GIVE UP!

Choosing an Affiliate Program

You'll want to set your own criteria for selecting a good program to sign up for. I'll share some of the important questions to which you'll want answers. After all is said and done, you'll want to make sure that the product you recommend will sell and that you're going to get paid.

My first question is always, "Is the company reputable?" The easiest way to make sure is to deal with a huge brand name like Eddie Bauer.

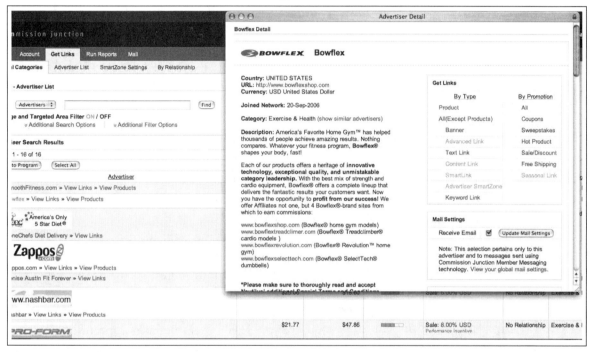

Figure 21-2. Through Commission Junction, one can ensure that a company is reputable

Another way to ensure that a company is reputable and that you're going to get paid is by going through an affiliate network like Commission Junction (Figure 21-2). In that case, the merchant has to put up a certain amount of cash based on expected affiliate payments, so the affiliate commissions are always kind of in the bank. That's a good guarantee that when you make a sale, you are going to get the payment.

You want to make sure that the affiliate program has an affiliate agreement in place. With Commission Junction, each merchant has individual agreements. You can read them on the site. You want to make sure that you read the agreement, because different merchants have different criteria.

For example, there are merchants that will not deal with affiliates outside of the United States, which is a problem for Canadian and other non-U.S.-based affiliates. Why that is, I don't know, because I'm promoting their product, and it doesn't matter where I'm promoting it from. But that's up to them. In essence, you want to look carefully at the conditions of the agreement.

You want to know if you can terminate the agreement. Now, that's usually more of a factor with independent merchants. Some of them will send out a form that you have to sign and return, and they'll try and get you committed to their program for a two- or three-year time frame. However, you should make sure you can get out of that agreement at any time. You definitely don't want to sign up for exclusive agreements. They bind you in such a way that you'll be stuck with them even if something better comes along.

> *You definitely don't want to sign up for exclusive agreements. They bind you in such a way that you'll be stuck with them even if something better comes along.*

You also want to make sure your site is eligible to join a program in terms of traffic or location. In addition, ask, "Is there a fee to join the program?" If there is a fee, generally speaking, it's not an affiliate program—it's an MLM, or multi-level marketing program, which has its own rules and parameters. And that's not something that I get into.

Of course, you need to know how much the commission is. That's an important question. Is the commission 8 percent? Is it 50 percent?

If a merchant is selling hard goods (something that needs to be shipped out), they're not going to pay you 50 percent of the take. After they've paid everything else associated with it, they can't afford to pay you 50 percent. But if it's an online service, such as a dating service—there are a variety of commissions being paid for dating service memberships; anywhere from 15 to 75 percent or even 100 percent. Some of them start off paying you 100 percent of the dating service membership in the first month, which is all fine and good. However, I would rather get paid 50 percent for each month that a person remains a member of the dating service to which I referred them. In fact, merchant programs that offer you recurring payments when applicable are the best kind! If you're selling web hosting or anything that requires ongoing monthly membership, you want to find a merchant that offers ongoing or recurring payments.

There's a factor called "lifetime commissions," and you are going to love this concept. Basically, there are affiliate programs that will pay you a commission for life on whatever your referred customer buys! So, for example, if I send a visitor to a merchant offering this program and they buy something, then that customer is mine for life. If the customer ends up buying anything else from that merchant, I will get the commission on that sale. So, although I may not have sold them that product directly, I still get credit for having sent them there in the first place.

Now that's a wonderful thing!

I gave you the most important questions to ask, but you can get the complete list of all 20 questions I ask my students at **www.moonlighting-ontheinternet.com/20questions.**

Read the Agreement

One of the first things you'll want to know is how often you're going to get paid. I've been stunned when merchants have owed me thousands of dollars and then I look back at the agreement to find out that they only pay twice a year. So, you *definitely* want to know how often you get paid. You'll also want to know the affiliate's minimum payment. I found a program once for which the minimum payment was $1,000. It can take awhile to get up there if you're not doing big numbers.

Incidentally, if you're wondering whether there are ways of knowing if an affiliate program *sells* before you sign up for it, that's another factor that makes **cj.com** a beautiful thing. They provide bar graphs of the EPCs, which are earnings per hundred clicks, over a three-month period and over a seven-day period. Here you can check how much the average affiliate earns by sending people to that merchant's site per hundred clicks. It's a good way to assess how much potential a program or a product has before you sign up for it, and certainly before you pay to advertise the program.

So, if you're deciding between two or three swimming pool accessory affiliate programs (you've got a pool site), then you'd look on CJ. You can see, for instance, that one site's EPC is $1.18 and the other site's is only 50 cents. Look at the numbers—how much easier could it be?

All right, what about the competition? It's a given that you're probably not going to be the only Eddie Bauer seller out there or the only one selling Sharper Image products. A lot will depend on the niche that you choose to work in. If you find a relatively underserviced niche, you might have little competition. However, even if there are thousands of sites selling the same product, it doesn't matter. There are thousands of dating service affiliates out there, and I still do good business in that niche. And there are even more dating service affiliates now, since so many people have read my book and they know how well I've done with dating services.

> *What you want to do is look at who's listed in the Google AdWords, which are located in the vertical bar along the right side of that page. They're your competition.*

But it doesn't matter. Because you know what? Your only real competition is on those first couple of pages of search engine results. What you want to do is look at who's listed in the Google AdWords, which are located in the vertical bar along the right side of that page. They're your competition.

What I'm going to suggest is that you buy pay-per-click advertising, which is cheaper than borscht, and put yourself alongside those other advertisers. That's how you get seen, and that's how you bring traffic to your site. After you've looked at the EPCs and assessed the conversion rate on your site, it's easy to see whether you can make money using AdWords and how much you can afford to spend on advertising.

The Business of Affiliate Marketing

Eventually, you may want to think about incorporating. I had all my business dealings separated from my personal income since the beginning. I was—what do you call that—a sole proprietor. I did that for about a year. I incorporated a year later, because I was making a lot of money and the tax implications as a sole proprietor on your personal income tax are much higher than they are for corporations. So it was worth my while to spend a little money and incorporate my business. For more info on incorporating and other considerations when starting your business, check out the business guide at **www.moonlightingontheinternet.com/bizguide**.

I think that anybody who starts making money should consult with an accountant. You can get going as a sole proprietor and not worry too much about it. But eventually, you'll want to check things out with a lawyer or accountant.

And, while you don't need your own web site to sell as an affiliate marketer, I recommend that you do, because the job of an affiliate is to presell the product, as opposed to selling the product.

Don't Sell, Presell

"Preselling" means endorsing a product. So that's what I am doing with the dating services. I talk about what it is that I like and dislike about the product. I'm honest about it. I show the advantages and disadvantages of different services, and compare and contrast them for my visitors. What that builds is credibility and trust, and people generally buy from people whom they trust.

If you don't have a site, you don't have that interaction with site visitors. You're sending them directly to the merchant site instead, which you can do using Google AdWords (which we talked about before). In that case, you miss out on the opportunity to have them sign up for your mailing list. That is integral to any business. You need to develop a list; otherwise, how do you get in touch with people, bring them back to your site, and have them buy more products from you? I think that's the difference between just doing a promotion and running a business or having something that is a tangible asset for you.

> *You need to develop a list; otherwise, how do you get in touch with people, bring them back to your site, and have them buy more products from you?*

You might want to pay a visit to one of my dating sites, **sage-hearts.com** (Figure 21-3)—it might make this picture clearer for you.

Moonlight on Janiss Garza

Janiss's Moonlighting Story

I created my first web site in 1997 and started doing it as a business in 2002. Currently I am a freelance writer and an author. The web site business thing began when I was the yoga guide for **about.com** in 2001—I went on to do my own mind-body-spirit fitness site in January 2002. The site, **www.allspiritfitness.com**, and an offshoot, **www.yourexercisedvds.com**, make money for me through affiliate marketing, Google AdSense, and some advertising revenue. A year after starting **allspirit fitness.com**, I decided I should start a web site for my then-six-month-old kitten Sparkle, and of course, my first thought was how to monetize her! So, in addition to her monthly diary and advice column, I added a store section for her to discuss cat products with the requisite affiliate links, and some Google AdSense, too, of course. Keep in mind that as a purebred Somali, Sparkle has expensive tastes, so the products she promotes tend to be big-ticket items, such as litterbox cabinets and designer cat trees. Because she is so photogenic—a kitty supermodel, if you will—I wound up giving Sparkle her own merchandise line via CafePress. Her store is **www.cafepress.com/designercat**.

I can say that having an online business has helped to keep me from having to get a J-O-B or struggling so hard to get my writing published. If there's a topic I REALLY want to write about, I can do a web site or a blog—I have the skills now to monetize most topics that interest me. And unless Sparkle happens to incur a big vet bill, she pretty much pays for her keep every month—food, cat litter, and toys—and she also supports the other two cats here that don't have their own web sites.

Beyond that, the web stuff just helps me stay home in this cool house working from my home office. Which makes Sparkle happy, because that means I am basically her full-time assistant. And I thought I didn't HAVE a J-O-B!

www.sparklecat.com

Janiss's Advice

My advice boils down to one five-letter word: NICHE! And don't be afraid to do something completely off-the-wall or foolish. I knew I was on the right track with Sparkle when I was at a marketing conference and I had two concepts I was promoting—Sparkle and another idea which I thought was really good. Well, all anyone wanted to talk to me about was Sparkle. That told me where to put my focus! I belong to Toastmasters—the worldwide organization that helps people learn public speaking—and one of my most popular talks was entitled "How to Make Your Cat Famous on the Internet." I may just turn that into a telecourse. Oh, and Sparkle says that if you use her story in your book, she will return the favor and send you a Paw-tographed copy of her own book, *Dear Sparkle: Advice From One Cat to Another!*

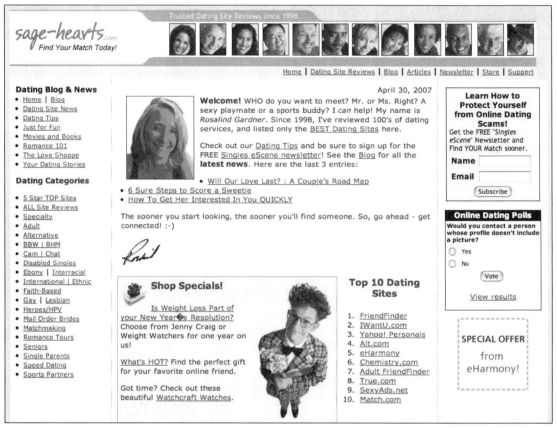

Figure 21-3. Sage-hearts.com dating site

I have an autoresponder series through which they can sign up for my newsletter called *The Singles E-Scene*. I try to keep people informed about changes in the industry and what's hot and new online, as well as giving them ideas for great first dates, how to stay safe online and off, and how to make sure you're not teeing up with an ax murderer.

KISS

It's a simple site—won't scare anyone off. I think it's a good indication that you don't need to have some fancy site to make a lot of money. I'm always telling people: "Forget the bells and whistles and the blinking-blinkings." I operate on the KISS premise ("keep it simple, sister"), and that's one of the reasons I like affiliate marketing—because it does keep things simple. You get the site up online, and that's it. You let it go. You let it make money. Simple is good. People appreciate simple.

And when it comes to start-up costs, we're talking less than $10 hosting, and you can register a domain name for another $8.95. It doesn't cost much to get into this game. But having your own domain makes you look like you're in it for real, not dabbling. And sometimes you won't get accepted as an affiliate if you don't have a web site for the merchant to see. They will only deal with credible affiliates—people who are serious about promoting their product.

If you have a site where you're obviously promoting other merchants' products and doing it well, you're more likely to get accepted by a wider range of merchants. It depends on the individual as to how soon you can start expecting to see some cash.

> *If you have a site where you're obviously promoting other merchants' products and doing it well, you're more likely to get accepted by a wider range of merchants.*

How much time have you got to put into it? Have you got a bit of money going into it to spend on advertising as well as that $8.95 to register the domain, and another $10 a month for hosting?

For somebody who's starting out, who maybe knows about HTML—actually, let's say somebody who knows how to build a simple web page, like the one that you saw at **sage-hearts.com**—they could have something making money by the end of a week.

These days, there are a lot of inexpensive HTML web site design programs and templates on the market for do-it-yourselfers. There's CoffeeCup, there's FrontPage. In addition, don't forget the resource page at **www.moonlightingontheinternet.com/resources**, where there's a template for you that is ready to go, along with other tools, checklists, etc.

Let's manage some expectations. For somebody who knows nothing about building a web site and where to go to find affiliate programs and anything else, give yourself a month, two months, three months. Take it nice and slow. Approach it step by step. Follow a plan. Affiliate marketing is the perfect business solution if you've only got 5 to 10 hours a week, but you will need to focus. Cut the surfing. Cut the instant messaging. Cut the checking your e-mail. Key word: focus!

Once again, I'm going to say that you should have a guide, whether it's this book, the blueprint on the Moonlighting site, or the Moonlighting coaching program (details at the back of the book). You should have a guide, and you need to focus on the task at hand.

Narrowing Your Focus

I notice that sometimes people get overwhelmed by all the choices they find when looking for merchants to affiliate with. They keep searching and searching and making longer lists of options. Wrong!

Do your homework and then narrow down your choices. Usually, the first thing you should do is choose a niche that you want to work in. Remember, you are not married to this choice, and you can always get into other niches, but it's important that you start somewhere and get the first one under your belt.

So, what are you interested in? Are you interested in travel? Do you play a sport? Are you into fitness? Cooking? Reading? You should probably build the first site around something that you're *really* interested in. And then it's step-by-step from there, given a guidebook—that's what you need to focus on. It's easy to lose precious time getting bogged down in surfing the internet or reading your e-mail.

Don't do it!

So turn off that e-mail or do whatever you need to do, and say, "I'm going to focus on finding a new affiliate program this week that I can promote," and go to work on that single task. Then, get your site up. Don't worry at first about how pretty it is or even how well it's written. You can tweak it later. Just get it up!

Driving Traffic

Once you have your site up, let's talk about some ways to drive traffic to the site and promote your affiliate program. I've already mentioned that you can expect to pay to advertise. You don't have to start out with a whole lot of money, but I've found that the most profitable way to market my site is by using the pay-per-click search engines. I got on that bandwagon as soon as they were available. **Goto.com**, which is now Yahoo! Search Marketing, was the very first one to come out. It sent my sales through the roof, because now I was driving targeted traffic.

So you understand what pay-per-click is, you advertise on "keywords" related to your business. So, if somebody's looking for a dating service online or if they're looking to meet people online, that's probably what they're going to type into the search engines. They would type in "singles," "online dating service," "dating," "meet men," whatever. I can bid on those phrases and those individual keywords at Yahoo! Search Marketing and 100 other pay-per-click search engines. Actually, I think there are probably as many as 500 or 600. I dollar-cost-average across a number of pay-per-click search engines to bring my average pay-per-click down to well below 10 cents. I have a title and a description that's listed on that search engine, and it may say, "Find your soul mate online. Come to online dating sites reviewed by blah, blah, blah." So if somebody's interested in that and they click on it, their visit costs me 5, 10, or 15 cents. And it only costs you money *when someone clicks*, which is the cool thing.

> *I dollar-cost-average across a number of pay-per-click search engines to bring my average pay-per-click down to well below 10 cents.*

And not only that, but people only click if they're interested. What you have to do is learn to write ads that pique people's interest and bring them to your site. It's not like waiting six months for search engine traffic, and when it comes, it turns out that the guy was interested in how to do carbon dating—because that's exactly what can happen if you're trying to go for the free search engine traffic. Sure, get it that way if you can. However, this is more direct, and let me tell you, it happens a lot faster! With Google AdWords, for example, you could be online today *and getting traffic today*. You can be set up in as little as 15 minutes on Google, driving targeted traffic directly to your site.

Other good ways to promote affiliate programs might include paying for a Yahoo listing or doing e-zine advertising, which is advertising your site in somebody else's online newsletter. Something that's more effective, however, is utilizing other people's newsletters by writing articles applicable to your site and offering them free to other newsletter owners. Make sure that you have a resource box at the bottom of the article that links back to your site. That will cost you nothing to bring traffic to your site— well, nothing but a little time to put together a little article with seven tips about seven great dates, or something like that. Then you send that out to a bunch of editors, and they pick it up and drive traffic to your site. Free traffic! That's neat. You can also reuse that content for your own newsletter or whatever people sign up for on your site.

And that is the next one. I don't place the value of my newsletter at this point. I place it as number two in terms of getting traffic, because if they sign up for my newsletter and they're on my list, getting in touch with my subscribers on a regular basis is one of the most profitable hours that I can spend in a week. With a good-sized list, it is possible to send out a newsletter and have it return $1,000, $5,000, $10,000 or more in an hour!

> *With a good-sized list, it is possible to send out a newsletter and have it return $1,000, $5,000, $10,000 or more in an hour!*

It's phenomenal how much revenue that generates. And it's basically free. All you're paying for is the cost of the autoresponder. So, you'll definitely want to have an autoresponder. The one I see many top internet marketers using because of how powerful it is also happens to be one of the easiest to set up and use. Check it out at **www.instantaweber.com**.

Since the autoresponders are automated, my promotions keep cycling through and going out at regular intervals unless I want to add something timely. Sometimes I'm promoting the affiliate products, just to remind people. Or the merchant might have a special. During February, they may have Valentine's Day specials going on, so that's a good time to remind your subscribers that they were at your site, they were interested, and they also signed up for your newsletter. Of course, you want to include content there to add value to it, and then link to the programs. In my case, what I'll link to sometimes is Sherry's Berries, which are fabulous. People who are single, of course, have a number of interests. They may have met somebody online, and they may want to send that person a gift. They may want to send themselves a gift. I send myself gifts all the time.

List + Autoresponder = Repeat Business

The biggest mistake you could make would be not having a mailing list. That is the number one mistake.

It's amazing how many affiliates think that because they're affiliate marketers, they don't have to have a mailing list. I don't understand that. They're letting dollars slip through their hands—and I do mean dollars—every time somebody who comes to their site doesn't sign up for their newsletter. They have no way of connecting with these people to promote either that product again or separate products, like Sherry's Berries.

You might be thinking, "Hey, that's a lot of work to put up some kind of newsletter." Not so.

A lot of people think they can't write. But, hey, I didn't write either before I got into this. I wasn't a writer, I was an air traffic controller. Air traffic controllers don't write prose. We write on little pieces of paper, and in cryptic language.

It's easy to gather content. There are writers who put out free content for the price of a resource link, which is what I recommend that you do in terms of putting your articles up on other people's sites. You can do the same thing in reverse, and put an article in your newsletter that somebody else has written. And for very little money, sometimes as little as $5, you can get somebody to write articles for you. Then, of course, you can put it on autoresponder.

> *It's easy to gather content. There are writers who put out free content for the price of a resource link.*

A secret that I love to use all the time is I that like to do stuff once and get paid over and over again. Sometimes what I do is this: when people come to my web site and sign up for a newsletter, they think they might be signing up and getting the most recent issue. But whenever they sign up, they're getting issue #1, and then issue #2 the next week—and it's all via an autoresponder, which is this e-mail drip thing that we talked about. It's like an e-mail robot. So you only have to write the content once. As long as it's all evergreen content, it doesn't change. And then you can have specials and things that you throw in for, say, Valentine's Day or something like that.

That's the difference between an autoresponder series and a broadcast message. And I've got one of those, too. I've got a few of those, as a matter of fact. Actually, the autoresponder series that I wrote for **sage-hearts.com** was written probably in 1998. Every so often, I go through it to make sure it's not too dated, but hey, it can run for years.

This is an almost mistake-proof business, with, I'd say, the only mistakes being not having a web site or a mailing list. If you want to get up and going fast and do the Google AdWords thing, that's great. For sure, you're going to make some money that way. But I think that the best money can be made by having a web site that promotes products through endorsements and a mailing list to which you can send autoresponders for repeat business.

I can't stress this enough: start small and simple and don't worry about perfect. That's not hard to do, as you've seen. My **sage-hearts.com** site is extremely simple. It's a box inside a box. And then I bought a CD of people pictures for relatively little money. I've been using those pictures over and over on various sites.

Moonlight on Anik Singal

Anik's Moonlighting Story

Well, a special thanks to Yanik, because he was the first real guru that cared enough to MEET with me and give me advice in person. That was a big deal to me, because it made the internet real for me, and also because I saw his car and knew he wasn't lying.

I got started when I was in college during my freshman year and I was 19—I won $100 at a Super Bowl party and REALLY wanted to start a business! But, unfortunately, you can't buy a McDonald's franchise for $100. So I started searching online to see what I could do, and I landed on the Ablake forum—little did I know that that would be the beginning of my multimillion-dollar online business! I found out that for $100 I could get a lot of stuff—I could get a domain name for $10 and hosting for $20, and then I bought software to help me build sites for the rest of it! Ablake became my home for the next year.

I didn't have money to buy information products, so I sat there and asked question after question. I almost immediately started making a little money at a time, but my first major affiliate success came in

www.affiliateclassroom.com

January 2005, when I fell on this idea of the affiliate upsell. What I would do is sell people's software as an affiliate. I'd offer them free e-mail support from me for buying through me. Then I would back-end them a $500 consulting service where I did all the work for them using the software. It only took me two hours, so I was making a LOT of money. That was when I finally started making $10,000+ a month, and I've never looked back since! I was still a junior in college then, and making more than almost all of my professors, working only about two to three hours a day usually.

My life is amazing today! As a matter of fact, I went through major health problems that had me in the hospital for three months one year. If I had a job, I'd have been fired and broke a long time ago. But my business continued to grow! I could run most of it from my cell phone, not to mention that all I needed was my laptop, even in the hospital! I was able to help my mom retire when I was 22 years old—now she enjoys her life without working at all. I have a very relaxed life. When my friends stress about getting up at six to go to work, I have ZERO stress—I'm my own boss and do what I want when I want! The thing I'm most proud of is that I've been able to help give back to my parents. In addition to helping my mom retire, I helped them renovate the house, and this year we're all taking a big vacation, and everyone is going business class! Sometimes I have to pinch myself to make sure it's real!

Anik's Advice

Life sucks when someone else tells you what to do. Being your own boss doesn't just improve your wallet, but every other part of your life as well. Your relationships, your happiness, your health—everything! My biggest "aha" is that I realized I was holding myself back by thinking I could do 10 things at a time. Now, I have a structured business plan: we have the entire year mapped out. We know exactly which products will be launched and when. NOTHING gets me off course—no distractions—and we NEVER work on more than one thing at a time!

Offline Marketing

There is no reason for you to be limited to marketing online. I have a friend who has an affiliate program, and he has a couple of affiliates that run display ads—tiny classified ads in magazines—and they do well. In fact, I've seen one of my affiliates advertising my book offline in a glossy magazine. I was so surprised—there I am, reading my own copy, and I'm thinking, "Huh?"

But if you're going to do offline, you should register your own domain name for it. Not only would you want to register your own domain name, you'd want to have a separate page specifically to see how many people are coming from that magazine ad or newspaper ad or whatever.

Another example—and I've seen these all over the place—is the 8½ x11 sheets of paper posted to telephone poles. If you have some extra time, I guess you could do it. You are only limited by your imagination; the important point is to realize that there are other ways of doing it besides online. My suggestion is to start online because it's super-easy, but feel free to experiment.

Tracking

Here's something I know a lot of people get to thinking about. How do I know I'm not going to get cheated by the merchant and not be paid what I should be getting paid? My answer is: Keep track. Even with independent merchants, but primarily with Commission Junction, most merchants have affiliate interfaces so you can check your sales stats in real time.

I remember when I first started—I don't know how many times a day I would check my stats to see if I made any sales. It was click, click, click, and refresh, refresh the page to see whether anybody had bought anything.

I would do the same thing on the pay-per-click to make sure I was on the black side of the equation. You can set up your own tracking, so you can independently verify that you're sending them 100 visitors and they're calculating it as 100 visitors. I employ minimal tracking. I operate on a simple accounting system. I confess, it's all working on the KISS principle, and it's like money in, money out.

I think that things like endless tracking and testing work well for an analytical mind. But you know what? I don't want to spend that much time on it. I would rather be outside playing with my friends. You can be doing simple things and still be making a ton of money.

Often, people also ask me if I have any cool advanced secrets or tips to give. Well, once again, I come back to the "keep it simple, sister" philosophy of life and affiliate programs. So, no, I keep everything very basic, very simple. I don't employ any tricks.

I will say one thing, however—I used to use Traffic Equalizer software to bring additional free search engine traffic to my site, and it worked for a while. I didn't do it for all of my sites, because I had to sit down for something like five minutes to get it set up. I'm lazy, but you should decide how much work you want to put in for yourself.

You can get as sophisticated as you want, but I invite you to start slowly and use the KISS principle to make getting started a piece of cake. Put up a basic site and take the time to craft your endorsement so that people want to buy. Keep things straightforward.

> *You can get as sophisticated as you want, but I invite you to start slowly and use the KISS principle to make getting started a piece of cake.*

If there's one thing I'd do differently if I were starting over, it would be to diversify more quickly. I always say one should choose a niche first. I worked *only* in the dating realm for the first four years. That was it. I didn't diversify. And now I tell people, "As soon as you can, as soon as that first site is making money and in the black, get on to the next niche and take advantage of that."

My site was making $5,000 a month by the end of the first year. I was so thrilled with all that it could bring me that I was taking advantage of it rather than spending time building new sites. I would not recommend doing it that way. Best to keep building one new Moonlighting affiliate machine after another.

So there you have it. You start small and focus on getting it done versus getting it perfect, because if you wait to get it perfect you'll never get anything done.

The last point I want to make is that you shouldn't get discouraged if your first check is small. Remember, my first check was for only $10.99, but by the time I wrote my book in 2002, I had made $436,797 for the previous year—and I make even more now!

Just do it!

Want more success story examples?

Go to **www.moonlightingontheinternet.com/success** to see more affiliate marketing success stories we couldn't fit in the book.

About Rosalind

In late 1997, Rosalind Gardner was working as an air traffic controller in Canada and didn't have a shred of business experience that might have helped her escape the inhuman ATC shift schedules OR the frozen north. However, a single click on a banner ad that read "Webmasters Make Money" changed her life completely for the better.

In 2002, Rosalind earned over $436,797 in commissions selling other people's stuff online, and since 2003, she's earned MUCH more than that selling everything from dating services to watches to webmaster tools!

Now she helps others do the same.

Author of *The Super Affiliate Handbook: How I Made $436,797 in One Year Selling Other People's Stuff Online*, "Affiliates Corner" columnist for *Revenue* magazine and *The Performance Marketing Standard* (the only glossy magazine representing affiliate marketing), and coauthor of *The Affiliate Business Blueprint*, Rosalind is recognized worldwide as a leading authority on the topic of affiliate marketing.

As a speaker, author, and consultant, Rosalind teaches her students how to create online businesses without having products of their own. She also teaches merchants how to use affiliate marketing to promote their products online for free. With her help, many of her clients are now earning their own hefty six-figure incomes.

Rosalind lives in the beautiful Okanagan Valley of British Columbia, Canada. Her online business affords her a healthy and active lifestyle that includes running, yoga, and only the finest of beers.

Part Four

Moonlighting on the Internet Method #4:
Yahoo! Stores and E-Commerce Stores

Developed by Andy Jenkins

For some people, this Moonlighting method is going to hit home.

Selling physical products and letting manufacturers drop-ship may be one of the easiest ways to get started online, especially since you don't have to go out and drum up demand.

Think about it: with the tools available now, you can immediately get going and set up your own store in virtually any marketplace for which you have a passion (or where you see trends occurring).

Imagine—your store sits out on the web 24/7, and once someone orders, you collect the money from your customer at retail prices; then you have 30 days to pay your drop-shipping vendor at the wholesale price. Not only do you make money, but it's like an interest-free loan for 30 days!

Moonlighting Online

Andy Jenkins is the guy I turn to when it comes to anything related to e-commerce stores, or more specifically, Yahoo! Stores. He's done it in a big way, starting from scratch across multiple marketplaces. That's always something I look for when seeking advice: has this person done it by himself or herself?

I've known Andy for quite a few years, and he's a guy who takes his business seriously, but not himself. In fact, he was even involved in an infamous chicken suit caper in Las Vegas with me and many of my internet buddies. (Once the statute of limitations runs out, I can talk about that!)

Let's drop in on Andy sharing his Yahoo! Store secrets …

… And to learn more about Andy personally, see his bio at the end of chapter 23.

Chapter 22

The Yahoo! Stores Phenomenon

My name is Andy Jenkins, and I am the CEO of A Squared Artifacts. My company owns and operates several e-commerce stores. I am also the author of *Online Store Profits* and *Stomping the Search Engines*. I'm going to share my secrets for operating an e-commerce business.

You are going to love this method, because, as you'll see, we can have all the benefits of owning our own retail stores in the largest mall on the planet with virtually zero risk. That means no rent or long-term leases, no employees, no utilities, no property insurance, etc., yet we keep all of the profit potential!

We're going to talk about online stores, specifically Yahoo! Stores. I'm excited to share this third way to quickly, easily, and legitimately make $300, $400, $500 a month or an even higher income for yourself, like clockwork, on a part-time basis. Try that with a retail shop!

The reason we can do this is because we're going to tap into the power of Yahoo!, the most recognized name on the internet and a top contender in the world of e-commerce. No joke—ask anybody and you'll be hard pressed to find a person on the planet not familiar with Yahoo! I can't think of a more recognizable brand, with the possible exceptions being AOL (they don't have AOL stores that I know of, but I believe they do have a shopping portal), Amazon, and eBay (which was covered in another chapter).

What's So Special about Yahoo!?

Well, the Yahoo! shopping network currently attracts 13 million shoppers to its portal every day. With your own Yahoo! Store, you can be right in front of these customers when they're ready to buy. And this is the best part: you can start with costs as low as $50/month, and you don't even need to own the inventory. This is exciting stuff. If you wisely choose your products and market them well, working part-time, your Yahoo! Store can quickly and easily give you that $300–500 a month or more.

It All Started with a Sword

I'll tell you about my old life before telling you how to get started in the e-commerce business. I used to work as a TV and film editor. At the time when I decided that I'd had enough of the daily grind—and I'll explain how that happened in a second—I was working on a feature film. It was a B-rated horror film about a bunch of teenagers running around a dark house at night, being killed by something. And it's in Blockbuster right now. You can go rent it. It's called *Killer Instinct*.

There was a scene where this pretty teenage girl was supposed to be impaled by this enormous sword (Figure 22-1). I was sitting around the set one day. I was the assistant director. Basically, I was in charge of everything except what the actors were supposed to say and where the camera was supposed to point.

The art director—he's the guy who would dress the sets and make them look creepy or fantastic or whatever the director called for—was walking around with this giant sword. And I'm like, "Boy, that is the coolest thing. Where did you get that? Did you have it made?" He goes, "No, I bought it online." I said, "You're kidding me!"

I used to be a big geek. "Used to be" is probably still an operative phrase. Back when I was in grade school and even high school, I used to play Dungeons and Dragons, and I thought that swords were the coolest

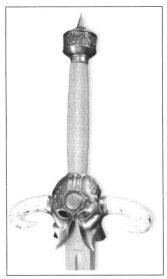

Figure 22-1. The sword

thing. Unfortunately, that particular scene ended up getting cut from the movie. Did I mention I was the editor on the film?

Anyway, that film about killed me, not only from an emotional standpoint, but also physiologically. It was then that I decided it was time to look for another means of supporting myself. Don't get me wrong—I love film and I'm still involved. I get to pick and choose what I do now. But at that point, I was doing it to make a buck. Did I mention it was low-budget?

Meanwhile, my partner, Audrey, worked at a significantly higher level in the film business. She was part of the production staff on M. Night Shyamalan's *Signs*, with Mel Gibson. What's interesting about that is that she had also decided she wanted to find an alternative way of generating some income.

About the time when we were getting ready to decide what to do, 9/11 happened. As you can imagine, all the movies in the area got shut down, and when we came back, everything was weird. It was almost to the point where a lot of the crew were leaving. The long side of it was that Audrey and I realized we were no longer meant for the business at that level. Film is tough. It's 16-, 18-, 20-hour days consistently. It's a lot of work that is totally draining, physically and emotionally.

We were ready for a change. The only question was, what to do?

While I was mulling this over one night, I remember thinking, "You know, if that guy can go and get a sword online, I bet you there are other people who want to buy swords online." So that's how it began. We decided, after some months of research, that we wanted to be able to sell cool things online (Figure 22-2). Our first attempt was a movie props e-commerce store, and this was before we discovered Yahoo!. It was a terrific failure. And that's okay, because we learned a lot.

> We decided, after some months of research, that we wanted to be able to sell cool things online.

Moonlighting on the Internet

Figure 22-2. We wanted to be able to sell cool things online

The reason it failed was because we were relying a lot on actual film and television prop houses on the east coast to supply us with stuff that they wanted to sell. They were rental houses, not places where we could reliably go and get inventory. So we would have a customer visit the site and say, "Hey, I want to buy this. This is the sword from *Blade*," and we'd call the prop facility and they'd go, "Oh no, we loaned that out for a shoot, for a music video." It was a terrible arrangement: they were unreliable and it wasn't even the business they were in. Lesson learned!

Moonlight on Amanda Raab

Amanda's Moonlighting Story

I launched my business while I was in graduate school at the University of Texas at Austin studying speech-language pathology. It was February 2004. I thought it would be more of a hobby project, but within one year, I knew I had to make a choice between the business I had built and my speech-language pathology career.

Today, three years later, my business is flourishing. It's **www.purepearls.com** a multi-million dollar company, and I receive new subscribers and customers every day. The business continues to grow as more and more people find out about **purepearls.com** and my business model. **Purepearls.com** experienced 300 percent growth in the second year of business. That is very exciting, and I'm thankful I have this amazing opportunity.

You should know that before I started moonlighting with **purepearls.com**, I was a graduate student trying to put myself through college. I was working to complete 350 clinical hours and taking 15 hours of courses so I could graduate ahead of schedule. At that same time, I was working on my graduate thesis and working 20 hours a week to try to pay my rent. I lived in a small, affordable apartment and had a reliable car and a computer. That was the extent of my possessions. To be honest, I was working so much that my personal life took a back seat.

Sometimes, I think I'm dreaming. I have been so fortunate. I have my dream business, a wonderful marriage, two custom homes, and my Range Rover. I have more freedom, and my husband and I love to travel all over the world. Before setting up my business, I didn't have the opportunity to travel. To be able to experience the world is something I will never take for granted! The most important thing to me is that I have fulfillment in my life. **Purepearls.com** has been a blessing in so many ways!

Amanda's Advice

The biggest advice I can give to readers is to quit putting your ideas and dreams on the back burner and start acting on them. I have found that so many people have great ideas, and they say they'll start their businesses in six months or a year when they have it all figured out. Why wait? It's all about taking it one step at a time and starting immediately.

I had the idea for **purepearls.com** at 2 a.m., and by 5 a.m., I already had a business plan. I launched my business within two months. Once you start your business, you can iron out the kinks and build on it. It's all about continually building on what you already have. The other thing that is incredibly important is networking. Networking provides wonderful opportunities for new business ventures, new resources, mentors, and inspiration! Much of my success can be attributed to this.

Getting Others to Do the Hard Work

As we moved along, we discovered this thing called drop-shipping, and that changed it all. "Drop-shipping," for those who don't know, means that the manufacturer will send the product directly to your customer so you do not need to buy inventory or store it. Anyway, don't get hung up on this, because I'll cover it in detail later, but it is important to get the gist of why this business is so desirable.

The last time I checked—and, of course, I've become fairly intimately involved with people who are drop-shipping experts—there are about a million products right now in the marketplace that you can have drop-shipped. But it was, I guess, three years ago that we went full-time with the whole thing.

At this time, we have a consistently six-figure-a-year store. That's not six-figure net; it's six-figure gross. But we consistently pull between 35 and 40 percent profitability out of the store. It's been going up as of late, because we've been creating our own products. We have custom swords made for our store, in which case we charge—and make—a little bit more, because they are custom and

At this time, we have a consistently six-figure-a-year store. That's not six-figure net; it's six-figure gross. But we consistently pull between 35 and 40 percent profitability.

unique. When you get to a certain level of volume with certain manufacturers and distributors, you start to have some pull.

It gets better. Once I'm confident that I've got a close rate on my site and people are interested in that product, if I want to make more money, I can buy it in bulk and save myself more money per cost of filling the sale. Essentially, that's how we've moved up from a standard drop-ship store to a store where we stock a little inventory, or even have that inventory at what's called a fulfillment center, which is a whole advanced thing.

Be aware that there are multiple levels on which you can do it. And to remind you, the Armory, right now, is a six-figure-per-year store. I think that last year, we had about $147,000 in gross sales without directly shipping anything. So, you can take this from as small as you want to as big as you want. For a list of drop-shippers, manufacturers, and fulfillment houses, go to **www.moonlightingontheinternet.com/dropship.**

> *Now, here's the great thing about this type of business: you don't pay until you make a sale!*

Now, here's the great thing about this type of business: you don't pay until you make a sale!

So we've got this store at A Square Armory that sells 576 products. I don't have any inventory in my house, except for the swords hanging on my wall. I don't have to pay for that inventory until I make a sale, as long as I have a good relationship with that drop-shipper. That's what they're designed to do. So, I can test out markets with little risk. I can find out whether there's even a sword market out there for me to invest time in.

I don't know what the U.S. Bureau of Labor Statistics says anymore about the median income for a middle-class family of four, but we're probably at about double that with one store—and we have 49 sites out there that all sell something. So it's been good.

Aside from the fact that we do this for a living, we also get to meet some fantastic people. I don't want to continue to wax poetic about how cool it is to have a store, but we've had our stuff on *Ripley's Believe It or Not*. Obviously, we come from the movie business, and we still have connections there. Last season, we supplied *Ripley's Believe It or Not* with every medieval replica they needed for their show. Pictures of the types of items we sell are shown throughout this and the next chapter (Figures 22-3 to 22-6, as well as all the images in Chapter 23).

We've been on *Trading Spaces* and *While You Were Out*, and we've been on Discovery and Home Channel shows. When they redo a room—whenever they do anything medieval—we're their first phone call! So it's cool. And I have to tell you, they always give us credit at the end of the show. And when they do, the next day is bedlam in terms of orders.

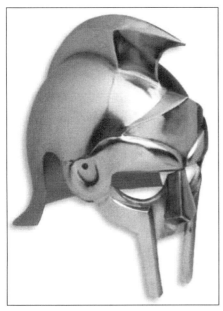

Figure 22-3. One of the cool items we sell

Sold on Yahoo! and How You Can Get Started

Hopefully you are starting to see the benefits of opening your own Yahoo! Store. I think it's a no-brainer, since I don't know many businesses you can get going with an investment of as little as $50 a month (try that with a retail shop), and you don't have to own the inventory. Your only other investment is a little time doing online research to determine what people are interested in buying.

When you decide that you're going to have a Yahoo! Store, one of the things that you can include in your store is the Yahoo! Store logo. Immediately, you're breaking down the barrier that people have against buying from someone they can't talk to or see. You build credibility right away.

There's more! Overture, which is probably one of the largest pay-per-click destinations on the web, has great deals with **shopping.com**, which is a shopping portal. Bizrate is another big shopping portal, and the Yahoo! Shopping Network, as mentioned above, gets about 13 million visitors a day. So you have all of these relationships that Yahoo! has. And if you want to get in and start paying for traffic right away, you can do that at a discount.

Everyone involved in these e-commerce shopping portals pays for traffic at some level. That's the standard. Everybody has to do it. Why not do it at a discount? When you join up with a Yahoo! Store, you get $50 worth of traffic free from Overture. That could equate to a couple of hundred visitors, which could lead to your first sale. We made our first sale about 27 hours after we opened our store.

Okay, I got ahead of myself there, but you have to admit this is exciting stuff.

So, how easy is it to set up one of these Yahoo! Stores and start making money? The biggest mental hurdle that a lot of people have to get past is the fact that they will have to set something up that other people can see on the web.

The second issue is that if you go with a company like Yahoo! Merchant Services, which is the official name of Yahoo! Stores, you can build a store right through your web browser. You don't have to have sophisticated software. It's point-and-click, drag-and-drop, press this to have it blue, and type this in to move it over. It's simple and it's scaleable. You can use the Yahoo! Store system to host a FrontPage or Dreamweaver or MySQL database site, whatever you want. It's very flexible. Bottom line: you don't have to be a technical wizard or a rocket scientist to do it.

Business License

While I am not a lawyer, my understanding is that there is no legal rite of passage to be an e-commerce store owner. There are some things you need to have, such as licenses—not to sell products to humans, but to get the good deals. First, you need a business license, which can be priced as high as $33. It takes a short time to get a business license from your county courthouse or appropriate agency. You're basically opening up a business (a sole proprietorship) with your county. For a complete list of agencies by state where you can get a business license, go to **www.moonlightingonthe internet.com/agencies**.

After you obtain your business license, you can apply online for a sales tax identification number. This enables you to buy from wholesalers. You might think that if you can go to any wholesaler and buy something at a wholesale price, why wouldn't everybody do that? Well, the reason that they

Moonlight on Kim Snyder

Kim's Moonlighting Story

I got started in 2004 after being in a car accident. I lost my job as an adult caretaker because it depended on me being able to lift people and I could not. I started with a simple site selling one item: nail polish.

I now have over 5,000 visitors a month, with a unique number of about half that. My traffic is increasing at the rate of about 300+ visitors a month. I blog often and get most of my return traffic from there. I have partnered with some big names in my business of beauty, which helps me with even more traffic. The sales are up and the subscribers to the newsletter are growing. This year, I have already doubled what I made last year.

www.overallbeauty.com

Kim's Advice

I think the best advice I can give is stick at it and don't give up, and give better customer service than you would want to receive. Trust in yourself and what you know you can do. Never stop learning, and there is a quote I heard that was my "aha"—"Success is not an accident." Biggest thing you must have: a blog!

don't sell to everybody is because they're depending on retailers to buy from them, so you need a sales tax identification number, which can cost anywhere from $7 to about $70, depending on what state you're in.

Once you have your business license and your tax identification number, the last thing you're going to need is a business checking account. You can normally set it up at the bank where you have your personal checking and savings accounts. There's no approval process, like there's no approval process for a tax ID or a business license. It's not like you're getting a credit card or a loan. You fill out some paperwork, and you take $100 from your checking account or your savings account and put it in your business checking account as the minimum deposit.

And that's all you need to do business with about anybody in the world. If you're going to do business online—whether you're going to sell information products or blue widgets to people in Florida—you should take these steps to set up your business.

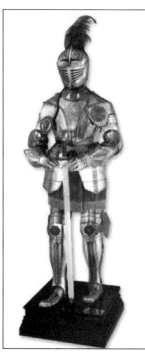

Figure 22-4. A suit of armor

You Are Going to Need a Web Site

This will be your online storefront, where people get to "walk in and check out" the merchandise. It doesn't need to be complicated, and in fact, you'll find that simpler is better. I suggest starting with a single one-page site. Trust me on this. Everybody thinks that is the trick—having the web site, I mean. That is a piece of cake.

The real trick that determines how much money you make will be getting people into your store. So you've got to spend time learning how to get them there. There are many ways to get people to come to your site—free search engines, the pay-per-clicks, shopping portals, and affiliate marketing, to name a few. Learning how to do it consistently is a bit of a trick. And the better and more efficient you are at that, the more sales you can make if you understand that once they're at your site, you still need to sell them. You've got to close the deal.

So put some time into building your site well. Then, as your site starts maturing, you might decide to build more onto it, or possibly build additional stores. For instance, you could build stores that sell maybe two or three things. They don't have to be giant Yahoo! Stores, low-maintenance stores that make money.

To download a fill-in-the-blanks template for a Yahoo! Store, go to **www.moonlightingontheinternet.com/storetemplate**.

Deciding What to Sell

If you are new to this, ask yourself this question: "What should I sell?" People can be paralyzed by not wanting to make a mistake. Please remember that this is a level of investment where no mistake is going to be financially catastrophic, because you're not buying inventory and you're going to use a drop-shipper.

There are two ways in which you should proceed. The first is to find something that you have some interest in, and this is why: As someone who

Figure 22-5. A cannon

sells both hard goods to consumers and information products, your close rates are always higher when you have a passion for the product. That is, people will come to your site and buy if you speak to them from a position of intimate knowledge about a product, and people who are hobbyists or have an interest in something can convey that better than others who don't.

If you're not that interested in anything, go where the money is. Sell into a market where there are buyers. There are many ways that are being discussed about how to find out whether a market is full of buyers and full of demand. You also have to find out what the competition is doing.

Checking Out the Competition

By competition, we're not talking about saturation—in other words, not about the number of people in the market. Because you'll quickly find that once you know what you're doing, you don't care about 99 percent of your competition. It's only the 1 percent that's smart and knows how to market that you have to be wary of.

There are ways to quickly determine what your competition is doing when you're looking into a market. You can look at who your competition is on the Yahoo! web site. Think about it for a second. If you were opening a brick-and-mortar store, you'd have to hop in the car and drive all over the state to find out who you were competing with.

If you surf around the Yahoo! Shopping Network, which is where most of the Yahoo! Stores live, you'll find a lot of stores sitting there doing nothing. There are ways where you can see what's happening with a store in terms of how it's being received by traffic on the web.

There's a service called Alexa, which keeps track of how many people with a certain program installed on Internet Explorer visit a certain site. You can search for the Alexa number of a site and see whether it is drawing any traffic. If not, it's not a competitor at this point, because to compete in a particular market, you have to take an active role.

> On the web, you can type in the keyword of the product you sell and look at who's coming up in the search engines, and right away, you know what your competition is doing.

On the web, you can type in the keyword of the product you sell and look at who's coming up in the search engines, and right away, you know what your competition is doing. So the short answer to that is, you want to sell something that you can convey an ownership experience about. If you're the kind of person people call to ask, "Hey, how's that cell phone that you bought?" or "You got that big-screen television?" or "How is the wood that you used for your deck?" chances are you can talk intelligently about any product.

But if you're a hobbyist—you play guitar, you knit, you paint, whatever—take a look into those markets first and see whether you can sell into them. Go into a market where there's a lot of demand and you can deal with the supply. Even though there might be a lot of demand, what about things like trying to compete head-to-head with someone like Best Buy or Circuit City for selling electronics, let's say? Suppose you want to sell CD players—there are going to be instances online where you are not going to be able to go into a market through the front door. That's how Best Buy gets people in through the front doors. They're often merchandise loss leaders, items such as blank CD-ROMs or printer cartridges or paper.

You may need an explanation of what a "loss leader" is. So, here goes: When you get that Best Buy flyer in the mail, there might be three items on the front of that flyer. One might be the most common product for the lowest price, such as a CD player or a cordless phone. They will also have consumable products that you need, such as printer cartridges or blank CD-ROMs. And then they'll have the hottest, coolest, sexiest product around, such as a 72-inch flat-screen plasma monitor.

So what they've done is encouraged you to come in and buy the $38 CD player, which they either lose money or break even on, so they can get a chance to sell you the material that you need over and over, which are blank CDs and blank DVDs and printer cartridges. On top of that, perhaps that day they're going to close a sale on a CD player that you want or

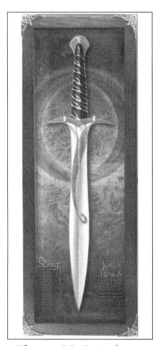

Figure 22-6. A dagger

even a plasma-screen monitor. You never know. So these people have that merchandising down to a science. They have huge reach because they buy an incredible volume. You can't compete with that. But why bother? You don't need to.

There are ways to go into competitive markets that are dominated by what are known as "brick-and-mortar" stores. Go in through the back door. If you want to sell an audiovisual receiver, don't sell the one for $300. Sell the one for $2,700, because chances are that when the same person goes into Best Buy and looks (and maybe Best Buy doesn't even carry such expensive receivers), they don't want the store clerk explaining to them why they want to buy that.

The internet has always been a place where people can go and get information. Before there was e-commerce, it was where you went to get information. So, if you are providing information and you're giving them a reason to spend money with you because you can speak intelligently about a product, you can still sell into that space. In that case, you need not try to compete head-to-head with a store like Best Buy.

Chapter 23

Establishing
Your Niche

You want to establish a niche. For instance, if you want to sell music, you don't want to be the Amazon or the CDNow of music. You may want to sell polka records.

Guitar Center and Sam Ash are the two huge online and brick-and-mortar retail stores that sell music equipment, and it would be pretty tough for you to create a store like that. It's not impossible, but pretty tough. What you could do is create a store that sells nothing but, say, electronic drum kits.

You can niche yourself out like that and be considered an expert in the field because that's all you sell. So people know they can go to Guitar Center and get that thing, but there must be something special about this guy who sells only electronic drums. That's his specialty. That's his niche. That word is thrown around a lot, but it's cost-effective on the internet. It's so cost-effective in terms of e-commerce that if you wanted to open a store that sold nothing but toothpaste, you could probably do it. But nobody's going to do that in the brick-and-mortar world, because you can go to the Wal-Mart or the Acme or the IGA to get that stuff.

Moonlighting on the Internet

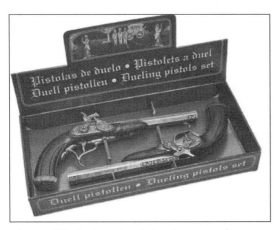

Figure 23-1. A pair of dueling pistols

Most people get scared when they talk about taking a niche, but it can work. There is a guy who has a site that only sells PDA jackets. He opened a store and had nothing in it. It was just a domain. He initially thought he needed a variety of products, but today he's doing a quarter of a million dollars a year just selling the covers for these personal data devices. And now he's selling them for the iPod and for the Napster MP3 player and even for laptops— he's diversifying all over the place.

Another example might be selling car accessories. What you really want to do is sell the fuzzy dice or the fuzzy seat covers, or you might want to sell the neon lights that go underneath. Be specific, or sell something specific for a particular model. Because when you're driving down the street and you see ABC Auto Parts, you know you can go in there and get car accessories. But when you're on the web, it's not passive like that. Very seldom— only maybe in the form of banner advertising or some of the pushed, spam-like e-mail that we get nowadays—will you be introduced to an idea of a shopping experience.

> *People on the internet look actively, so they're not going to type in "car accessories" when they're shopping.*

People on the internet look actively, so they're not going to type in "car accessories" when they're shopping. They want the neon under-light. They want the 22-inch chrome bling-bling. They want the fuzzy dice. That's the way that people shop online. So that's the way you should sell.

Here's another example of establishing a niche. There is a guy who has a store that sells wedding favors—the paper, the little candies that have lace on them, the wine wedding favors, and the golf wedding favors. He's not selling dresses or tuxedos. He's selling one small component of a wedding. But apparently, everybody who gets married needs these things. His average cost per item was about $1.85. We're talking about the price of a couple of cheeseurgers. Last month, he made $168,000. This illustrates that on the internet, volume is easy, especially if you're drop-shipping.

Moonlight on Ricky Breslin

Ricky's Moonlighting Story

My wife and I started online in March 2004 selling instructional videos that teach you how to do hair. I saw a problem when my wife would order videos and all the videos were of terrible quality. We decided that we could do much better, as well as price our products better, and fill this void in our market.

Today, we recieve around 65,000 unique hits per month. We average between $35,000 and $50,000 per month in sales, about half of which is profit. We are growing every month. We currently get around 100 opt-ins per day, and that will continue to grow as our traffic increases.

www.braidsbybreslin.com

The business is going great, and we love working on it and helping thousands of people learn the skill of braiding and weaving. We now have two children, are completely debt–free, and can pretty much do whatever we want. We try to fly to Las Vegas twice a year and really just enjoy our new lifestyle.

Ricky's Advice

Focus on one thing and don't get caught up in a lot of other business. We were NOT going to let Braids By Breslin fail: we were determined. You have to expand within your niche. You have to develop different income streams inside your business, each selling one item, such as nail polish.

Marketing to Your Niche

You need to learn how to market your products. Everything else is secondary; and that should be good news. Because in the same way that Yahoo! has made the process of creating a store in the browser easy, there's so much good information online about marketing and driving traffic to your site. Also, when you have a store with a drop-shipper involved, you generally get all kinds of product literature from them. You get a picture of the product from them, and you set your price based on what your competition is doing.

One of the first things to do is to make sure that your site "closes," which means writing some good sales copy. Good sales copy makes people understand what it would be like to own your product and how your product is going to help them. You want to write in terms of the benefits of owning your product.

Then start running traffic through it by marketing with pay-per-click search engines and shopping portals, such as Bizrate, DealTime, or NextTag. Go after off-the-beaten-path keywords—meaning, if you're selling a CD player, don't bid for *CD player*, bid for the most specific keyword phrase that you can think of, such as *Yamaha SL1Z 5-Disk CD player*. Do this because you're paying for traffic. You want it to be qualified to allow you to get traffic into your site.

> *One of the positives is that no one's going to knock off your information product. The negative is: why is someone going to buy from you when Joe Blow down the way has got it for 32 cents cheaper?*

One of the positives is that no one's going to knock off your information product. The negative is: why is someone going to buy from you when Joe Blow down the way has got it for 32 cents cheaper? The answer to that question is that you want to be so in that visitor's face when they're looking for you that they don't get a chance to see Joe Blow. And if they did, you want to convey a feeling and environment of expertise. In other words, make your web site an environment where a transaction of value can take place. That means speaking to the customer's needs.

When someone is looking for a particular product, they want it to fulfill a need they have. And the only way to make them understand how a product is going to fulfill their need is to understand what it would be like to own it. Think about what a vacuum cleaner does—it turns on, it's got hoses, and it's self-propelled. That's not the ownership experience. The ownership experience is that your carpet will be fresh and clean, keeping your house smelling wonderful. It's all the benefits of using that product. What matters is how your product is going to make their life better when they use it. If it's a product like a sword, you probably have to fall back on describing the features of the product. But you have to think about the best way to pitch your product, no matter what it is. Just make sure you describe all the benefits you can think of.

Once you've made sure that people want to buy something from you, because you've worked on your sales copy, then invest some time in it.

When you first start out, you have to trade time rather than money for moving forward. You don't want to spend a bunch of money in order to move forward. This is where search engines come in. Once you know how to pick the right keyword, you can make money from it, because it will show up on the first page or the first two pages in the search engine results. What will happen is that you will spend time to make your store well ranked and well liked in the search engines. It's easier than people would have you believe, because they want you to spend $2,500 a month to have them optimize your store. Bottom line: once you know your site is selling, spend some time getting it up in the free search engines, which can be a profound traffic generator. In addition, you can open an affiliate program through Commission Junction, which has got to be one of the largest affiliate networks on the planet. Then you can start to leverage other people's ability to market into commission sales for your store.

Just know that once you've reached a higher level with Yahoo!, it's fairly expensive. But there are other turnkey store services where an affiliate program will only cost you an extra $10 a month.

One of the biggest fallacies ever stated was this: "If you build it, they will come." Building it has gotten to the point where it is easy. The challenge, and the difference between a mediocre success and a stunning success online, is in how you're able to market it. Whether it is a Yahoo! Store or a store from Monster Commerce, there's always going to be competition. And because there's competition in the marketplace, there's probably money being made there. So they're just waiting for you to come in and be better.

> *… because there's competition in the marketplace, there's probably money being made there. So they're just waiting for you to come in and be better.*

Drop-Shipping in Depth

We covered this a bit earlier, but you are going to want to know the nitty-gritty.

As far as how big an investment you need to start selling online with one of these stores, this is where drop-shipping comes into play. Drop-shipping can make the difference between spending almost no money to get started and spending and possibly wasting thousands of dollars.

Especially if you want to do this to make supplemental income, you don't want to invest all kinds of capital.

Figure 23-2. More swords

"Drop-shipping" is basically a relationship that you create with someone who is selling a product in a wholesale environment. It could be the manufacturer of the product, it could be a regional distributor of the product, or less specifically, it could be someone who's in the business of drop-shipping. They've decided that they're going to put their warehouse space to good use to drop-ship for a customer.

And here's what happens. For example, you would call up one of your drop-shippers and say, "Jay, we need the replica Scottish flintlock sent to John Smith at 123 Main Street, Anywhere, USA." And Jay will tell his warehouse person to pack up those flintlocks and send them out, but make sure that it's from whatever the name of your store is. So when the customer gets the package, they get a package from you.

Here's the great thing about it: you don't pay until you make a sale. So when you've got a store, you can have many products, but keep no inventory in-house. You don't have to pay for that inventory at the drop-shipper's location until you make a sale, as long as you have a good relationship with that drop-shipper. That's what they're designed to do. I love it!

In point of fact, you can test out markets with little risk. As I have already stated, you can find out whether there's a sword market out there before spending time trying to market swords. In other words, you can go out and run a couple of hundred people through your store with Google AdWords, not own any inventory, and if you get a bite, great. You can ship the advertised product just by making sure you have a good relationship with your drop-shipper.

(For people who don't know, "Google AdWords" are those little ads that appear on the right side of the page whenever you type a search into Google.) Therefore, you can be the one advertising and driving people to your site, and paying as little as 5 cents per click every time someone clicks

Figure 23-3. Lord of the Rings

Figure 23-4. Tapestry

on your link. It's traffic on demand, and it's also product on demand.

Be aware, though, that one of the disadvantages of drop-shipping is that you usually pay a little more than you would if you bought a pallet of goods, and there's usually a drop-ship fee associated with it. So, once you're confident that you've got a good close rate on your site and that people are interested in that product, if you want to make more money, you can buy it in bulk and save yourself money per cost of filling the sale. Essentially, that's how you can move up from a standard drop-ship store to a store where you stock a little inventory or even use a fulfillment center, as mentioned earlier. I stress again that it's up to you how big you want your business to be. At any rate, you won't have to ship any products yourself.

There are tons of products on the market that you can drop-ship, and people from the manufacturing and distribution sectors have also realized that they should get involved in e-commerce, so they're making it easier for e-retailers to create drop-shipping relationships.

There may be instances where you're not going to be able to find every item or any item for drop-shipping. There are going to be certain consumable items, such as cell phone batteries, that are too small for a drop-shipper to package individually and ship out. In any case, you should only buy inventory because you want a better deal.

There are lots of ways to determine whether an item you want to sell is going to be a hot seller. Maybe you should go where there's a hot market first. People in the business counsel others about what they should do when they decide to look for a particular drop-shipper, and about whether they should pony up the money for inventory if they can't find that drop-shipper.

Beware of Middlemen

I wasn't going to mention this, but it has become enough of a problem that I'd be doing you a disservice if I didn't. Be aware that there are a lot of scams going on with drop-shipping. A lot of times, what will happen is that middlemen will get in touch with the drop-shippers, and they will be the front end and advertise themselves as the source, charging you $39, $69, or $99 a month to come into their database. And you would place an order online. But they don't want you to be in touch with the person doing the shipping. So they get a customer record, they charge your credit card, and what do you think they do? They turn around and they send that order to a drop-shipper on your behalf.

What they're doing is essentially creating a membership site, where they're charging you for the privilege of getting access to the drop-shippers they have relationships with. And they've marked up the wholesale drop-ship prices by as much as 30 percent. So you could be drop-shipping a product that you're paying nearly retail for, but because it has a banner that says "drop-shipper" across the top of it, you think you're getting a good deal. Stay away from something like that. In other words, stay away from the middlemen!

Taking Payments

Early on in the business, taking payments was a big deal. There were whole e-books about how to take credit card payments through the internet. It used to be a big deal, but not anymore.

Set yourself up to take credit cards (Visa, MasterCard, Discover) and payments through PayPal. PayPal is an electronic payment service that has become easy, convenient, and standard, thanks to eBay.

Moonlight on Ross Malaga

Ross's Moonlighting Story

I purchased this site in August 2005. The previous owner was running it as an affiliate site. I did the research and realized that he had not really done much search engine optimization. In addition, there were a number of good lingerie drop-shippers that provided keystone markup.

www.lingeriediva.com

After taking over, I switched to a real e-commerce store. I embarked on an aggressive SEO campaign and saw some immediate results.

Ross's Advice

The big thing for me was learning about drop-shipping. I had wanted to sell online but did not want to deal with storing items, picking, packing, etc. I also did not want to invest a lot of money in upfront inventory. The main thing—and I pass this on to my students—is that you can get started with very little money.

You can also accept something called Yahoo! Wallet, which is similar to MSN Microsoft Passport. You must have a positive credit report to do this, because when you get a merchant account, essentially you're being entrusted with fulfilling a service when you get the money. So, in some ways, it's like qualifying for a small loan, although it is less intrusive. You have to fill out a short application, sign it, and fax it. Of course, the terms of service are very long.

But you will be in a position where someone's going to take a look at your credit. Because, just like with a mortgage, a car loan, or other kind of financing, there are programs to help people move forward. Maybe you start out with a merchant account limit of $1,500 a month, and then they'll say, "We'll see how it goes." Or they will take something called a "rolling reserve," where they'll hold back 5 percent of each sale to make sure that if something goes wrong, they're not going to be liable for the entire sale. But this is rare.

When you sign up with Yahoo!, there is a service called Payment Tech, for which there is no setup fee. The problem with Payment Tech is that it charges a lot per month for its service. So if you want to minimize your initial expense, go with Payment Tech. Because in a month—you never know—you could be into profitability.

But what you're going to want to do is go with a company like Advanced Credit Systems, which has one of the lowest rates on the internet. They will let you put multiple stores under one merchant account, which is great, because if you have more than one store you often have to open up a separate merchant account for each one and pay a monthly fee for each.

You generally don't charge the credit card until you ship the product. You will have an accumulation of orders sitting in your Yahoo! shopping cart. I've found that it is easiest to copy the information out of the shopping cart, open up your e-mail program, paste it in, and send it to your drop-shipper. When your drop-shipper says the product is on its way, you charge the card. Have the drop-shipper send the tracking number to you and your customer when the product ships.

> When your drop-shipper says the product is on its way, you charge the card. Have the drop-shipper send the tracking number to you and your customer when the product ships.

There are times when you might be the middleman and you will have to do the shipping communication. Sometimes a customer has a shipping issue. At Christmastime, it can be insane, but in a good way. So ultimately, you could be getting paid, say, $35 to spend about 3½ minutes taking one e-mail and turning it into another one. And that's really passive income generation. That's why e-stores are so effective in generating income for very little investment, both time-wise and financially. I will again advocate that once you know your site is selling, you should spend some time getting it up in the free search engines, because that can be a profound traffic generator.

Running a Part-Time Store

If you want your store to be a part-time thing where you make $500 or $1,000 or $2,000 a month, it is possible. But what you will find, no matter what level of income you want to achieve, is that you're going to be doing the same things over and over, no matter what you're selling. That is, you're going to be learning how to drive customers who are looking for what you're selling right to your store. So to make $500 a month, that could mean two or three sales. If you start to look at it in terms of the economics—if you're selling wedding favors, for example—that might mean selling

1,000 wedding favors. But maybe you only have to sell to five people, because they buy them 200 at a time.

If you just want to make a couple hundred bucks and you know what you're doing, it's not difficult to run your store as a part-time business. It's definitely different from creating your own product, which is covered in the first section of this book.

There are also communities out on the web (such as eLance) where you can hire people on a piecemeal basis to take care of your orders for you. They'll charge you $4, $5, $6 an order and they'll take care of everything. They expedite orders from store to drop-shipper.

Traffic Value of Suppliers and Affiliates

If you find a great supplier with five or six products that you want to put on your site and you don't want to open a whole store around them, fill out your store with affiliate products. Go to Amazon or Commission Junction. Make sure that your flagship products are the products that you have control over, but at the bottom of the page or maybe in a little section, it wouldn't hurt to have a couple of Amazon products there. Here's why: search engines like big sites, not because they're big, but because they have a lot to them.

Generally, it's easier to get a decent ranking, especially in Yahoo!, if you have a site that has 30 pages versus a site that has one page. It gives you 30 chances to get a position in the search engine, because search engines rank pages, not sites. So, even if you only have five or six products from a drop-shipper, that doesn't mean you should have five or six pages.

For example, if you want to sell home theater equipment and you can only find the guy who's going to sell you the speakers, there's a great place in Commission Junction, an advertiser called Vans, that sells every single home theater receiver ever made. So you could be this home theater super-store and know that you're going to feature speakers. But if they don't want to buy a speaker this time, maybe they'll exit through your affiliate link and buy a $2,000 receiver.

Adding Your Own Affiliate Programs

Affiliate marketing is hot, and this is the reason why huge affiliate sites like Commission Junction, ClickBank, BeFree, and LinkShare have grown so dramatically. If you want other people to get out there and sell your products, start an affiliate program. Besides, there are people who do nothing but affiliate marketing. Wouldn't you rather have someone besides you out there, utilizing all their expertise to market your products?

Figure 23-6. King Arthur tapestry

We started an affiliate program with our tapestry store. We wanted to go into some of those portals where people sign up with affiliate programs. So we started a "two-tier affiliate program," which means that someone can join up, and if someone joins under them in the affiliate program, they get credit for the sale. In fact, Audrey and I were featured in a book by a cancer survivor because we sent her a tapestry from the Baio tapestry line. She had the tapestry next to her hospital bed. So we're now in an epilogue in a book!

The next day, I went out to all of the affiliate portals to register our affiliate program, and when I checked, I saw that our store was already registered. The affiliates out there had all the bookmarks together and all the forms ready to fill out; they saturated the affiliate market for us.

As an aside, if you use **finestshops.com**'s affiliate program, it costs around $9 a month to manage.

Moonlight on Mark McCoid

Mark's Moonlighting Story

I started in 1998 with a couple of pages created in FrontPage. I was doing it on the side, mainly to get free demos of the CDs I was selling! Well, about a month into it, a check for $14.99 rolled in the door, and I was hooked. I accepted only checks for the first year and made next to nothing, but it was fun. Then I started accepting credit cards, and I started making about $1,000 per month. All from about three hours of work a week.

In 2004, I discovered internet marketing. I started getting newsletters from gurus such as Dan Kennedy and Yanik Silver, and guess what happened? In 2005 I had gross sales of $45K!

Mark's Advice

Chill out and really look at what you want to create. When I started making some money with my business, I started thinking about quitting my job, and that stressed me out. Once I sat down and thought about it, I realized I liked my job and I liked running my web business and I liked the money. What is there to stress about? Also, make a list of what you are going to accomplish each day. Otherwise you will find yourself reading e-mail or surfing the web and doing nothing.

www.healingproducts.com

Repeat Sales

Another great thing that happens when you have an e-commerce store is that you have the ability to legitimately market to someone after a sale. For example, as an information product seller, when you send an e-mail to someone, you have to be careful to include something of interest or value in that e-mail besides an offer. When someone signs up for your store newsletter or your catalog or your alert list, you don't have to have that pretense. They signed up to find out about new products. They signed up to find out about sales.

So when you market to your store customers, you would say, "On sale right now," or "New sword, new tapestries, new claw-foot tub, new inflatable boat," whatever it is. You go to them with an offer, because that's why they signed up. Guess what that means to you? You don't have to slave over great content for a newsletter and then get reported to a spam cop. Because you're an e-commerce store, customers expect you to send them offers.

Some people say that as much as 33 percent of their income is derived from repeat sales. And customers usually don't come back on their own: they come back because you let them know what is on sale or what is new that they might be interested in.

The important secret is that you need some way to capture customers' information, either for a sale or to provide updates. That's communicating with your customers. And this is probably obvious to people who have experience in internet marketing or any kind of marketing.

> *The important secret is that you need some way to capture customers' information, either for a sale or to provide updates. That's communicating with your customers.*

It's always most expensive to make the sale the first time. The next time, the only thing it takes is the electricity that keeps your computer on while Outlook is open, while you're typing your mail, and paying the hosting fee for the store. That's about it. The next time you contact those people, it costs practically nothing. At first, you might be in a position to break even or maybe even lose a little bit on the first transaction with a customer. If they buy from you once, there's a likelihood that you're going to get them again, and the next time it's going to bring you an even higher percentage.

Cross-Selling

When someone comes to your store and buys a portable CD player, if you don't try to sell them batteries, you're missing the boat. If someone comes to your store and buys a printer, if you don't try to sell them printer cartridges, you're missing the boat. You should be cross-selling all the time.

One thing will hold true for all internet sales: people are annoyed by shipping, so they try to combine shopping trips. They only want to buy from one place, because in many cases there's a discount associated with buying multiple products in that one place. They also pay less for shipping. So, if they're going to buy something that might require an accessory, you should try to sell that to them during the checkout process.

Think about it.

They decided that they're going to buy the printer. They've already got their credit card out. Maybe their information is already filled in. Why not ask them if they need ink to go along with it? Or how about a stand, or some paper? Or you could go off the beaten path and offer a laptop computer to go with the printer.

There are many ways to cross-sell into many markets and increase your visitor value without much effort, and this is getting more true for every kind of e-commerce store.

One other thing you can do is sell gift certificates online. We have gift certificates available in $50 increments. When you're in a niche market, especially during the holiday season, this is very helpful: the customer may know that her grandson wants a sword, but she doesn't know if it's the Excalibur sword, the Braveheart sword, or the Glamdring sword. So she might get him an e-gift certificate. That can be good, because you don't have to ship anything until they come back—and usually they don't come back until after Christmas, which is a great thing.

Moonlight on Jay McGrath

Jay's Moonlighting Story

While selling about 30 percent of my golf mats online through my web site, **www.realfeelgolfmats.com**, and on eBay, I've been building a valuable e-mail list to which I market golf accessories and golf training aids. Before this time, my business could only have been described as steady, and not until I cracked the internet code thanks to Cory Rudl and Yanik Silver did I start to see real growth. Last year, my business was up 35 percent over the previous year.

Jay's Advice

I don't remember who said it, but it was "Make your first dollar." Once you make one sale, you realize that it is all possible and more will follow.

www.realfeelgolfmats.com

Exclusive Packages

The one last thing you could do that's interesting, and we talked about this earlier, is this: let's say there is competition and other people are selling the same thing. What you should do is put together an exclusive package. You can do this in a lot of ways.

If I'm going to sell a sword, I should be selling the sword, the scabbard, the stand, and the plaque. Because, number one, when I sell all of that for $297 and Joe Blow Swords down the way is selling just the sword for $197 and selling the plaque or stand separately, customers can't compare apples to oranges. So, in this way, you eliminate price shopping—which is an important thing to do online, because how hard is it to go online and get the lowest price for a product? It may require more clicks on their part, but if you've got a way to infuse value into a common product by offering it in a package, you're increasing the benefit, you're increasing the sale, and you're eliminating price shopping.

And, you know what? When you're making more volume, when you're making more dollars per sale in a gross fashion, you generally have more flexibility in your price. Usually, you don't see a product sitting by itself. Usually, the blank CDs at Best Buy are sitting right next to the CD burners. So paying attention to packaging and merchandising is a great way to go.

It is an excellent idea to include your own report on something—that is, to package a report along with the product you're selling. If you're selling swords, for example, you could provide two kinds of reports: how to buy a sword or how to take care of your sword. We do this for our information products. We capture 15 to 18 percent of people who arrive at our site the first time by getting them involved with some sort of freebie. It's been tested, and it works.

We're giving away stuff this year when customers come in so we can get them on our list and follow up with them all through Christmas. It's going to cost some money, but we have been in the business long enough to be in a position to do that. So we're going to do it, because the concept is sound. And we're counting on increasing sales over last year by about 20 percent.

Finally …

There are some things that you can't control. Recently, I had a fellow from Utah order something, and we shipped it to the UK because he got a letter wrong: instead of *UT*, he wrote *UK*. After everything was said and done, we had to laugh about it. But we were looking west and the package was going east. It took awhile to figure that out.

Also, there are people who are creepy, for lack of a better term. You're never going to satisfy them, and they're always going to want something for nothing. That's what happens when you deal with the public!

Now, it's your turn!

Want more successful examples?

Go to **www.moonlightingontheinternet.com/success** to see more success stories we couldn't fit in the book.

About Andy

Andrew (Andy) Jenkins is the founder of StomperNet, FreeIQ, and A2Artifacts.

With 16 years of experience in video, television, and feature film production, as well as 7 years of e-commerce and affiliate marketing experience, Andy brings strong media convergence skills to the internet marketing and training industry.

After graduating with honors from the prestigious NYU Film School, Andy served in the capacity of production manager for one of America's most-watched soap operas. As an editor and postproduction supervisor, Andy has worked with Tier 1 advertising agencies such as BBDO, J. Walter Thompson, and Saatchi & Saatchi. Andy received an Emmy award for editing; he is a sought-after talent in all areas of creative television advertising and feature film postproduction.

In 1994, Andy co-founded America's Interactive Production Network, which produced a nationally syndicated job search television show. After only its second year of production, the show received three Telly awards and one Regional Emmy award.

Andy holds credits for four full-length motion pictures, 22 direct response infomercials, and over 190 nationally broadcast ad spots.

His most recent feature work was with Haxan Films, the creators of *The Blair Witch Project*. On *Altered*, he served as associate producer and postproduction supervisor, as well as equity investor. The film is currently in distribution with Universal Pictures.

Moonlighting on the Internet

In 2000, Andy started his first e-commerce web site, leading to an electronic information product that quickly became a bestseller in the internet marketing community.

Since 2000, Andy has owned and operated 30 e-commerce web sites with revenues in the seven-figure range. His online publishing credits include *Yahoo! Store Profits*, *Stomping the Search Engines*, and most recently, StomperNet, a members-only entrepreneurial training portal.

Moonlighting on the Internet Method #5: Blogging

Developed by Darren Rowse

Imagine a totally part-time web site that lets you share your ideas and thoughts on topics you love with others and get paid for it. Pretty cool, right?

Well, if you like communicating and writing, blogging might be ideal for you.

I was lucky enough to get Darren Rowse to give you his thoughts in this chapter. I "met" Darren online when I heard about his success with blogs in all sorts of areas, such as digital photography, printer reviews, camera phones, spirituality, and even the Athens Olympics.

Darren started a hobby blog, and in less than two years he was making a solid six-figure income (while working only two days per week because of church commitments and a previous job).

Moonlighting on the Internet

Because of his unique story and background, I flew Darren in from Melbourne, Australia at my expense to present to attendees at my Underground™ Online Seminar III.

Make no mistake, Darren is the real deal when it comes to blogging and not just teaching "how to make money blogging" in the same way as others who have made a couple of bucks doing it and then make all their money teaching. Luckily, I managed to twist Darren's arm and get him to grudgingly reveal his simple yet profitable formula for legitimate blogging sites you can start on a shoestring budget ...

Pay attention to what Darren shares on:

◆ How to choose which topics are the biggest evergreen moneymakers for blogging and how to create compelling content around each of these topics. (Hint: You do not have to write it yourself.)

◆ How to take advantage of your blog's natural "search engine magnet" to get lots of traffic to your site. (According to the Technorati blog search engine, Darren's blog is listed in the top 50 blogs in the world.)

◆ The best ways to get paid from your blog, and much more!

To find out more about Darren, see his bio at the end of chapter 26.

Chapter 24

Why Blogging?

In this section, I will be taking you on a short journey through the wonderful world of blogging so that you can learn to blog for fun and profit.

I'll echo what's been said in other sections: this process can be as simple or as complex as you want it to be. And while I want to offer information that is useful for beginners and advanced internet folks alike, most of the material comes from the questions I receive from novices, because the basics are where all the action is.

So, a quick word about your guide in this section: My name is Darren Rowse and I'm the guy behind **problogger.net**, which has become one of the leading sources of information about making money from blogs. That means you're in good hands.

I'm a full-time blogger, so I practice what I preach and have been doing so for the last few years. As well as being the original ProBlogger, I'm one of the founders of b5media, a blog network, where I am the VP of training.

What Is a Blog?

We hear that term everywhere these days, so what does it mean?

In the simplest terms, a blog is nothing more than a type of web site where the content (also referred to as entries or posts) is organized in chronological order going from the most current to the oldest. Think of it as an online journal that you start reading from the most recent entry.

Now, it may sound kind of odd that it flows backward, but blogs are meant to be read on a regular basis. That way, when someone checks in to see what is new, the newest or freshest content is top, front, and center. A person new to the blog can go back and read forward to see a story or chain of events unfold.

If you want a rule of thumb, blogs tend to be written by one person on a specific topic and updated regularly, so they have a journal or diary feel to them. The topics can be pretty much anything: hobbies, cooking recipes, spirituality, photography, actual diaries—you name it!

> What's neat about some blogs is that if they resonate with the readers, they tend to become centers or gathering places, commonly referred to as online communities.

What's neat about some blogs is that if they resonate with the readers, they tend to become centers or gathering places, commonly referred to as online communities. People in these communities get together online to exchange ideas, learn from each other, debate issues, and plug in to other people from all around the world because of a common interest.

There are two other elements worth mentioning: archives and comments.

Archives

At first glance, the front page of a blog may look like there is very little going on. Keep in mind that this is typically the most recent entry or entries, so you are seeing only the tip of the iceberg, which makes a lot of sense when you consider the purpose of a blog. However, look beyond the surface and you'll find the archives that make up the history, or all previous posts on that blog.

The best way to explain this is—imagine that a friend has been sending you pages from her diary as she writes them. When they arrive, you put them on top of your desk to read. Once you've gone through each entry, you file it away in a cabinet. To the casual observer looking at your desk, they would only see a few of the most recent pages from your friend's diary and might assume that was all she wrote. If they only knew!

Comments

While this isn't a requirement for a blog, many do have a comment section where readers can—are you ready for this?—leave comments! In many cases, this makes a blog come to life as the readers provide feedback, ask questions, critique, etc. While this is beyond the scope of our discussion, I hope that you appreciate the value and power comments add to a blog by making it more valuable to readers and contributing content without any effort on the blog author's part.

I could go on and on describing blogs, but I think it's easier for you to just check out a few of them. It's like soccer—sure, I could tell you what it is, but you'll learn a lot more by seeing it on TV or going to a park and playing for a few minutes.

Rather than giving you a laundry list of blogs (don't worry, I'll be giving you plenty of examples as we go along), I suggest checking out a blog on something that interests you. Go to **www.google.com**, type in a hobby or anything that interests you, and then add the word *blog*. Hit "submit" and you should get a list of blogs on that topic.

Moonlight on Taylore Vance

Taylore's Moonlighting Story

I started building a blog only six weeks ago, and now I'm number three on Google search! I never thought it would be so easy to add articles and comments for my energy healing blog. It was 100 percent free, too. While looking up information on how to blog, I found a list of directories where I could submit my new blog. I submitted to about 20 directories. Within a few days, my keyword was found in the number three position on Google!

www.reikiranch.blogspot.com

Taylore's Advice

Just start a blog! With Google, you can get a fine free blogger site and start building it. Next, list your blog at all the directories you can find.

Qualities of an Ideal Blogger

This list is the ideal scenario. The qualities are more useful than essential. Having them does not guarantee success, and not having them does not guarantee failure. We don't live in a perfect world, so don't sweat it if you don't have all the qualities. Hopefully, they will provide some clarity so you can make smarter decisions about how to start blogging.

- **Good communication skills.** You don't need to be Winston Churchill, but it helps if you can communicate your thoughts and ideas. A quick word about writing skills—they are useful but not entirely necessary, as there are alternative types of media including audio blogs (like podcasting) and video blogs.

- **Having something to say**, preferably about a topic people are interested in.

- **Being passionate about that topic.** This will help in many ways: passion is contagious, so it will make your blog more interesting, and you'll need to keep up with it and keep it going.

- **Enjoy the limelight.** If your blog takes off in a big way, you'll become somewhat of a celebrity in the arena. Even with moderate success, your readers will want to know more about you.

- **A certain degree of ego-toughness.** You say something in your blog and it is there for people to see. Some will agree and become your fans, while others will disagree and become your critics. Are you okay with that? I don't want you to think that half your audience will be adversarial; in reality, most folks that disagree with you will leave and not frequent your blog—but you need to be aware that the more passionate people are about a topic, the more vocal they become.

- **A sense of humor.**

- **See blogging as a journey** rather than a destination. Your blog is an extension of who you are; as you learn, evolve, and change, so should your blog.

- **Reading is fundamental.** There is an expression, "Readers are leaders"—well, "bloggers are readers." Blogging is a two-way street, and you'll find that reading and taking in information is as essential as giving it away.

- **Participating in your online community.** While there are ways to do a blog and be unreachable by your readers, blogs that have a social

component where readers feel like they have a relationship with the blogger tend to do better.

- **Outside-the-box thinking.** A bit of creativity can be a compelling reason for people to visit your blog.

- **Integrity.** If you are doing a blog for the long haul, and I hope you are, honesty will be your best policy.

- **Working hard** (this is a subjective term—harder than surfing, but certainly easier than a second job) in exchange for your ultimate goals and objectives is necessary.

Getting Started

Now let's focus on where to begin.

Choose a Niche Topic for Your Blog

Some questions to help you decide on a suitable topic are:

Are You Interested in a Particular Topic Already? The easiest place to start is right where you are. So, make a list of all the topics that interest you and rate them on a scale from 1 to 10 in terms of how much they energize you (where 1 is a topic you are mildly interested in and 10 is super-fired up about it). You may be tempted to go out and pick a topic based on what is popular and has high traffic value. While that is a viable approach in other online money-making endeavors, it has some serious drawbacks in the blogging arena. For starters, it is difficult to fake passion for a topic you are not into, and even if you could, would you want to keep faking it for the long haul? Blog readers tend to be some of the most passionate people on the web, and they can smell when something is off. There are easier ways to make money than blogging about something you don't care about and participating in a community you do not enjoy.

> *Blog readers tend to be some of the most passionate people on the web, and they can smell when something is off.*

Is the Topic Popular? If you are doing a blog as a hobby, this won't matter. But if you hope to make some money from it, you'll want to make sure that enough other people are interested in it, too. You don't need millions of interested folks—enough to make it financially viable. I can't give you hard rules about this, since it will vary by topic, industry, passion index, your income model (i.e., how you bring in money, which we'll cover shortly), etc.

Where Is the Topic on the Growth Curve: Upward Slope or Downward Slope? Sure, some topics are evergreen, but most are dynamic and experiencing a growth or decline in popularity. The more in touch you happen to be with your topic, the better you'll be able to gauge what is happening in that area. Otherwise, you'll have to do more homework to get a better feel for where things are going and be ahead of the curve. Become a trend detective.

What Competition Is There? A certain amount of competition is desirable; it validates that you do indeed have a viable topic. However, while some competition is healthy, too much competition means you'll have to work hard to get penetration and pay more for marketing costs.

A common mistake is to find a market with zero competition and think you have found the Holy Grail. While it is possible that you have discovered a truly untapped and virgin marketplace, odds are that others have tried that market and found it unresponsive, unprofitable, or both. Don't worry—I'll show you how to figure out what you have and make money even from lackluster topics.

What Are the Opportunity Gaps? Okay, this goes into Marketing 101 and locating opportunity gaps within your chosen marketplace. That means finding out what needs or wants other blogs are not satisfying. Domino's Pizza penetrated a crowded pizza market by doing something every other pizza place did badly, which was delivery. The easiest way to do this in blogs is by going deeper into a topic or sub-niching. For example, there may be many blogs for BMW owners, but you can always go deeper and create a blog for BMW M3 owners.

Do You Have an Ample Supply of Content? Ultimately, you have to have enough stuff to write about to keep your blog fresh and current so readers will want to keep coming back.

Your two main sources will be the information that you already have (in your head) and information that you can get from external sources such

as Google News, Topix, Yahoo! News, Bloglines, Technorati, and Blog Pulse (among others).

Does the Topic Lend Itself to Income Streams? Once again, this will not be an issue for those who are blogging as a hobby, but we are here to make a paycheck, so it is a concern for us. There are too many factors that affect income potential, so I won't go into it here, but it is something to keep in mind. As you'll see, there are many ways to make money with your blog; all, some, or none may work for a particular topic, so let's leave it at that.

If you've made your list and done a bit of homework, you've decided on a topic for your blog. That means it is time to take the next step.

Moonlight on Rebecca Hilbert

Rebecca's Moonlighting Story

I started about two years ago when I was sick to death of paying someone else to tell me what trades to place. I trade options on the stock market, so I decided to do my own online trading diary FREE for all who wanted to see what I was doing, and it has taken off!

I'm a mum with two small boys, and I get to spend time with my kids by working from home, as my business runs itself and I only spend about an hour a day on the PC, no weekends! I don't have to pay for child care and I've completely replaced my income.

www.marketmum.com

I can tell you that we have been able to buy multiple investment properties as well as a new Mercedes M-class.

Rebecca's Advice

Get your mindset right! You have to believe you deserve to be profitable, abundant, and happy! You have to know you can have anything and everything you want, as long as you ask for it and be happy! As soon as I stopped focusing on what I DIDN'T want and started focusing on what I DID want, everything changed!

Deciding on a Blog Platform

If your content is the "what," then the platform will be the "where," as in where your blog will exist.

The two main camps of blog platforms are hosted platforms and stand-alone platforms.

Hosted Blog Platforms

These are the best starting point for most people, as they allow you to get your feet wet quickly and easily with services you are probably familiar with, such as **blogger.com**, **wordpress.com** (Figure 24-1), **myspace.com**, and MSN Spaces. It helps that most of the services are free! All you'll need to do is register, and they will provide you with the URL of where your blog will be.

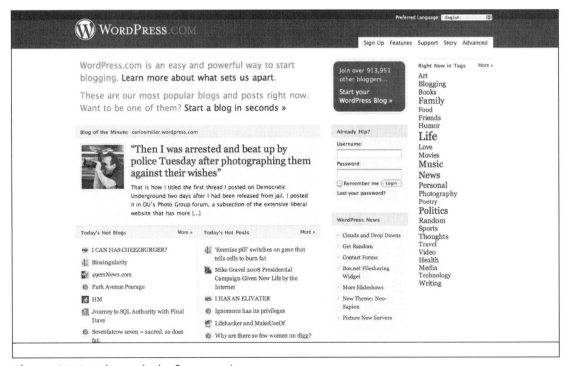

Figure 24-1. A hosted platform service

Why Blogging?

These services allow your blog to reside on their servers, which is why they are referred to as "hosted." Take a look at the popular WordPress blog for AtariBoy at **atariboy.wordpress.com**. That tells you Atariboy's blog is hosted, because it is hosted by **wordpress.com**.

Standalone Blog Platforms

As you can guess from the name, this platform is one that you host yourself, meaning on your own domain or URL. You'll need to use platform standard software such as WordPress, Movable Type, PMachine, Greymatter, B2Evolution, TextPattern, or Expression Engine (to name a few).

If you are serious about treating your blog as a business venture, this is the platform of choice. It will be worthwhile to become fluent in the technology and develop the skills necessary to exploit all the capabilities that your blog can offer.

That is not meant to dissuade you from using a hosted blog for your income-producing venture or to imply that hosted accounts are not capable, but merely to point out that once you become a pro, you'll probably want something more robust. And if you ever go through it, you'll learn that moving platforms is a royal pain in the you-know-what.

Chapter 25

How to Set Up a Blog

This will be a piece of cake. You are going to answer some questions on a form with wizards and you'll be set. Let's walk through it.

Five Steps to Setting Up a Hosted Blog at Wordpress.com

1. Head over to **wordpress.com/signup**.

2. Enter a username. This will be the name you use to log in, but can also be the first part of your blog's web address, e.g., **username .wordpress.com**. When you have filled out the form, hit "Next."

3. Next, you will be asked to choose or confirm a blog domain, the title for your blog, your language, and if you want your blog to be discoverable by search engines (yes!). If you are happy with your selections, click "Sign up."

4. An e-mail will be sent to your address for you to confirm your account. You will be asked for your full name. Once you have clicked the confirmation link in the e-mail, you will be provided a password. Another e-mail will arrive letting you know your blog is set up and giving you a reminder of your password.

5. That's it—you are set up and ready to blog! You might want to choose

a new look for your blog. Log in. Click "My Dashboard" in the top menu, then "Presentation." You will be able to choose from a variety of themes. Happy blogging!

Set Up a Custom Standalone Blog Using One-Click-Install

That was easy, no? Okay, setting up a standalone blog can be a little trickier, but as I said, it's worth the effort in the long run. We are going to use a shortcut by picking a hosting company that features "one-click-install" of WordPress, sometimes advertised as the "Fantastico" system. The company I use is Dreamhost (Figure 25-1), partly for this reason.

1. First you will sign up at **dreamhost.com/signup** and decide if you want to pay annually or monthly. Also, you will need to choose a domain name (see the next section for things to think about). This will be a proper domain in the form **www.myblog.com**, so choose carefully and consider its potential to bring in revenue (read further for more about that). It's a long form, but it looks more complicated than it really is. Just take it slowly.

2. You will be asked for your payment details. How long this process takes will depend on a number of factors, but eventually an e-mail receipt will arrive, followed by an e-mail confirming your new account. Other e-mails may inform you of various services that are ready to use.

3. At this point, you will have a hosting account and a domain registration. Your domain might not be visible for 24 to 48 hours, but that will not stop you from setting up your blog, and most people find it doesn't take that long.

4. When you log in to your account, you should see a list of options down the left side. Under "Goodies" you will find the "One-Click-Install" option.

5. You will need to select "WordPress" and the domain you wish to install it on. It will ask you for database and database host details; this is the database the system needs to create in order to store your blog posts. Don't worry about getting this wrong—just put in the name of your blog and do the same for a new MySQL for the new hostname.

Figure 25-1. Dreamhost

6. After 5 to 10 minutes, you will receive an e-mail that tells you your blog has been set up. Simply go to the web address you requested.

7. When you visit your domain, you will see a message from your blog. Click the "install.php" link.

8. You will be asked for a blog title and your e-mail address.

9. The next screen will let you know if the setup was successful and show your temporary password (it will also be e-mailed to you). You only need this password to get in the first time; it can be changed to something more memorable later.

10. After logging in, you will see your dashboard, just as with the **wordpress .com setup**, and like before, you will be able to select a template. Switch the template by clicking on the one you like.

11. While your blog is now set up, you might want to take a look through the "Options" menu to configure your blog the way you want it. Pay particular attention to "General," where you will want to set your tagline and date/time settings, and "Permalinks," where you can set WordPress to use a friendlier URL structure (e.g., **myblog.com/post-name** rather than **myblog.com/?p=123**).

Your Own Domain Name

> *A well-chosen domain name will aid in your efforts to create credibility, help people find you, and possibly enhance search engine rankings.*

I recommend that you get one. There is no reason I can think of not to have one, and for about $10–20, the benefits are amazing. A well-chosen domain name will aid in your efforts to create credibility, help people find you, and possibly enhance search engine rankings. It may also prove useful in branding and gives you the option of having e-mail addresses with that same domain.

Considerations When Choosing a Domain Name

This is much like picking a name for a baby: you can do it by the rules or just go with whatever you want and be done with it. I say "rules" loosely, as there is much debate about what makes a domain name work, but then again, there are successful domains that break all the rules.

Ultimately, you'll have to decide for yourself, and it isn't a make-or-break proposition. Having said that, why not stack as many odds in your favor as possible? You may want to consider the following:

◆ Is the domain name in line with your long-term goals for your blog?

◆ Does it telegraph to the reader what your blog topic is?

- Who is your target audience, and does the domain name resonate with them (young, old, motorheads, the in-crowd)?
- What is the tone of your blog (professional, humorous, news)?
- Where are they coming from (different sources of traffic)?

Thinking of the Future

If you don't consider the future, how can you future-proof your blog? I don't expect you to have a crystal ball, and there are certainly things that you can't possibly predict. But it doesn't take long to think about where things are going and make some assumptions about the future.

I speak from experience and have made this mistake myself. One of my blogs on digital cameras is on my **livingroom.org.au** domain. It does well, but I often wonder how well it would be doing if I had considered the future a bit more.

An example I like to share with my students is **www.about.com**. They have numerous blogs running from that one domain, but what an appropriate domain name it is!

Another caveat for future-proofing your name is not to pick a domain that is time-specific; you are in it for the long haul, remember? So, names like **www.y2ksoftware.com**, **www.election2008.com**, or even **www.bestgolfcoursesof2019.com** would not be good.

Other Considerations

Dot-com names are the gold standard, but the .net and .org names are becoming more common. I don't think it is worth sweating over; any one of those three would be fine.

I don't have any hard proof, but it makes sense to me that the easier a name is to remember, pronounce, and type, the easier it will make it for readers to get to your blog.

Avoid trademarked names.

Check out previously used domain names to make sure they were not used by spammers and are not blacklisted by the search engines.

Blog Design

While you do not need to be an artist, you'll get some good mileage out of creating an appropriate look and feel for your blog. Keep in mind that people do judge a book by its cover—at least initially. I don't put it in the make-or-break category, but we do want the highest probability to make money, and this is one area where care and work can pay off.

The questions to answer for design are similar to the ones for picking a name. Do you see a pattern?

◆ So, what is the purpose of your blog (sell directly, generate ad revenue, become a celebrity)? As you'll see when I cover the revenue models, some models dictate design cues, such as leaving space for advertisements.

◆ Who is your target audience? Obviously, something aimed at the corporate crowd will call for different design elements (color, structure, tone, etc.) than a site geared for hip-hop skateboarding youth.

◆ What specific functions does the site need? Here are some standard features you need to consider and allow space for: contact details, "about" or bio details/photo, advertising, archives by category and/or date, logo, subscription buttons, newsletter signup, search, blogroll, and recent posts list.

Moonlight on Mary Bogdanski

Mary's Moonlighting Story

February 2007 was when I decided to generate traffic by blogging. I have had **www.horsemoms.com** up for a short time, but it is generating tons of traffic to my two money sites. One is **www.equus-rx.com**, where I sell nutritional software for horses, and the other is **www.horsemomssupplements.com**, where I sell the horse supplements. Rather than trying to sell the stuff, I get people to visit and

www.horsemoms.com

get comfortable. I educate them first, and then they go ahead and buy my nutritional products. Now, thanks to the short time I've been blogging, my traffic and my sales have doubled.

Mary's Advice

The internet is about trust. It's tough to sell to someone. It's easier to get a customer after they get to know you!

Tools of the Trade

It seems that a new blogging tool or service is being released every day to help bloggers add a feature to their blog. It can become overwhelming to choose from them all.

I asked ProBlogger readers to come up with a list of the blog services and tools they use, and they came up with some great resources. Unfortunately, the problem with putting that list in a book is that some of those resources might have changed, evolved, or been replaced by something better by the time you get to them.

Fortunately, the internet is a great way to keep things current, and you can see that list in its most up-to-date format at **www.moonlightingonthe-internet.com/blogtools**.

Writing Good Content

If there is a make-or-break component to blogging, content may be it. Think about it: your content determines whether your blog gets read, or whether people subscribe and return to read it again. It also determines the value of your information. It is such an important piece of the blog equation that "Content is King" has become the mantra of many bloggers.

We are left with the question, "What constitutes good content?" Ultimately, the target audience will decide and cast their votes with their readership and loyalty. So perhaps the better question is, "What would make people want to read my blog and return to it?"

Usefulness and Uniqueness

Put yourself into the mind of your audience and think about that question. You'll probably come up with many things, but you'll notice two qualities beginning to emerge: usefulness and uniqueness.

What Makes for Useful Content?

It could be any of the following:

◆ **Entertainment Value.** People gather there to have fun, laugh, and be amused. Might think of this as the new water cooler.

- ◆ **Educational Value.** Readers can learn about a particular area of interest, like fishing.

- ◆ **Information Value.** Could be similar to the previous example, depending on how we define information, but clearly there is a distinction between learning how to fish and going to a blog to get information about the best fishing spots.

- ◆ **News Value.** Readers want to be kept up on what is happening in a particular area of interest.

- ◆ **Community or Social Value.** Obviously, providing a venue for people to connect and belong.

- ◆ **Intellectual Value.** I'd consider this similar to the previous example, but the emphasis is on expressing a position, flexing mental muscle, debating an issue.

- ◆ **And sometimes many of the above at the same time.**

What Makes for Unique Content?

As you can imagine, it is difficult if not impossible to be the only blog on the web with some specific information, or the only humorous blog, or the only blog offering people a place to connect. So, we are faced with the challenge of how to get readers to pick our blog over other blogs on the same topic.

Distinguish Yourself. The easiest way to do this is to check out the competition and look for the opportunity gap. Chances are good that they'll all be using a similar style, voice, and tone to present their content. With that homework under your belt, you can find a way to set yourself apart from the crowd. If their approach is a "just the facts" news-related tone like that of a TV anchorperson, you can take a humorous approach like Howard Stern's or a more opinionated approach like Bill O'Reilly's. Just be certain that your approach is appropriate for your target audience.

Other ways to distinguish yourself are sub-niching (which I already mentioned in the BMW example) or presenting in a distinct voice. Take a look at Manolo's blog at **www.problogger.net/archives/2005/09/23/shoe-blogs-six-figure-blogger** for an example of an anonymous blogger who has grown a cult audience by writing about an odd combination of topics in the third person.

Original Content. This can be confusing to some folks, but the take-home point is that you can quote other people (giving them proper credit, of course) and by adding comments, create unique content.

Other Considerations

Post Length. This is one of those funky questions like, "How long should a man's legs be?" Long enough to touch the ground, right? So, while the general consensus is about 250 words, a post should be long enough to communicate a complete thought, but not so long that it bores the reader.

Posting Frequency. This depends on personal preference (how much time do you want to commit to your blog?), your audience's preferences, and the topic you are posting on. Posting for the sake of posting is a bad idea, but you need some frequency to maintain the relationship. Also, keep in mind that some topics lend themselves to a higher frequency. For example, what is happening in the stock market may be worth a daily post, but trading currency options may warrant several posts a day.

Visitor Type. Regular readers tend to have more patience, while new folks who found you because of a search engine or link tend to have shorter attention spans.

The Title of Your Post. This is like the headline on a newspaper or the subject line of an e-mail. Put some thought into it, as it will have a strong influence on readership.

Scannable Content. One study found that only 16 percent of people read word for word when they are online, and another found that the average person only comprehends about 60 percent of what he or she reads. The average web user will scan a web site, quickly determine if there is anything of value, and decide to leave or stay. It is like meeting a member of the opposite sex: you have a few seconds to make a good impression. That buys you maybe 2 minutes, and if that goes well you may get 15 minutes, then a phone number. After that, if you go on a first date, and if all goes well you get a second date, and so on.

That's how the web game works. You have a few seconds to catch their attention, then a little longer to wow them with some useful and unique content. Maybe they'll read more, and if you keep wowing them, you'll end up with a loyal reader.

So, the first challenge at hand is the first impression. Put another way, it does us no good to have the best content on the planet if we do not catch their attention in those first few seconds.

Fortunately, we know they are scanning for visual cues and key words and phrases. And there are ways to optimize our sites to be scan-friendly:

- **Lists.** Everybody loves lists. Who doesn't know Letterman's Top Ten lists? They get attention and you can scan them in the blink of an eye.

- **Pictures.** I like pictures on blogs, as they break up copy and make the page more interesting. Make sure the pictures are appropriate and relevant. A picture may say a thousand words, but don't forget a photo caption.

- **Formatting.** Make use of **bold**, CAPITALS, *italics*, underlining (be careful with underlining, as it is also commonly used to indicate that text is a link), and bullets to emphasize points. Don't go overboard, as you run the risk of frustrating your reader.

- **Short Paragraphs.** Make it easy to read by breaking up the copy and putting the meat of your message front and center. Remember, if you are saving your sense of humor and charming personality for the second date, you may not get a phone number.

Using Images on Blogs

Using your own images is never a problem, and I encourage you to do so. Once again, I'll remind you that you want the images to be appropriate and relevant for your target audience.

But what about someone else's images? This should not be an issue, as most countries have "fair use" exceptions in their copyright laws and using an image for a post seems to be fine. Make sure to cite your sources. Images from commercial sites should normally be avoided unless you are certain that you have a case for fair use or they are explicitly there for your purpose. That said, do realize that I am not an attorney and if you have doubts about your local laws, you are best served by getting a qualified legal opinion. Moreover, from a point of common sense, you can always ask for permission to use something that isn't yours. You can also license the material for your use by paying the owner.

Moonlight on John Clark

John's Moonlighting Story

I got started in 2002 with a vision to provide good-quality personal development information on the Internet. I joined several affiliate programs from some of the people whom I liked and started to use their articles to feed my blogs. I was getting commission checks here and there and started to build a list of subscribers using forms on my site to capture names and e-mail addresses.

Today, across my blog sites I get several hundred unique visitors with about a hundred repeat visitors daily. I am monetizing my web sites using Google AdSense and the affiliate programs that produce the better conversions. I also have seasonal affiliate programs that I utilize to increase the chances of conversion. I average about $500–800 profit per month between the affiliate sites and AdSense. I am profitable with the business model, and it's growing daily without increasing expense. Although the numbers are not huge, they are grow-

www.lifetosuccess.com

ing monthly, which gives me hope for the future.

I am more upbeat in my daily life knowing that I have a system set up that generates an income without my presence. When I wake up and see income that has been produced while I was sleeping, it's exciting. I have made some key contacts and friends in the niche that I have chosen to do online. It has made me look at work a lot differently. I am constantly looking for ways to better utilize the contacts I have and to make their lives easier with the information I provide online. It's nice to be able to use my extra income to do things for the ones I love.

John's Advice

If you concentrate your efforts on looking for solutions to common problems that people have and present them in a way that makes sense to those who need them, your dreams will fall into place.

Different Styles of Blog Posts

There is a blog to fit every type of person and objective. Here are some I came up with (certainly not an exhaustive list):

1. Lists. This is my favorite type of blog post. Let me show you why:

Five reasons why I like lists for blogging:

◆ Lists are easy to write.

◆ Lists are scan-friendly.

◆ Lists are persuasive.

◆ Lists are easy to link to.

◆ Lists make the writing look neat and organized.

See what I mean?

2. Instructional. Tell people how to do something, such as how to fix a faucet or pick a ripe fruit.

3. Informational. Dispense information on a particular topic, such as where the next marathon will take place or what happened to a particular stock.

4. Reviews. Provide useful opinions on any product or service you can imagine. Can be from peers (for example, **Amazon.com**'s book reviews) or a single source, such as *Consumer Reports*.

5. Interviews. Give readers exposure to a celebrity or expert. A "build your own patio" blog could interview Bob Vila.

6. Case Studies. Provide useful models based on an objective. A restaurant blog could do a case study showing how Subway repositioned itself from a fast food chain to a healthy diet alternative.

7. Profiles. Similar to case studies, but focus on a particular person. Cable television's A&E network show *Biography* runs a theme every week. For example, when they do comedians, they would profile Jerry Seinfeld.

8. Link Posts. This type of blog post is popular because of how easy it is to do. You basically find other posts or blogs you find interesting and link to them. You make them unique by adding your own comments, remember?

9. Contrasting Two Options. Similar to reviewing posts, but with a wider focus. Usually involves comparing two products in a shootout manner. For example, "Which is better: the Windows or Apple operating system?"

10. Rant. This is personality-driven because you need to be uber-passionate and uncensored; stir the pot and light a fire under some controversy.

11. Inspirational. This is the anti-rant, where the messages are inspirational and motivational.

12. Satirical. Not a rant or anti-rant, as it is less about the message and more about the style of presenting the message. Wit, humor, and strong writing skills are particularly useful here.

13. Prediction and Review Posts. The prediction part is self-explanatory, but I want to be clear that we are not talking about reviews as in comparing products or services, but more in a chronological sense. You'll see these pop up as things start or end, like the "year in review" or "race to the White House"-type of posts.

14. Critique Posts. Not sure if these started with movie critics, but people seem naturally drawn to a good critique. Topics such as how a quarterback threw the ball or how well the President handled a crisis are good examples.

15. Debate. The online version of a fight after school. Debates can be between the blogger and another person, the blogger and anyone who wants in, or the blogger presenting point and counterpoint. For example: Who is faster, Superman or Flash?

16. Hypothetical Posts. Basically a post on different "what if" scenarios. This would refer to stuff such as "What if Bill Gates became president?" or "What if the polar ice caps melt?"

17. Research. While taking more time and effort than other types of posts, this can be worthwhile if the research yields some exciting results.

Miscellaneous Content Writing Tips

- **Involve or engage your readers.**
- **Copyright.** Same as the rules for using images. Give proper credit, remember fair use, and consult a qualified attorney if you have any doubts.
- **Names are important.** 42 percent of SE searches are for product, brand, and/or company names. That tells you that it may be worthwhile to give names some thought.

Chapter 26

Making Money with Blogs

It is amazing how something that was once on the outer fringes of the internet is now front and center. I can't say for sure what it was that fueled the incredible growth in blogging: perhaps it was exposure to social sites such as **myspace.com**, the evolution of the tools that made it as easy as opening an e-mail account, a greater comfort around all things on the web, or something entirely different.

I may not know the reason why it happened, but I do know that more people are blogging than ever before, and they are starting to figure out more ways to make money with these blogs. I did my bit of research and found that 100 percent of the top 30 blogs had some sort of income stream from their blogging.

One more point before I get into the income methods: yes, you can make money from blogging and there are examples of people making a lot of money from it. Just don't make the mistake of thinking that this is a get-rich-quick plan.

Okay, so on to making money.

All of the methods for generating income fall into one of two categories: direct and indirect.

1. **Direct Income Earning Methods.** The blogger earns an income directly from the blog.
2. **Indirect Income Earning Methods.** The blogger makes his or her money because of the blog.

Direct Income Earning Methods for Bloggers

Advertising

There are an infinite number of permutations for generating advertising income with your blog, but these are the most popular ones:

Contextual Advertising. Programs like AdSense, YPN (beta), and MSN are popular with bloggers and are probably the most common income streams used today. The way these programs work is that they scan the content of your blog to ascertain what its topic is and attempt to put contextually relevant ads (text and image) onto your blog. They are generally simple to use and involve pasting some code into your blog's templates. Payment is on a per-click basis (referred to as CPC, or "cost per click" ads). Contextual ads work well with a blog that has a particular niche topic, especially if it has some sort of commercial angle (i.e., it has products and services associated with it).

Other CPC Advertising. There are a variety of other ad systems that pay on a per-click basis and are *not contextual* in nature (which is important, as systems such as AdSense do not allow you to run contextual ads on the same page as them).

BlogAds. These have become something of an institution when it comes to advertising on blogs. They traditionally have focused on monetizing political blogs, but are expanding their focus lately.

The beauty of these ads is that bloggers set their own rates and can accept or reject advertisers that apply to be featured on their blogs. BlogAds put control over what ads show and how much they earn into the hands of the blogger. It is basically rent for space on your blog.

Text Ads. Another increasingly popular way to sell ads on your blog is to look into text links. The beauty of these is that they don't take much room, and depending on the system you choose to run them on, you can control which advertisers you accept and reject.

Other Ad Systems. In addition to the above systems (most of which I've used myself), there are many advertising options that I do not have experience with. I'm sure they are worth experimenting with, however, as I see many of them being used by bloggers every day. You'll find a complete list on the resources page at **www.moonlightingontheinternet.com/blogtools**.

Sponsorship

Another form of advertising that a smaller number of bloggers are using is finding their own advertisers. All of the above systems have the advantage of finding advertisers for you (or at least assisting in the automation of ads to your blog), but as your blog grows in profile and influence, you might find that other options for private deals come up.

> *Another form of advertising that a smaller number of bloggers are using is finding their own advertisers.*

The big blog networks have people dedicated to the task of finding advertisers (often working through ad agencies), but smaller bloggers might find this worthwhile, as well. I've been selling ads on my digital camera blog for two years, and as I've been doing so, it's grown in traffic and profile and managed to attract larger companies willing to pay more for space. Currently, the blog features ads from Adobe, which has bought a combination of banner, newsletter, and text ads.

If you take this approach, the key is to target advertisers in your niche that have products closely related to what you're writing about. There are a variety of ad forms that you can offer them, including banner ads, buttons, text links, mentions in newsletters, and even individual post sponsorships. I recommend that you always make it clear to readers that your post is a sponsored one when you're writing a sponsored post.

Affiliate Programs

"Affiliate programs" are where you take a commission for referring a reader who purchases a product or service to a company. Probably the most common for bloggers is **Amazon.com**, which has tens of thousands of products you can link to. Other affiliate programs that represent many companies and products include Linkshare, Commission Junction, and ClickBank. Affiliate programs take some work if you want to get the most out of them (perhaps more work than advertising), but can be lucrative if you match the right program with the right blog or topic.

Donations and Tip Jars

A small number of blogs have a history of making good money with these. To be successful asking for money from readers, you'll need a large and loyal readership (and a rich one might help, too). Most bloggers don't have the critical mass or the cult following to make it work.

Selling/Flipping Blogs

The idea of selling (or flipping) your blog is one that many bloggers have in the back of their minds for "one day," but in reality, it is not overly common … yet. (I think this is changing.) Probably the largest sale is that of Weblogs, Inc. (a network of blogs), which sold to AOL for a reported $25 million.

Merchandise

Another method that some blogs use to reasonable effect is selling T-shirts, mugs, stickers, and other merchandise with the blog's name, logo, and/or tagline on it. This is another idea that probably only works if you have a brilliantly designed merchandise range and/or you have a cult-like status as a blogger with some fanatical readers who are obsessive about your blog. Some blog topics lend themselves to this more than others.

Selling Subscriptions

The idea of charging readers for content is one that surfaces from time to time. While there are numerous web sites that do this successfully (community membership sites), I've yet to see many (or rather, any) blogs do it well. The problem is that most topics that you could think to start a blog about already have free sites available. To make it succeed, you would need to have some sort of premium or exclusive content and/or real expertise on a topic.

Blog Networks

Another emerging income source for bloggers is blog networks. There are two ways to make money here. First, you can start a network and contract with bloggers to write for you, or second, you might join a blog network as a writer. There are many networks, and all have their own strengths and weaknesses. I'll write more later on what to think about when you're considering joining a network.

Indirect Income Earning Methods for Bloggers

As you can see, there is no shortage of people making money using direct methods. So, you'll be pleasantly surprised that there is even more potential in employing the indirect methods.

The only caveat is that the following methods are positioning strategies and rely on your expertise in a particular subject to be used correctly. Once again, I'll remind you that this is not an overnight miracle solution and will take time.

Consulting

When someone says he or she is a top _____ (fill in the blank with just about any profession—hairdresser, architect, painter, etc.), there is a tendency to be skeptical. However, when you find out the person wrote a book on the subject, things change and he or she is seen as a bona fide expert. Being the author of a popular blog can have a similar effect, enabling you not only to attract clients but also to charge higher fees.

Offline Writing Gigs

Manolo from Shoeblogs (the third-party voice guy) landed a writing gig with the *Washington Post Express* after he was discovered via his blog. These types of opportunities can come from newspapers, magazines, trade publications, etc.

Online Writing Gigs

I am seeing more bloggers leveraging their blogging experiences and turning them into writing-for-hire gigs or even creating their own products for their particular niches. I guess that could qualify as direct or indirect, depending on how you do it.

Speaking Opportunities

This is similar to the consulting example. Authoring a book has been opening doors to the speaking world for a long time. Now, blogging opens those same doors, with opportunities to speak at conferences, workshops, and seminars on the blogger's topic of choice.

How Much Money Can a Blog Earn?

This is a tricky question, much like "How long should a piece of string be?"

Don't get me wrong—there is some validity to it; if you're going to put time and energy into building something, it'd be great to know up front what rewards might be awaiting you. It's an impossible question to answer, because there are so many factors to take into consideration.

The answer is: It depends.

I can share some of my personal experiences—and keep in mind that I am involved with over 100 blogs. I know you want numbers, so here are three examples:

Blog A: For a particular month, one blog had around 20,000 page views from about half that number of visitors (i.e., they viewed two pages each). The total earnings of this blog (all from contextual advertising) were $790.91.

Blog B: Another blog had just over 40,000 page views over the month, this time from about 13,000 visitors. Its total earnings from contextual advertising (same number of ad units per page as Blog A) were only $99.08. It also earned $35 from an affiliate program.

Blog C: Our last example is a blog that had around 160,000 page views over the month from around 80,000 visitors. It earned $515.12 from contextual ads and somewhere in the vicinity of $2,500 from affiliate programs.

As you can see in my examples, the monthly income varies with each blog from a low of $134.08 to as much as $3,015.12.

If you are curious about just how well someone can do, Yanik interviewed Steve Pavlina from **www.stevepavlina.com** and got him to describe how he generates $40,000 a month from his blog without selling any of his own products. This exclusive interview was only for members of Yanik's Secret Society (a monthly newsletter dedicated to bringing its members leading-edge, under-the-radar "make money on the internet" news, techniques, and strategies), but Yanik has made the transcript of the entire interview available for Moonlight readers. You can get a free copy at **www.moonlightingontheinternet.com/BlogSecrets**.

So, How Much Can I Earn?

I don't know, because I don't know your skill sets, your work ethic, the topic you'll choose, etc. However, I do know that if you never get started, the answer is a big fat donut. On the other hand, if you take advantage of multiple blogs, choose your niches wisely, and utilize as many income streams as possible, you should do at least as well as I have, or possibly better. While I have made it a rule not to disclose my exact earnings, I will say I am earning over six figures per year from the following income streams (earnings from b5media, products, speaking, and consulting are not included):

Chitika. While they don't work on every blog (for example, I don't use them on ProBlogger) and there is a traffic minimum to be accepted by them, Chitika (Figure 26-1) continues to be my highest earner.

AdSense. The most popular form of advertising on blogs is AdSense (according to a few studies I've seen), and for me it's a reliable earner that brings in a significant level of income (just under what Chitika pulls in each month). While I use referrals and their search product on some of my sites, I find that normal ad units are producing the best income for me—particularly rectangle (250 x 300 pixels) ones placed close to content with a blended design.

Text Link Ads. Perhaps the biggest mover for me over the last 12 months in terms of earnings has come from TLA. While they have a ceiling in regard to what they earn per site, they are another solid earner for me.

Amazon Associates. The fourth quarter of each year tends to be a good one for me when it comes to commissions from Amazon. The last quarter is a time when people are in a buying mode in the lead-up to Christmas, so smart placement (deep linking inside posts) can bring great conversions.

Figure 26-1. Chitika

The key is picking relevant products to promote.

Private Ad Deals. I don't do a lot of private ad deals (it's something I should focus on more, but there are only so many hours in the day), but when they come in they can be significant (if you have decent traffic). I've just signed two deals on my digital photography blog with Apple and Adobe for the next couple of months, so I suspect this one will leap up in the next quarter.

Miscellaneous Affiliate Programs. My blogs have a variety of smaller affiliate programs running from them. I try to find quality products related to my topics that I can genuinely recommend, often via reviews. Some of the better converting products that I've recommended this last quarter included Digital Photography Secrets (a camera technique series), Pro Photo Secrets (a Photoshop product), and SEO Book (Aaron's legendary resource).

ProBlogger Job Boards. Not spectacular earnings, but growing. I see this more as a service to readers than an income stream at this point; however, it does pay for itself and brings in a few hundred dollars each month.

BlogAds. I don't use them much these days, but they do bring in a little cash each month. I noticed that BlogAds decreased in performance for me around the time they went to the new version. I'm not sure if it's my problem or theirs, but apart from one blog, I rarely see any sales these days.

What Factors Contribute to a Blog's Earnings?

There are many factors that impact how much you can earn from each of your blogs, but here are the most common ones to consider:

Traffic Levels. While we can't look at traffic levels alone to determine the income potential, they are a significant component of the income equation. All things being equal, increasing traffic increases income.

Source of Traffic. Not all traffic is equal, and you'll have to consider the impact if it is weighted more favorably toward loyal readers, referred traffic, or folks who found your blog via a search engine.

Income Stream. The actual method you use to generate income will impact your earnings. Pretty straightforward, but it suggests having multiple streams of income or utilizing multiple methods.

Topic. This is kind of obvious, as some topics lend themselves better to producing income than others. This creates huge income fluctuations in contextual ad programs, as some keywords will generate more money than others. Likewise, affiliate programs are subject to the same topic biases. Consider a blog about books using Amazon's affiliate program—the payout will be small, since it is only 5 to 8 percent and the average book may cost only $20. Contrast that with publishers in the financial web site game, who use affiliate programs that can pay out $100 per sale.

I suspect it is the main difference in income from my earlier three blog examples:

Blog A has a specialized topic that not many would be interested in (hence its lower traffic). On the other side of things, it has well-paying ads in YPN on a per-click basis and triggers ads that are relevant to the topic. As a result, despite its low traffic, it earns well.

Blog B has a popular topic, but there are few advertisers interested in buying ads with those keywords in contextual ad systems. As a result, its Click Through Rate (CTR) is low, and click values are also low. Furthermore, it has yet to generate enough traffic to make much from impression-based ads (although there is potential here—it's a reasonably new blog). As a result, while it has more traffic than Blog A, it's earning considerably less.

Blog C is on a popular topic that doesn't convert brilliantly into contextual ads in terms of CTR and ad value. It does have a reasonable reputation in its niche, and affiliate recommendations are responded to well by readers (plus the fact that they have a good value per sale, which doesn't hurt).

In addition, let's not forget that the topic will play a role in the indirect methods of producing income. As we've seen with my blogs, different niches offer different income opportunities from different sources. So, while a book review blogger may not be in much demand for consulting work, he could find a way to syndicate his blog to magazines or newspapers. Similarly, while another blogger with a good profile in the PR industry might not get picked up as a writer in magazines, she could land a well-paying job or gain an opportunity to do some consulting.

Age of Blog. Typically, good blogs get better with age as they develop an ever-larger base of loyal readers and eventually reach critical mass. From there they'll be fine and at least maintain their position in the market unless they do something to alienate their readers or a major shift in their marketplace changes the playing field. Blogs can rise out of nowhere and become dominant players, but that is the exception and not the rule.

Moonlight on Caterina Christakos

Caterina's Moonlighting Story

I started blogging a little over a year ago and the obsession hasn't stopped. It started as a fun hobby and grew into an even more fun business for me in a lot of ways. I have reached a Google #3 ranking with little effort. I use this blog to generate sales for my dating book site, **seductiondiva.com**. I also gain revenue from Google AdSense, affiliate links, and paid blog sites.

www.stillagirl.com/journal

Caterina's Advice

I realized that I was juggling too many potential businesses online. When I focused on just the one or two that I was passionate about, my sales took off and new ideas about how to make my business successful started to flow to me.

How Much Do I Spend?

When I am asked how much I spend to generate traffic for my sites, my answer is "very little." I have experimented with using AdWords to promote my blogs, but never on a large scale because I did not have the time or patience to test it properly. I will tell you, however, that my biggest AdWords month ever was $100 (just over $3 a day). I don't do any paid promotional activities, and my costs are hosting-related and the normal ISP and office costs.

Ad Relevancy

Pay-per-click advertising programs, such as AdSense, YPN, and Chitika, rely heavily on the positioning and design of their ads when it comes to performance, but ad relevancy may be the more important factor. The principle is simple: readers come to your blog in search of content on a particular topic, and if they see an ad that relates to that topic, they are more likely to both notice it and respond to it. Irrelevant ads will almost always convert poorly, so in the same way that publishers work on the design and positioning of ads, they should consider making sure that ads are as relevant as possible to the content positioned near them. Keep in mind that each ad system will have different methods of making ads more relevant.

Ten Tips for Using Affiliate Programs on Your Blog

Everything so far has been geared toward advertising programs, but affiliate programs can create a substantial income stream, so they deserve some attention. Note that there will be some similarities. Here are my 10 tips for using affiliate programs on your blog:

1. Consider Your Audience. This should already be drilled into your brain, because knowing your readers will not only help you with the content of your blog, but will help you figure out the answers to these questions: Are they shopping for specific products? Might they be looking for related products or accessories? What would get them to buy? By starting with your reader in mind rather than the product, you'll be serving your readers as well as making a few dollars on the side.

2. Genuine Recommendations and Personal Endorsements Always Work Best. There are literally hundreds of thousands of products and services for

> *Your blog's readers come back to your blog day after day because something about you resonates with them.*

you to choose from to recommend to your blog's readers, but making money from them is not as simple as randomly adding links to them from your blog. Your blog's readers come back to your blog day after day because something about you resonates with them. They have at least some level of trust and respect for you, and perhaps the quickest way to destroy this is to recommend they buy something that you don't fully believe will benefit them.

3. Link to Quality Products. We all like to make sure we're buying the best products money can buy; your readers are no different and are more likely to make a purchase if you've found the best product for them. Choose products and companies with good reputations and quality sales pages.

4. Contextual Deep Links Work Best. When I started using the Amazon Associate Program, I naively thought that all I had to do was place an Amazon banner ad (that linked to Amazon's front page) at the top of my blog. I thought that my readers would see it and surf over to Amazon and buy up big, thereby making me a rich man. Nothing could have been further from reality. I was deluding myself.

5. Consider Positioning of Links. One of the things I go on about with AdSense optimization is the positioning of ads. I tell bloggers to position their ads in the hot spots on their blog pages (like the top of a left sidebar, inside content, at the end of posts above comments, etc.). The same principles are true for affiliate advertising.

6. Traffic Levels Are Important. While this is not the only factor, traffic levels are key when it comes to making money from any online activity. The more people see your well-placed, relevant, and well-designed affiliate links, the more likely it is that one of them will make a purchase. So don't just work on your links—work on building a readership. Not only this, but consider how you might direct traffic on your blog toward pages where readers are more likely to see your affiliate links.

7. Diversify without Clutter. Don't put all your affiliate efforts into one basket. There are plenty of products to link to, so there is no need to just work on one. At the same time, you shouldn't clutter your blog with too many affiliate program links. If you do, you run the risk of diluting the effectiveness of your links, and it could disillusion your readership.

8. Be Transparent. Don't try to fool your readers into clicking links that could make you money. While it may not always feasible to label all affiliate links, I think that some attempt should be made to let people know what type of link they are clicking on. I also think that consistency is important with this, so that readers of your blog know what to expect. For example, at ProBlogger, I usually put a note beside or under affiliate links to let readers know what they are clicking on. On my digital camera blog, I don't do this because the text around the majority of such links makes it clear that clicking on them will take them to some sort of shop or information where a purchase is possible (i.e., a link may say "buy the XXX product" or "get the latest product on XXX").

9. Combine with Other Revenue Streams. Affiliate programs and advertising programs are not mutually exclusive. I've come across a few people who have said that they don't want to do affiliate linking because it will take the focus off their AdSense ads. While there is potential for one to take the focus off the other, there is also potential for both to work hand in hand, as different readers will respond to different approaches. You should consider the impact that your affiliate links have on other revenue streams, but don't let one stop the other.

10. Track Results. Most affiliate programs have some type of tracking or statistics package that will allow you to watch which links are effective. Some packages are better than others, but most will allow you to see what is selling and what isn't. Watching your results can help you plan future affiliate efforts. Keep track of what positions for links work well, which products sell, what wording around links works well, etc., and use the information you collect as you plan future affiliate strategies.

What else is there to say? There you have it—a crash course to turn you into a pro blogger! Now, just do it!

For a complete list of the resources Darren uses and recommends, go to **www.moonlightingontheinternet.com/blogguide**.

About Darren

Darren Rowse started his first blog in 2002 and quickly grew it into a network of entrepreneurial blogs, which today forms the basis his business and provides him with a full-time income.

Darren is best known for founding **problogger.net**, a blog dedicated to helping bloggers earn money through blogging. ProBlogger covers a wide array of topics useful for bloggers, including writing content, search engine optimization, finding readers and blog marketing, affiliate marketing, ad optimization tips, and much more.

Darren is the co-founder of the Six Figure Blogging Course (**sixfigure-blogging.com**), a six-session course that examines in detail how to monetize blogs. He is also the founder of the successful Digital Photography School blog (**digital-photography-school.com/blog**).

Darren comes well qualified to train bloggers, not only because he's been blogging full-time for three years, but because he is the VP of training for the b5media blog network—a network that he co-founded, which now has 200 blogs and over 100 bloggers.

He lives in Melbourne, Australia with his wife and son.

What Am I Doing Now?

Now you've got the five road maps for making $500–5,000+ per month online like clockwork in your spare time. These are five proven ways to earn a second paycheck online without another daily nine-to-five grind. What are you going to do about it?

Are you truly committed to taking the next step?

People from all over the globe are taking back control of their lives and building little (or big) online businesses that keep spitting out cash no matter what they're doing or where they live.

Why not you?

You can throw out any excuse you want and there's somebody in the book who didn't let that stop them. Are you too old? Too young? Too experienced? Too inexperienced? You can keep making excuses, or you can go out and get to work moonlighting in your spare time. Remember, nobody started off as an expert—not even me. They all stumbled around for the answers. (Note: Be sure to watch the accompanying CD-ROM to save a lot of that pain with more proven advice and help.)

In a few short months, I've achieved the ultimate Internet fantasy of making a lot of money from a simple (almost primitive) web site that runs itself virtually on complete autopilot. Starting from scratch, I banked over

$51,351.94 during my first 6½ months online, working part-time out of the corner of my living room.

Today, at age 33, I've gone on to earn over seven figures.

How did I go from a standing start to banking mega-profits?

To do that, what I think you need to know are these inner secrets to mega internet success. This has nothing to do with search engines or pay-per-clicks. It doesn't have anything to do with the tactical stuff. It's all about stuff that goes on in your head.

Secret #1: Cheerful Expectancy

One of my mentors is Earl Nightingale. He passed away several years ago, but you need to get everything he recorded at **nightingale.com**. He has a program called "Lead the Field" and another called "The Strangest Secret." Just listen to that thing. He talks about "cheerful expectancy."

There's a big difference between having expectancy and hoping or wishing something is going to occur. When you have cheerful expectancy, you know it's going to occur. And that doesn't come from being "Pollyanna-ish" or having rose-colored glasses.

It comes from having knowledge. And you get that knowledge from studying your field, whatever it is. It could be internet marketing, or it could be neurology. That means reading, studying, and buying everything related to it and immersing yourself in it.

> *I learned from Earl Nightingale that if you want to be an expert, you spend an hour a day reading about whatever subject you want to be an expert on.*

I learned from Earl Nightingale that if you want to be an expert, you spend an hour a day reading about whatever subject you want to be an expert on. So I said, "Well, what would happen if I read for three hours a day?" I started learning as much as I could, and that knowledge gives you the confidence to know that you have that positive expectancy. Your expectations determine your results.

Secret #2: Do One Proactive Thing a Day

You don't need to do 100 things a day. Just get that one proactive thing a day. So each little brick builds a big wall for you. Trust me, it's easy to be overwhelmed with hundreds of tasks. You're like, "Oh, we need to do e-zine ads and free-for-alls and pay-per-click search engines, and I need to do all this other stuff."

Ahhhhhhhhhhhh!

Just relax and do one task a day.

Your single action will create more action for you. You need to commit to one proactive thing a day no matter what. Even if you're dead tired and worked a 14-hour day, come home and mail one letter or send out one joint venture proposal. I'm telling you—these little proactive things will have an immense impact.

Most everyone has heard of the 80/20 rule, or the Pareto Principle. It says that 20 percent of your actions produce 80 percent of your results, and the other way around: 80 percent of your work only creates 20 percent of your results.

So go back and look where your successes came from, and I know that they're from a little group of actions. If you go ahead with the one proactive thing a day (from the 20 percent group) that is going to propel you further, that's going to bring you wherever you want to be.

> *If you go ahead with the one proactive thing a day ... that is going to propel you further, that's going to bring you wherever you want to be.*

Make it a point to focus on those 20-percent activities. Stephen Covey, in his famous work *The Seven Habits of Highly Effective People*, calls these activities "important but not urgent."

Several years back, I decided to create an "Apprentice" program (yes, even before Trump), and I was pleased that nearly 100 percent of my apprentices got online ventures up and running.

One of my apprentices, Peter Woodhead, from the UK, is a perfect example of doing one proactive thing a day. A lot of apprentices bolted out of the gate during our one-year program, but Peter was an internet newbie and he had a full-time job, so he was slower getting started. However, he took my advice and managed to do one proactive thing every day, no matter how big or how small. It could be writing one autoresponder message, or it might have been writing 50 headlines. No matter the day, Peter was moving ahead. And not surprisingly, his project was completed before many of the other apprentices were finished.

Secret #3: Decision

This is a big point. A lot of people have problems with decision making. That's because they don't like it, to narrow one's options means to cut off other options. But frankly, that's exactly what you want. You want to cut off other options.

One of our top apprentices, Cindy Kappler, had no other option but to succeed because she quit her job. I'm not encouraging you to do that if you have a real job, but it does prove that if you cut off your options, you're more motivated. Successful people make decisions quickly. Oh, and I forgot to mention, she was pregnant with child #5 when she was working on her project.

There's a magic of attraction when you make your decision. However, when you're hemming and hawing, you don't experience this magic. I don't want to get into too much metaphysical or spiritual stuff.

But there's this magic of attraction. I can't explain it. When you set your mind that you're going to do this, all of a sudden, at the next dinner party you're attending, you meet somebody who can help you get to where you want to go. Is that luck, or is that something else? I don't think it's luck. It's like, once the decision is made, your mind is tuned into the solution and all kinds of "freaky" coincidences and occurrences happen.

And that brings me to another important point about decisions—fail quickly. Don't be afraid of failure. A lot of people are so afraid of making a mistake that they are frozen. Who cares? I screw up all the time. And you want to fail quickly.

That's the great part about the internet. You want to find out if your dumb idea is going to work. You can do it in days instead of months—sometimes hours—and if it doesn't work, you move on. You say, "Next!"

Look, I know a lot of people who have been working on their products for the last two, three, four years. Get the darned thing out! You make it better as you go along.

Instantsalesletters.com, my first product, was not where it is now. We've added a ton of stuff to it and made it better. But I wanted to see if the thing was going to sell. It wasn't complete and utter rubbish, as my British friends say, but it was enough that it made the point. It helped me find out if there was a marketplace for it. So find out what will work for you.

Secret #4: Deadline

I've thought about my most successful students and come to a striking conclusion that will be worth a lot of money to you if you heed it. There was one key aspect that got them off their butts and making money, and it came down to one thing …

A deadline!

As simple as that sounds, once a firm deadline was established, that was when the rubber met the road and all obstacles melted away like snowflakes in a frying pan. I'll give you a perfect example of how this happened for one apprentice. We were going back and forth, tidying up some finishing touches on the project and trying to get it out the door. Many times people can try to make everything perfect and it never gets out and starts making money, so we said we were going to launch this project at the LIVE Apprentice Summit. That was it and that was final.

The date of the summit was getting closer, and I could see this apprentice start to sweat a bit. But I made him make the commitment to this deadline publicly during our group call, and he couldn't back out.

Fast forward to the day of his launch. He had multiple obstacles that would normally have put the project on hold or swept it away, but not in this case. With the firm deadline in place and the opportunity for him to be embarrassed, our apprentice finished his project. We hit the "send" button and he made a tidy sum from a tiny list over the weekend. And this was just the start, because his project has made well into the five figures already. And why did it get finished?

The deadline.

What's your deadline for your first project or your next project?

Is it something that's in your head? Not a good idea. It's easy to keep moving that forward or letting other things take precedence.

Who knows about your deadline, and who's going to hold you to it? In some cases it's not a good idea to share your deadline or goal with another person, especially if they're the kind of energy vampire a lot of well-meaning friends and family sometimes are. But if you've got a group of colleagues who share the same thinking, use them. This works especially well if you don't want to look like an idiot in front of them and they are people you respect.

I'll tell you what works for me, and maybe it'll work for you, too.

> *Personally, I work best when I absolutely have to perform.*

Personally, I work best when I absolutely have to perform.

For instance, my first product on internet marketing might never have been made (or at least it would have taken much longer) if I hadn't sold it before it was done. In 2000, when I started marketing online, a lot of people wanted to know what I did and how I started making money so fast.

Well, I got my first opportunity to share my story in Atlanta at an internet seminar. I was nervous and my heart was almost beating out of my chest when I knew I was to talk in front of 100 strangers. I gave my presentation, and then I sold this product (yet to be created).

I told people it would be delivered in a few weeks, so they knew it was a prepublication offer. I walked away with ten orders at $200. All well and good, except that I couldn't charge anyone until the manual was done—even though it was only $2,000 worth (less what I had to pay the promoter).

I knew that at least people wanted this information and I could keep selling it once I finished it. I probably had a week or two of three o'clock in the morning work sessions, but I finally completed the project and charged the cards. I was under pressure to get the manual done because these people had paid me (although I hadn't charged them) and I owed them the material.

What Am I Doing Now?

Since then, I've updated my course material and it's brought in earnings well into the six figures, because I had to do it.

How can you set something like this up for yourself?

Once you've set your deadline for anything, you'll "magically" see certain resources fall into place. Trust me, it can feel a little eerie, but when it occurs every time you set a deadline, you know there's something to it. Just making the decision sets these events in motion for you. It's also because what you focus on becomes your reality.

> *Once you've set your deadline for anything, you'll "magically" see certain resources fall into place.*

Your perception has changed. Your internal "radar" is now attuned to resources, allies, and other positives that can help you get your project completed.

Now I leave you with one more secret: set "mini-deadlines."

When you're looking at the whole task of setting up an internet business (or anything, really), it's easy to get overwhelmed. But if you break everything into small tasks with their own deadlines, you'll be at your destination before you know it. I promise it'll work for you. In fact, that's one of the reasons I like Franklin planner systems (now Franklin Covey). I've been using them since 1998, and that was when I first started making significant changes in my life.

Even though I hate ad slogans (they don't work), this one should become your mantra for the year: "Just Do It." As clichéd and overused as it is, that's all it comes down to—whether you're willing to roll the dice and put yourself out there. I promise that whatever worst-case scenario you're thinking about is far from the reality.

I can't remember the author who said, "If you show me what a person does in his spare time, I'll show you the type of person he'll become." What are you doing with your spare time?

◆ Watching TV or reading?

◆ Napping or practicing your copywriting?

◆ Yakking to your friends or studying direct marketing?

Moonlighting on the Internet

You need to turn off the TV and stop checking e-mails, surfing aimlessly, and watching silly videos on YouTube. The time you might be "wasting" somewhere could be used to build yourself an extra paycheck moonlighting online.

It all comes down to the choices we make every day. In fact, you shouldn't let one day go by without making sure you take at least one proactive step toward your own independence. Just because the thought of you doing what you want when you want may seem far away, don't let that stop you from taking those baby steps every day. That's one of my rules, and I hope you'll adopt it.

Now here's the warning. With all this said, don't get fooled by the idea nearly everyone gets. It goes something like this: "Well, if I can create 10 products, each making $1,000/month, I'll make $10,000 every month." Yes, that's a great thought, but what happens is you get sidetracked and lose focus working on more than one project at once.

Your best bet is to focus on product #1 first, and *only* after you have that securely in place should you move along to product #2. Trust me. I realize there are so many opportunities available online that you want to grab each one, but the only thing you'll do is run around like a headless chicken.

You can see from my examples that my multiple revenue streams consist of information products. I love info products, but your multiple revenue streams could come in any or all of the five proven ways shown in this book. And remember, head over to **www.moonlightingontheinternet.com** to stay connected with your fellow "Mooners," because you're not alone.

Index

A

Ablake, 206
Abuse-recovery-and-marriage-counseling.com, 19
Acethatjob.com, 46–47
Adjectives, avoiding in eBay titles, 151, 153
AdSense, 272, 277
Advanced Credit Systems, 236
Advertising
    affiliate programs as, 184
    in e-newsletters, 203–204
    minimal needs for, 6–7
    with search engines, 36, 197, 198, 202–204
    via blogging, 272–273, 276, 277, 278, 281
AdWords
    affiliate marketing competitors in, 197
    direct link to merchant sites through, 198
    effectiveness of, 203
    promoting blogs in, 281
    test marketing with, 232
Affiliateclassroom.com, 206–207
Affiliate marketing
    business setup for, 197–198
    driving web traffic via, 202–204, 231, 237–238
    elements of, 181–184
    finding and choosing programs, 191–197
    narrowing focus in, 202
    offline, 207–208
    payment methods, 185–186
    preselling in, 198–200
    repeat business in, 205–206
    Rosalind Gardner's entry into, 187–190
    simplicity of, 200–202
    tracking sales in, 208–209, 284
    via blogging, 273–274, 277, 278–279, 282–284
Affiliate networks, 191–192
Ages of blogs, 280
Agreements, affiliate marketing, 194–197
Air traffic controllers, 187, 188–189
Alexa, 223–224
Alibris.com, 74, 75, 76
Allen, Lance, 106, 107–108
Allspirit fitness.com, 199
Altered, 243–244
Amazon.com
    affiliate program, 273, 277, 279
    book sales rankings, 39–40
    harvesting ideas from, 40–41

Index

America's Interactive Production Network, 243

Anatomy and Drawing, 82–83, 103

Andrewlock.com, 128

AOL Instant Messenger, 28

Apprentice program, 287–288

Archives, 248

Art grants, 103–104

Articles as bonuses, 102

AtariBoy blog, 255

Auction counters, 149

Auction durations, 132, 162–163

Auction Genius Course, 180

Auction management software, 166–167, 168

Audio files, 11, 55

Auto accessories, 228

Autoresponders, 96–97, 200, 204, 205–206

Aweber.com, 96

B

Backup service for web sites, 95

Backward marketing, 137

Bad headlines, 152

Bandwidth, 94

Barnum, P. T., 71–72

Baseball card auctions, 143

Benefits, in domain names, 89

Best Buy, 224, 225

B5media, 247, 284

Bids, encouraging, 160–162

Biography, 268

BlogAds, 272, 279

Blogging

    affiliate marketing via, 273–274, 277, 278–279, 282–284

    basic elements, 247–249

    costs, 281

    design for, 262

    direct income from, 272–275

    income potential from, 276–280

    indirect income from, 275–276

    personal requirements, 249–251

    platform selection, 254–255

    setup tasks, 257–262

    styles of, 268–269

    topic selection, 251–253, 279–280

    writing and content tips, 252–253, 263–270

Blog networks, 274–275

Blogs, finding, 249

Bodybuilding products, 120–121

Bogdanski, Mary, 262

Bonus offers

    in eBay marketing, 144–146, 153

    in information marketing, 102–104, 108

Books. *See also* E-books; Public domain information

    auctioning first editions, 143, 176–177

    licensing, 61–63

    sales rankings, 39–40

    searching for, 74, 75, 76

Braidsbybreslin.com, 229

Brainstorming offers, 108

Brainstorming project ideas, 28–29

Breslin, Ricky, 229

Brooklyn Bridge, 186

Bullet points, 119–120

Business checking accounts, 221

Business forms, 197–198

Business licenses, 220–221

Business plans, 130

Business topics, 21–22

Buy It Now option, 165

C

Camtasia, 12, 41

Canadian pharmacy site, 186

Caples, John, 118

Car accessories, 228

Carroll, Alex, 56

Case studies in blogs, 268

Index

Catch-wrestling book, 85–86
Categories (eBay), testing, 150
Cat sites, 199
Certification exam prep services, 54–55
CGI scripts, 94–95
Chat rooms, 187
Checking accounts, 221
Cheerful expectancy, 286
Chitika, 277, 278
Christakos, Caterina, 281
Clark, John, 267
Clearing rights, 75–81
Clickbank.com, 41–42, 98, 99
Clientmagnets.com, 99
Closeout merchandise, 135–136
Clothing, seasonal, 139
Collier, Robert, 22, 117–118
Comment sections, 249
Commission Junction
    basic features, 191–192
    driving e-commerce traffic via, 231
    earnings data on, 196–197
    reputability of programs, 194–195
    tracking sales in, 208
Commissions, 195–196. *See also* Affiliate
    marketing
Communication skills for blogging, 250
Competition
    beating in eBay marketing, 144–148
    in blogging, 252, 264
    endorsing, 45
    researching, 44–45, 138, 223–225
Computer games, 31–32
Consulting by bloggers, 275
Consumerreports.com, 15
Contact times, 173
Content for blogs, 252–253, 263–270
Contextual advertising, 272, 276, 282
Contrasting opinions in blogs, 269
Copyright.gov web site, 77–79

Copyright office, 81
Copyright protection
    for blogging, 270
    clearing for public domain works, 75–81
    identifying public domain material, 72–74
    for information marketing, 4
    licensing and, 61–64
Cornell, Lee, 17–18
Cost per click ads, 272
Counters, 149
Covey, Stephen, 287
Credit card affiliate programs, 186
Credit card payments
    in e-commerce, 234, 236
    methods of accepting, 98–99
    via PayPal, 98, 173
    when to process, 236
Credit reports, 235
Critiques in blogs, 269
Cron software, 95
Cross-selling, 240–241

D
Dating books, 281
Dating services
    number of affiliates, 197
    potential commissions, 195
    preselling, 198
    Rosalind Gardner's entry into, 187–188
    Sage-hearts.com example, 200
Davies, Wayne, 20–21
Deadlines, 289–292
Dean, Joe, 109
Debates in blogs, 269
Decision making, 288–289
Derivative works, 74, 84
Dermatologists' manual, 12–14
Design of blogs, 262
Design of web sites, 6, 111–112, 201
Dickbank.com, 24
Diet topics, 22–23

Index

Digital information products, 3–7. *See also* Information marketing
Digital Photography School blog, 284
Direct income from blogging, 272–275
Directories, 11
Discussion boards, 44
Disk space on servers, 94
Diversification in affiliate marketing, 209
DNS information, 91–92
Domain names
    for blogging, 258, 260–261
    creating for information marketing, 89–90
    importance for offline marketing, 208
    selling, 147
Domain registration, 89–90, 91, 258
Domains, multiple, 95
Domino's Pizza, 252
Donations for blogs, 274
Dot-com domain names, 89, 147, 261
Doyle, Bernadette, 99
D-publishing.jp, 64
Dreamhost, 258, 259
Drop-shipping
    in eBay marketing, 134–135, 156
    in e-commerce, 211, 217–219, 231–234
    scams, 234
Ducati motorcycles, 154–155, 156
Dutch auctions, 162–163

E

Easyprofitauctions.com, 149
eBay marketing
    affiliate program, 184
    auction durations, 132, 162–163
    auction management software, 166–167, 168
    beating competitors, 144–148
    buyer motives, 133–134
    Buy It Now option, 165
    encouraging bids, 160–162
    featured items, 163–164
    feedback, 166, 170–172, 176
    follow-up on sales, 141–142, 168–169, 173–174
    headline selection, 148–149, 151–154
    keyword selection, 148–150
    managing orders, 173–174
    obtaining products for, 129–132, 134–136, 137–140
    payments, 165, 169–170, 172–173
    potential of, 123–125
    setting up business, 131–133
    shipping products, 136, 165, 168–169, 174
    specialization in, 158–159
    success strategies, 140–144, 175–179
    Sydney Johnson's entry into, 125–127
    tips for strengthening listings, 153–158, 178–179
E-books. *See also* Information marketing
    as bonuses, 102
    car engines, 30–31
    defined, 9
    fitness, 23
    tax savings, 20–21
    wedding toasts, 24
E-classes, 85
E-commerce
    Andy Jenkins's entry into, 214–216
    drop-shipping with, 217–219, 231–234
    exclusive packages, 241–242
    getting started in, 219–223
    middlemen, 234
    niche marketing importance, 227–229
    niche marketing methods, 229–231
    overview, 211–214
    part-time stores, 236–237
    payment methods, 234–236
    repeat sales and cross-selling, 239–241
    researching competitors, 223–225
    use of affiliate marketing, 231, 237–238
80/20 rule, 287

Index

Elance.com, 56
E-mail address collection
    for eBay repeat sales, 141–142
    for e-commerce, 239–240
    for information marketing, 97, 98
E-mail autoresponders, 96–97
E-mail messages to auction winners, 167
Employees, 5
Endorsements in blogs, 282
Engine swap e-books, 30–31
Entertainment topics, 25
EPCs, 196
Epinions.com, 15
Even-Esh, Zach, 23
Exam prep services, 54–55
Exclusive affiliate agreements, 195
Exclusive packages, 241–242
Expectancy, 286
Expertise, developing, 286
Expired domains, 90

F

Failures, learning from, 32, 288
Family therapy, 19
Fantastico add-on, 95, 258
Farmer Burns, 85–86
Featured items (eBay), 163–164
Federal publications, 72
Feedback (eBay), 166, 170–172, 176
Fees
    for affiliate marketing programs, 195
    eBay, 152, 157, 161
Figure Drawing Secrets, 83, 103–105
Film business, 214–215
Filmspecific.com, 105–106
Final value fees, 161
Financial topics, 20–21
Fine, Rebecca, 84–85
Finestshops.com, 238
First Class Flyer, 11
First edition books, 143, 176–177

Fitness membership site, 10
Fitness products, 67–68, 120–121
Fitness topics, 22–23
Flash, 147
Flipping blogs, 274
"Flood" method, 137, 159
Focus in affiliate marketing, 202
Foreign publications, 73
Formatting text in blogs, 266
Formerly copyrighted works, 72
Franklin planners, 291
Freeware, 104–105
Frequency of blogs, 265
FTP programs, 92
Fulfillment houses, 136, 168, 218
Full Record Display option, 79, 80
Furey, Matt, 85–86
Futterer, Shawn, 54–55
Future-proofing domain names, 261

G

Gainmuscleandlosefat.com, 120–121
Galloway, Paul, 90
Game sales, 31–32
Garage sales, 130
Gardner, Rosalind, 181–182, 210
Garza, Janiss, 199
Generic public information, 71–72
"Get Fit While You Sit," 67–68, 112, 113
Ghostwriters, 55–56
Gibbons, Dale, 83–84
Gift certificates, 241
Golf mats, 241
Good Keywords software, 35
Google AdWords. *See* AdWords
Google.com
    ads on, 36, 197, 198, 203
    market research using, 44–45
    test marketing with, 232–233
Goto.com, 203
Government grants, 103–104

Index

Government publications, 72
Government web sites, 75
Guitar Center, 227

H

Haibeck, Tom, 24
Hammacher Schlemmer, 184, 185
Harricharan, John, 106
Haxan Films, 243
Headlines
    for eBay marketing, 148–149, 151–154
    in information marketing, 117–120
Healingproducts.com, 239
Health topics, 22–23. *See also* Fitness products
Hendricks, Andre, 46–47
Hidden counters, 149
High-end items on eBay, 143
Hilbert, Rebecca, 253
Hirschhorn, Debby, 19
Holland, Michael, 39
Horsemoms.com, 262
Hosted blog platforms, 254–255, 257–258
Hosting web sites, 90–95
How-to topics, 17–19
How to Write Letters That Win, 82
Hynak & Associates, 81
Hypothetical posts, 269

I

Ideas for products
    evaluating, 43–47
    generating, 6, 27–33, 40–42
    "stealing," 59–60
Idictate.com, 55
Images in blogs, 266–267
Immediate payment option (eBay), 170, 171
Important but not urgent activities, 287
Incorporation, 197–198
Indirect income from blogging, 275–276
Informational blogging, 268
Information lists from wholesalers, 137

Information marketing
    advantages, 4–5
    best topics for, 17–25
    choosing products for, 6, 27–33, 40–42
    discovery of, 12–16
    earning potential, 7
    elements of, 9–12
    joint ventures, 65–69
    licensing for, 61–64
    market research, 35–42
    need for, 3–4, 5
    product creation, 49–57
    product packaging, 101–106
    product pricing, 106–108
    things not needed for, 6–7
Information overload, 15
Inserts, 168–169
The Insider's Guide to Film Distribution, 105
Inspirational blogs, 269
Instantsalesletters.com
    growth of, 57, 289
    headlines, 117
    origins of, 14
    packaging options, 82, 101–102
    templates on, 10
Instructional blogging, 268
Internet Marketer's Little Black Book, 90
Interviews in blogs, 268
Inventories, drop-shipping from, 218, 232, 233
itunes.com, 11

J

Jackson, Dean, 65–66
Jeffreys, Alex, 149
Jenkins, Andy, 212, 213, 243–244
Job boards, 279
Jobsearchbootcamp.com, 193
Johnson, Sydney, 124, 180
Joint ventures, 65–69
Jordan, James, 120–121

Index

K

Kappler, Cindy, 288
Keywords
    for pay-per-click ads, 203
    researching use of, 35–36
    selecting for eBay marketing, 148–150
    selecting for e-commerce, 231
Killer Instinct, 214

L

Labeling affiliate links, 283
Leads, paying for, 185
LeClear, Matt, 84
Lee, Ryan, 9, 10
Length of blogging posts, 265
Levis, Daniel, 21–22
Libraries, 74
Library of Congress web site, 77–79
Licensing, 61–64, 220–221
Life magazines, 127
Lifestyle topics, 25
Lifetime commissions, 196
Lifetosuccess.com, 267
Lingeriediva.com, 235
Link positioning in blogs, 283
Link posts, 268
Listing fees, 161
Listings (eBay), enhancing, 153–158,
    178–179
Lists in blogs, 266, 268
Livingston, Glenn, 37–39
Lock, Andrew, 128
Lord of the Rings merchandise, 139, 233
Loss leaders, 224
Low-cost marketing, 6–7
Low starting bids, 160–162

M

Macro recorders, 41
Madscienceindustries.com, 30–33
Mailing lists
    for affiliate marketing, 198, 200, 204–206

for e-commerce, 239–240
Malaga, Ross, 235
Managing orders in eBay marketing,
    173–174
Manolo, 264–265, 275
Marketmum.com, 253
Market research. *See* Research
Maverickphotographer.com, 172
McCoid, Mark, 239
McGrath, Jay, 241
Mckay, Brian, 186
Membership sites, 9, 10, 93
Merchandising blogs, 274
Merchant accounts, 98–99, 235–236
Microsoft Word, 92
Middlemen, 234
Mind mapping, 52–53, 55
Mini-deadlines, 291
Minimum payments, 196
Moneymaking topics, 21–22
Morris, Nathan, 30–33
Motorcycles, 154–155, 156
Movie making, 214–215
Mp3 files, 11
MSN Microsoft Passport, 235
Multiple domains, 95
Music equipment, 227
Music files, 11
MySQL database software, 95
Myszak, Mark, 25

N

Nameboy.com, 90
Nameserver settings, 92
Names in blogs, 270
Names of domains. *See* Domain names
Needs fulfillment, 230
Negative feedback, 171, 176
New-in-box products, 152, 153
Newsletters
    advertising via, 203–204

Newsletters (*continued*)
  to build mailing lists, 200, 204
  as information products, 11
Niche marketing, 227–231
Niche topics for blogging, 251–253
Nightingale, Earl, 286
Non-paying buyers, 169–170
No reserve auctions, 160–162

O
Offers
  brainstorming, 108
  in e-commerce, 239
  headlines, 117–120
  strengthening, 102–103
  template for, 114–116
Offline marketing, 207–208
Ogawa, Tadahiro, 63–64
Omidyar, Pierre, 127
One and Only dating service, 187
Online auctions. *See* eBay marketing
Online book searches, 74, 75, 76
Online communities, 250–251
Online dating services. *See* Dating services
Online learning, 12
Online membership sites, 9, 10
Online newsletters. *See* Newsletters
Online stock trading, 253
Opinions in blogs, 269
Opportunity gaps, 252
Ordering systems, 3–4
Order management in eBay marketing, 173–174
Outlining, 50–51
Overallbeauty.com, 221
Overdelivery, 171–172
Overhead, minimizing in eBay marketing, 152, 157
Overture, 35–36, 219–220

P
Packaging information products, 101–106

Paragraphs in blogs, 266
Pareto Principle, 287
Parks, Stacey, 105–106
Parrot training keyword search, 35–36, 39–40
Part-time e-stores, 236–237
Passion for blog topics, 250, 251
Pavlina, Steve, 276
Payments
  in affiliate marketing, 185–186, 196
  for digital information products, 97–99
  in eBay marketing, 165, 169–170, 172–173
  in e-commerce, 234–236
Payment Tech, 235
PayPal
  use in eBay marketing, 165, 172–173
  use in e-commerce, 234
  use in information marketing, 98
Pay-per-click advertising, 197, 202–204
Pay-per-click programs, 185
Pay-per-lead programs, 185
PDA jackets, 228
Pedal cars, 127
Personal development information, 267
Personal endorsements in blogs, 282
Personalizing eBay listings, 153–156
PHP software, 95
Pickup101.com, 107
Pictures, 157, 266–267
Plank, Robert, 68–69
Platforms, blogging, 254–255
Poker player training, 25
Popularity of blog topics, 251–252
Positioning links in blogs, 283
Powerpause.com, 106
Prediction and review blogs, 269
Preselling, 198–200
Price shopping, 242
Price wars, 144
Pricing information products, 106–108
Print magazines, affiliate marketing in, 207–208

Index

Priority Mail, 174
Private ad deals for bloggers, 278
Private membership sites, 9, 10
Proactive behavior, 287–288
Problogger.net, 247, 279, 284
Product creation, 49–57, 101–106
Product knowledge, 223, 225
Product selection
    for eBay marketing, 129–131
    for e-commerce, 222–223
    for information marketing, 6, 27–33,
        40–42
Profiles in blogs, 268
Profits from digital information products, 4
Project management certification exam prep,
    54–55
Public domain information
    clearing rights to, 75–81
    creating products from, 81–86
    identifying, 72–74
    potential of, 6
    searching for, 74–76
    types available, 71–72
Publishers, licensing books from, 61–63
Purepearls.com, 216–217

Q
Qualifying e-commerce traffic, 230
Questexperiences.com, 109
Questions for choosing products, 27–28

R
Raab, Amanda, 216–217
Rants, 269
Reading, importance to blogging, 250
Realfeelgolfmats.com, 241
Recurring payments, 195–196
Registering domains, 89–90, 91
Registration numbers (copyright), 77
Reikiranch.blogspot.com, 249
Relationship topics, 19
Relevancy of ads in blogs, 281

Reliability of web servers, 94
Relisting, 141
Renewal of copyright, 77, 79, 80–81
Repeat business
    in affiliate marketing, 205–206
    in eBay marketing, 141–142, 168–169
    in e-commerce, 239–240
Reports, packaging with merchandise, 242
Reputable affiliate programs, 194
Research
    for eBay marketing, 137
    for e-commerce, 223–225
    for marketable product ideas, 35–42
    presenting in blogs, 269
    target market selection, 43–44
    using search engines in, 44–45
Resilience for blogging, 250
Reviews in blogs, 268
Ripley's Believe It or Not, 218
Rolling reserves, 235
Rowse, Darren, 245–246, 284

S
Sales letters. *See also* Instantsalesletters.com
    templates for, 10, 14, 114–116
    web sites as, 111–112
Salespagetactics.com, 68–69
Sales pitches
    brainstorming, 108
    for e-commerce, 229–230
    Figure Drawing Secrets example, 103–105
    headlines, 117–120
    starting product development with, 68
    strengthening, 102–103
    template for, 114–116
    web design versus, 111–112
Sales tax ID numbers, 131–132, 220–221
Sam Ash, 227
Satirical blogs, 269
Scannable content in blogs, 265–266
Scanning services, 82

The Science of Getting Rich, 84
Search engines
    driving affiliate marketing traffic via, 202–204, 209
    driving e-commerce traffic via, 230, 231, 236
    using for online market research, 44–45
Search firms, 81
Seasonal items, 139
Second Chance Offers, 170
Seductiondiva.com, 281
Seeingwithoutglasses.com, 62–63
Self-help topics, 19
Selling blogs, 274
Selling Manager PRO, 166, 168
Sellingtohumannature.com, 21–22
Seven-day auctions, 162–163
Shared hosting, 95
Sherry's Berries, 204
Shipping products, 136, 165, 168–169, 174
Shopping cart software, 93, 99
Shopping.com, 219
Shopping comparison sites, 178
Shopping portals, 219
Shulenski, Stephen, 172
Singal, Anik, 206–207
Six Figure Blogging Course, 284
Skills improvement topics, 24
Smartholdempoker.com, 25
Snyder, Kim, 221
Software
    affiliate marketing of, 206–207
    auction management, 166–167, 168
    blogging, 255, 258, 260
    as bonuses, 102, 104
    search engine traffic, 209
    web design, 33, 92, 201
    web hosting, 93, 95
Software sales, 12
Sole proprietorships, 197–198
Spare time, using, 291–292

Sparklecat.com, 199
Speaking opportunities, generating with blogs, 276
Specialization, 158–159, 227–229
Spelling in eBay listings, 157
Sponsorships for blogs, 273
Standalone blog platforms, 254–255, 258–260
Start-up costs, 5, 201
State documents, 75
"Stealing" ideas, 59–60
Stephensonandcompany.com/medifast, 193
Stephenson, Brian, 193
Stillagirl.com/journal, 281
Stock options trading, 253
"Stop Your Divorce," 65–66
Stove-top grills, 144–146
Styles of blogging, 268–269
Subscriptions, 97, 98, 274
The Super Affiliate Handbook, 189–190
Support for web servers, 94

T
Tape-recording, 55
Tapestries, 238
Target markets, selecting, 43–44
Tax ID numbers, 131–132
Tax savings, 20–21
Templates
    as bonuses, 102–103
    for sales pitches, 114–116
    selling, 10–11, 14
Terminating affiliate marketing agreements, 195
Test marketing
    for eBay sales, 140–141, 149–150, 162, 175
    in e-commerce, 232
Text formatting in blogs, 266
Text link ads in blogs, 272–273, 277
Thank-you letter templates, 11
Themed events, 109

Index

Thomson and Thomson, 81
Timing
    auction durations, 132, 162–163
    for eBay order management, 173–174
    for marketing seasonal items, 139
Tip jars, 274
Titles. *See* Headlines
Titles of blogs, 265
Tools and templates as bonuses, 102–103
Topics
    best for information marketing, 17–25
    selecting for blogs, 251–253, 279–280
Torso Tracks, 153–154, 156
Tracking affiliate sales, 208–209, 284
Traffic Equalizer software, 209
Training topics, 24
Transcription, 55
Travel topics, 25
Trust, building, 198
Turbo Lister, 166, 167
Two-tier affiliate programs, 238

U
Undergroundstrengthcoach.com, 23
Unique content in blogs, 264–265
Unix/Linux servers, 93, 94–95
Uploading files, 92
Upselling, 142
Uscanadianpharmacy.com, 186
Used book stores, 74
Useful content in blogs, 263–264

V
Vance, Taylore, 249
Ventriloquism101.com, 17–18
Verdugo, Ernesto, 62–63
Video courses, 86
Vintage clothing, 139
Vitale, Joe, 22
Voice, in blogging, 264–265, 269

W
Walker, Jeff, 65
Web design software, 33, 92
Web Hosting Talk forum, 94
Weblogs, Inc., 274
Web sites
    advantages for affiliate marketing, 198
    autoresponders, 96–97, 200, 204, 205–206
    benefits of simplicity, 200–202
    bringing traffic to, 202–204, 230
    building with Yahoo! Store system, 220, 222
    collecting payments via, 97–99
    designing, 6, 111–112, 201
    hosting and setup, 90–95, 201
    keeping simple, 32
    registering domains, 89–90, 91
    selling designs for, 146–147
Wedding favors, 228–229
Weddingtoasts.com, 24
Weight loss topics, 22–23
Welcome e-mails, 91–92
Wholesalers, 131–132, 136, 137
Woodhead, Peter, 287–288
Wordpress.com service, 254, 257–258
WordPress software, 258, 260
Writing assignments, generating with blogs, 275
Writing blogs, 263–270
Written product creation process, 49–55

X
Xboxes, 162

Y
Yahoo! Search Marketing, 203
Yahoo! Stores, 213–214, 219–220. *See also* E-commerce
Yahoo! Wallet, 235
Yousaveontaxes.com, 20–21

Moonlighting On The Internet
Charter Membership Acceptance Form

Enjoy three FREE months of membership with all of these benefits:

◆ Three months of the Moonlighting Monthly Newsletter

◆ Three months of audio interviews with experts and other Moonlighting members

◆ Three months of Moonlight Alerts (the internet moves fast and you'll be the first to know of any new opportunities and pitfalls to watch out for)

◆ Access to Member's Only area

◆ And much, much more!

There is a one-time charge of $4.95 to cover postage for your first three issues of your newsletter. For your convenience and to prevent any interruption of your membership once the three month trial period is up, the low $39.97 ($49.97 outside U.S.) monthly membership dues will be billed automatically. You are under no obligation and can cancel your membership at any time.

Copy and fax to (301) 770-1096 or go to
www.MoonlightingOnTheInternet.com

Name: _____

Business name: _____

Address: _____

City/state/zip: _____

E-mail: _____

Phone: _____

Fax: _____

Credit card: ❑ Visa   ❑ MC   ❑ Amex

Credit Card #: _____ Exp: _____

Signature _____ Date _____

Providing this information constitutes your permission for Moonlighting On The Internet to contact you regarding related information via the above listed means.

Free Resources to Help You Succeed

Here's Your Fast Track
to Moonlighting On The Internet!

Instantly, get all of your free bonuses, resources and tools right here:

www.MoonlightingOnTheInternet.com/resources

◆ Every resource mentioned throughout this book·

◆ FREE Email Course with the latest info!·

◆ Hundreds of Internet Money-Making Tips & Tricks.

◆ FREE step by step video tutorials·

◆ FREE Mindset of a Millionaire audio·

◆ PLUS many other resourcesAre all waiting for you at:

www.MoonlightingOnTheInternet.com/resourcesAccess

your resources right now to get on the fast track

and start Moonlighting On The Internet!

Two Additional Exclusive Bonuses!

($350.00 Value)

1. "Look Over My Shoulder" Expert Video Training

This is the closest thing to having a "Moonlighting On The Internet" expert personally coach you in your home. Your most pressing questions get answered in these step by step videos covering the everything from A to Z on making money online:

- How to register a domain
- Setting up an autoresponder
- Getting vistors to your site
- Setting up a blog
- Hosting a site
- Processing orders while you sleep
- And much much more!

Just look over our shoulders as we perform a specific task or teach you a money-making technique right on your computer screen.

You no longer have any excuse not to succeed!

See how easy it really is at:

www.MoonlightingOnTheInternet.com/bonus

2. "Steal Yanik's Brain" Audio

How easy would it be to duplicate Yanik's success if you not only had his know-how but his actual mindset (how he thinks about making money online).

You'll practically be able to get inside his head and hear what he thinks about when he starts a project, how he manages his time, how he decides what is a worthwhile idea, and lots more.

None of these secrets are "technical" (Yanik still can't build a website if his life depended on it) but he considers them absolutely vital to achieving the internet lifestyle.

Listen to this audio right now and discover the secrets at:

www.MoonlightingOnTheInternet.com/bonus